Scots on the Chesapeake
1607-1830

Scots
on the
Chesapeake

1607–1830

Compiled by
David Dobson

Introduction

here has been a Scottish element in the population of the Chesapeake since the foundation of Jamestown in 1607. Initially the region attracted relatively few Scots—probably 200 by 1645—but their numbers were substantially increased by Oliver Cromwell who exiled 900 Scots prisoners of war around 1650. Economic links, which would have led to subsequent settlement, were established as early as 1626 with the voyage of the *Golden Lion of Dundee*, but such links were terminated by the introduction of the English "Navigation Acts" during the 1660s which effectively made trade between Scotland and the English colonies illegal.

During the 1660s the Scots government followed the practice of England by transporting criminals and religious or political undesirables to the American plantations. Many of these transportees were Covenanters—militant Presbyterians who opposed the religious policies of the Stuart kings. The records of the Scottish Privy Council contain numerous requests from shipmasters for prisoners for shipment to Virginia, but of course not all of these men or women ever reached America; for example, 200 Covenanter prisoners on board the *Crown of London* perished when the ship was wrecked off the Orkney Islands in 1679. This period ended in 1689 when William and Mary acceded to the thrones of Scotland and England. The subsequent demise of the Episcopal Church in Scotland prompted many Scots clergymen, such as James Blair, to seek opportunities in Virginia and Maryland as tutors, schoolmasters and ministers.

The political union of Scotland and England in 1707 removed all restrictions on trade between Scotland and the American colonies. Soon burghs such as Glasgow were establishing or expanding economic links with the Chesapeake. However, the first major group of Scottish "emigrants" to arrive were Jacobite prisoners captured after the Siege of Preston in 1715 and subsequently banished to America. Similarly, in 1746 the failure of the '45 led to shiploads of Jacobite prisoners being landed in Virginia and Maryland for sale as indentured servants. And throughout the eighteenth century there was a steady stream of criminals being shipped from Scotland for sale as indentured servants on the Chesapeake. At the same time there was a constant flow of indentured servants sailing via English ports to Virginia or Maryland. However, the single most important factor stimulating Scottish emigration to Virginia or Maryland was the rapid growth and expansion of the tobacco trade. By 1740 Glasgow had begun to dominate the tobacco trade between America and Great Britain, partly for geo-strategic reasons and partly for efficiency of operations. This resulted in a proliferation of Scottish merchants, factors, and their servants throughout the region. From towns like Norfolk and Portsmouth the Scots factors controlled operations throughout the Chesapeake. This, however, depended on the continuance of the Navigation Acts which required colonial produce to go directly to Great Britain rather than to European markets. The success of the American Revolution brought the system to an end, and although Scottish immigrants still arrived, the emphasis on settlement was elsewhere in the Americas.

While tradition and historical sources indicate a continuous link between the Chesapeake and Scotland from the early seventeenth century, and the fact that thousands of Scots settled permanently or temporarily in Virginia and Maryland, the specific data that genealogists require is far from complete; possibly in many cases it never existed, while in others it has perished. This book attempts to bring together all available references to Scots in Virginia and Maryland from sources scattered throughout Great Britain and North America. In order to develop the information research was carried out over many years in major archives and libraries in Scotland, England, Canada and the United States with emphasis on primary sources such as probate records, court records, indenture agreements, jail registers, family papers, contemporary newspapers and magazines, naturalization papers, Loyalist claims, church registers, militia papers, gravestone inscriptions, government documents, and census returns. This research in primary sources has been supplemented by the inclusion of additional material located in secondary published sources such as family or local histories. While the historic records of Virginia and Maryland contain a substantial number of references to people bearing Scottish names, only those who can be positively identified as Scots or were highly likely to have been born in Scotland have been selected for inclusion in this work.

David Dobson

Sources

AA	American Ancestry (Albany, 1887-1895)
AABB	Matthew's American Armory and Blue Book (London, 1905)
ABR	Aberdeen Burgh Records
ACA	Ayrshire Collections (series) (Ayr, 1947-)
AGB	Americans of Gentle Birth : H. Pitman (Baltimore, 1970)
AHR	American Historical Review
AJ	Aberdeen Journal (Aberdeen, 1748-)
ANE	Aberdeen and North East Scotland Family History Society
ANY	Biographical Register of the St Andrews Society of New York : W. McBean (New York, 1925)
AOF	An Old Family : R. Seton (New York, 1899)
AP	The St Andrews Society of Philadelphia 1749-1907 (Philadelphia, 1907)
APB	Aberdeen Propinquity Book MS
APC	American Presbyterianism : C. A. Briggs (Edinburgh, 1885)
BAF BLG	Burke's Landed Gentry incl. American Families : P. Townsend (London, 1939)
BD	The Book of the Duffs : A. & H. Tayler (Aberdeen, 1914)
BGBE	The Roll of the Burgesses and Guildbrethren of Edinburgh : C. Boog-Watson (Edinburgh, 1930)
BGBG	The Roll of the Burgesses and Guildbrethren of Glasgow : J. R. Anderson (Edinburgh, 1925)
BM	Blackwood's Magazine (Edinburgh)
BOM	The Book of Mackay : A. Mackay (Edinburgh, 1906)
BRO	Bristol Record Office
BS	Bermuda Settlers of the Seventeenth Century : J. Mercer (Baltimore, 1983)
C	US Census, 1850
CAG	Compendium of American Genealogy

CBK	The Court Book of Kirkintilloch 1658-1694 : G. S. Pryde (Edinburgh, 1963)
CCAI	Clan Cameron Ancestral Index (Raleigh)
CCMC	Colonial Clergy of the Middle Colonies : F. L. Weis (Baltimore, 1978)
CCMDG	Colonial Clergy of Maryland, Delaware and Georgia : F. L. Weis (Lancaster, Pa., 1950)
CCS/USA	Clan Campbell Society, USA
CCVC	Colonial Clergy of Virginia , North and South Carolina : F. L. Weis (Boston, 1955)
CF	Colonial Families of USA : G. Mackenzie (Baltimore, 1966)
CLRO	City of London Record Office
CMR	Canongate Marriage Register : F. J. Grant (Edinburgh, 1915)
CPD	Consistorial Processes and Decreets : F. J. Grant (Edinburgh, 1909)
CTB	Calendar of Treasury Books (London, 1904 -) series
DAB	Dictionary of American Biography : A. Johnson (London, 1928)
DAI	Dictionary of the American War of Independence : M. M. Boatman (London, 1973)
DPCA	Dundee, Perth and Cupar Advertiser (Dundee, 1803-1861)
DR	The Douglas Register : W. M. Jones (Baltimore, 1985)
DU	Duke University, North Carolina
EA	Edinburgh Advertiser (Edinburgh, 1764-1859)
EBR	Extracts from the Burgh Records of Edinburgh : M. Wood (Edinburgh, 1938)
EEC	Edinburgh Evening Courant (Edinburgh, 1718-1859)
EMA	A List of Emigrant Ministers to America, 1696-1811 : G. Fothergill (London, 1904)
ETR	Extracts from the Records of the Old Tolbooth 1657-1686 : J. A. Fairley (Edinburgh, 1923)
F	Fastii Ecclesiae Scoticanae : H. Scott (Edinburgh, 1928)
F.Ab.	Fasti Aberdonensis 1494-1854 : C. Innes (Aberdeen, 1854)
FBO	Family of Black of Over Abington 1694-1923 : W. G Black (Glasgow, 1924)
FD	Family of Dallas : J. Dallas (Edinburgh, 1921)

FEA	Founders of Early American Families, 1607-1657 (Cleveland, 1975)
FKC	From Kintyre to Carolina (Glasgow, 1976)
FOS	Family of Seton : G. Seton (Edinburgh, 1896)
FPA	Fulham Papers in the Lambeth Palace Library : W. W. Manross (Oxford, 1965)
GC	Glasgow Courier (Glasgow, 1791-1860)
GGE	Genealogical Gleanings in England (Baltimore, 1965)
GHH	General History of the Halliburton Family : W. K. Rutherford (Lexington, 1983)
GKF	Genealogy of Kentucky Families (Baltimore, 1981)
GM	Gentleman's Magazine (London, 1731 -1868)
GR	Extracts from the Records of the Burgh of Glasgow : R. Renwick (Glasgow, 1908)
HAF	History of Ayrshire and its Families : J. Paterson (Ayr, 1847)
HAW	History of Ayr and Wigtown : J. Paterson (Edinburgh, 1863)
HF	Honeyman Families : A. V. Honeyman (New Jersey, 1909)
HFV	Hunter Family of Virginia (Denver, 1934)
HGM	Historic Graves of Maryland and the D.C. (New York, 1908)
HHG	History of Hutcheson's Hospital, Glasgow : G. Hutcheson (Glasgow, 1881)
HKK	History of Kemp and Kempe Families : F. H. Kemp (London, 1902)
HM	History of Maryland : J. T. Scharf (Hatsboro, 1880)
HWC	History of Washington County, Maryland (Maryland, 1906)
INSH	Scottish Colonial Schemes : G. P. Insh (Glasgow, 1922)
JAB	Jacobites of Aberdeen and Banff : A. M. Taylor (Aberdeen, 1934)
JRA	Justiciary Records of Argyll and The Isles : J. Imrie (Edinburgh, 1969)
KCA	Officers and Graduates of King's College, Aberdeen : P. J. Anderson (Aberdeen, 1893)
KFR	Kincaid Family Records (Edinburgh MS)
L	Virginia Colonial Soldiers : L. Bockstruck (Baltimore, 1988)
LC	Lamont Clan : H. McKechnie (Edinburgh, 1938)

LCW	Library of Congress, Washington D.C.
LIM	The Lyon in Mourning : H. Paton (Edinburgh, 1895)
LJ	Letters and Journals 1663-1889 : J. G. Dunlop (London, 1953)
LNA	Lower Norfolk County Antiquary (New York, 1951)
LNS	Loyalists in Nova Scotia : D. Wetmore (Hantsport, 1983)
LOM	The Loyalists of Massachusetts : J. H. Stark (London, 1933)
LRO	Liverpool Record Office
MAGU	Matriculation Albums of Glasgow University 1727-1858 W. I. Addison (Glasgow,1913)
MCA	Records of Marischal College : P. J. Anderson (Aberdeen, 1898)
Md Gaz	Maryland Gazette
MHS	Maryland Historical Society, Baltimore
MOM	Memorials of the Montgomeries : W. Fraser (Edinburgh, 1859)
MR	The Muster Roll of Prince Charles Edward Stuart's Army 1746 : A. Livingstone (Aberdeen, 1984)
MSA	Maryland State Archives, Annapolis
NA	National Archives, Washington D.C.
Nat. Int.	National Intelligencer
NEHGS	New England Historic Genealogical Society
NGSQ	National Genealogical Society Quarterly
NLS	National Library of Scotland, Edinburgh
NMC	Notes on the Maryland Clergy
NY Gaz	New York Gazette
OD	Scots in the Old Dominion : C. Haws (Edinburgh, 1980)
OPW	Original Patentees of Land in Washington prior to 1710 : B. W. Gahn (Maryland, 1936)
OVG	Ohio Valley Genealogies : C. A. Hanna (Baltimore, 1989)
OWC	Of Whom I Came (Greenville, 1963)

P	Prisoners of the '45 : B. G. Seton (Edinburgh, 1929)
PA	Passenger Arrivals in US, 1819-1820 : (Baltimore, 1971)
PAL	Princess Anne County, Loose Papers, 1700-1789 : J. H. Creecy (Richmond, 1954)
PC	Register of the Privy Council of Scotland (Edinburgh, 1899-1970)
PCC	Prerogative Court of Canterbury, London
PF	Patullo Families : M. C. Crosse (Fort Worth, 1972)
PMA	Perth Museum Archives
PRO	Public Record Office, London
RAV	Register of Ancestors in Virginia (Richmond, 1979)
REA	Register of Edinburgh Apprentices : M. Wood (Edinburgh, 1926)
RSM	Records of the Synod of Moray : W. Cramond (Elgin, 1906)
RSA	Rose Steele Anthology (Richmond, 1982)
S	The Scotsman (Edinburgh, 1817 -)
SA	Scotus Americanus : W. R. Brock (Edinburgh, 1982)
SC	The Scots in Canada : J. M. Gibbon (Toronto, 1911)
SCHR	Scottish Church History Records (Edinburgh, 1926-)
SCI	Saint Clair of the Isles : R. W. Saint Clair (Auckland, 1898)
SCM	Stewart Clan Magazine
SEV	Some Emigrants to Virginia : W. G. Stanard (Baltimore, 1953)
SFV	A Scottish Firm in Virginia 1767-1777 : T. Devine (Edinburgh, 1984)
SG	The Scottish Genealogist (Edinburgh, 1948-)
SHC	The Scottish House of Christie : C. Rogers (London, 1878)
SM	Scots Magazine (Edinburgh, 1739-)
SN	The Scottish Nation : W. Anderson (Edinburgh, 1869)
SNQ	Scottish Notes and Queries (Aberdeen, 1887-)
SOF	Some Old Families : H. B. McCall (Birmingham, 1890)

SOP	Setons of Parbroath : R. Seton (New York, 1890)
SOS	Surnames of Scotland : G. F. Black (New York, 1946)
SP	The Scots Peerage : J. B. Paul (Edinburgh, 1904)
SPC	Calendar of State Papers Colonial, America and the West Indies (London, 1880-)
SPG	Calendar of Letters of the Society for the Propagation of the Gospel 1721-1793 (London, 1972)
SRA	Strathclyde Regional Archives, Glasgow
SRO	Scottish Record Office, Edinburgh
TM	Terra Mariae : E. D. Neill (Philadelphia, 1867)
TMR	Membership Roster of the Tennessee Society of DAR 1894/1960 : C. R. Whitby (Tennessee, 1961)
TOF	Thanage of Fermertyn : W. Temple (Aberdeen, 1894)
TQ	Tyler's Quarterly
TSA	The Scots in America : P. Ross (New York, 1896)
UNC	University of North Carolina
Va Gaz	Virginia Gazette
VG	Virginia Genealogies : E. Hayden (Wilkes Barre, 1891)
VMHB	Virginia Magazine of History and Biography
VSA	Virginia State Archives, Richmond
VSL	Virginia State Library, Richmond
VSP	Virginia State Papers
WA	Who was Who in America 1607 -1899 (Chicago, 1967)
WMQ	William and Mary Quarterly
1812	British Aliens in the US During the War of 1812 : K. Scott (Baltimore, 1979)

Abbreviations

arr	arrived
b	born/baptised
bd	buried
Co	county
d	died
da	daughter
edu	educated
fa	father
fr	from
g/s	gravestone
m	married
mo	mother
nat	naturalized
ph	parish
pro	probate
res	residence
s	son
sett	settled
sh	shipped
tr	transported
Uni	University

SCOTS ON THE CHESAPEAKE
1607 - 1830

ABBOT, FREDERICK, Jacobite, tr. 29 June 1716, fr. Liverpool to Va or Jamaica, on *Elizabeth and Anne*. (SPC.1716.310)

ABERCROMBY, JOHN, res. Skeith, Banffshire, Jacobite, tr. 29 June 1716, fr. Liverpool to Va or Jamaica, on *Elizabeth and Anne*. (SPC.1716.310)

ABERNETHY, JANET, res. Foveran, Aberdeenshire, da. of William Abernethy, thief, tr.1772, arr. James River, Va, 29 Apr. 1772. (SRO.JC27.10.3)

ABERNETHY, JOHN, res. Haddington, East Lothian, storekeeper in Va pre 1776, Loyalist. (PRO.AO13.30.473)

ADAM, JOHN, b. 1729, sett. Caroline Co, Va, militiaman in Va Regt 1757. (VMHB.1)(L)

ADAM, JOHN L., b. 1808 gentleman, arr. Baltimore 1826. (NA.M596)

ADAM, ROBERT, b. 1731 Kirkbride, s. of Rev. John Adam and Janet Campbell, sett Alexandria, Va. (SEV.7)

ADAM, WILLIAM, b. 1751, runaway indentured servant, Loudoun Co, Va, 1770. (VaGaz.27.9.1770)

ADAMS, ROBERT, sh. 1708, sett. Albemarle Co, Va, m. Penelope Lynch, fa. of Robert. (BLG.2533)

ADAMSON, JAMES, indentured servant, sh. 1714, fr. Glasgow to the Potomac River, on ` *The American Merchant* . (TM202)

ADAMSON, JOHN. b. 1705, res. Largo, Fife, sh. Aug. 1723, fr. London to Md. (CLRO/AIA)

ADAMSON, THOMAS, b. 1754, tanner, sh. July 1775, fr. Bristol to Md, on *Fortune* (PRO.T47.9\11)

ADDISON, ROBERT, goldsmith in Va 1778. (SRO.CS16.1.173)

AFFLECK, JAMES, b. 1800, farmer, sh. pre 1830, m. Catherine -, fa. of Margaret, Jane, Nancy, James, Marion, John, and Ellen, sett. Winchester, Frederick Co , Va. (NA.M932\982)

AFFLECK, PETER, b. 1733, shoemaker, sett. Isle of Wight Co, Va pre 1753, militiaman in Va Regt 1757. (VMHB.1)(L)

AFFLECK, ROBERT, b. 1805, farmer, sh. pre 1829, m. Jane -, fa. of Mary, sett. Frederick Co, Va. (NA.M932\982)

AGNEW, ANDREW, sh. 2 Nov. 1674, to St Mary's Co, Md, on *Bachelor of Bristol* (MSA.ESB.152)

AGNEW, ANDREW, clergyman, sh. 1706 to Jamaica, sett. Va. (EMA10)

AGNEW, JAMES, b. 1737 in Galloway, merchant in Portsmouth, Va pre 1776, Loyalist, sett. Stranraer, Wigtownshire. (PRO.AO12.99.204)(PRO.AO13.27.15)

AGNEW, JOHN, b. 1727 in Wigtownshire, clergyman, sh. 1753, sett. Suffolk, Nansemond Co, Va, fa. of Stair, Loyalist, sett. New Brunswick, d. 1812. (EMA10)(PRO.AO13.27.7\10)

AGNEW, STAIR, s. of Rev. John Agnew, sett. Va pre 1776. (PRO.AO13.27.171\5)

AIKEN, DAVID, b. 1717, sh. 1752 on brig *Molly*, arr. Hampden River, Va, Oct 1752, runaway. (VaGaz6.10.1752)

AIKEN, JOHN, sett. Pincader Meeting House, Newcastle Co, Va(?), pre 1773. (SRO.CS16.1.154)

AIKMAN, FRANCIS, merchant in Edinburgh, sh. pre 1669, sett. Va. (EBR.3.63)

AINSLEY, JOHN, b. 1728, sailcloth weaver, sh. Feb. 1774, fr. London to Md, on *Mermaid*. (PRO.T47.9/11)

AINSLEY, THOMAS, b. 1701, carpenter, res. Jedburgh, Roxburghshire, sh. Aug. 1720, fr. London to Md. (CLRO/AIA)

AIREY, THOMAS, clergyman, sh. 1726, sett. Dorchester Co, Md. (EMA10)

AITCHESON, SAMUEL, merchant, sh. pre 1773, sett. Northampton, Va. (SRA.T76.6.3)

AITCHISON, THOMAS, merchant, res. Glasgow, sett. Va pre 1764. (SRO.CS16.1.120)

AITCHISON, THOMAS, merchant, sett. Norfolk, Va, m. Rebecca Ellegood, fa. of William, Loyalist, d. 1776. (VaGaz4.4.1766)(PRO.AO13.27.205/25)(WMQ.8.287) (WMQ.2.22.532)(PRO.AO12..54.273)(PRO.AO12.109.74)(PRO.AO13.27.207)

AITKEN, MATTHEW, sett. Md pre 1772. (SRO.CS16.1.151)

AITKEN, WILLIAM, b. 1727, impost waiter, res. Edinburgh, Jacobite, tr. 24 Feb. 1747 fr. Liverpool to Virginia, on *Gildart* , arr. Port North Potomac, Md, 5 Aug. 1747. (PRO.T1.328)(MR50)

ALEXANDER, ALEXANDER JOHN, s. of Provost William Alexander of Glasgow, sh. to Va 1756, sett. West Indies 1763. (NLS.525.8/9)

ALEXANDER, ARCHIBALD, b. 1708, m. (1) Margaret Parks (2) Jane McClure, sett. Augusta Co, Va, d. 1779. (RAV1)

ALEXANDER, BOYD, s. of Claud Alexander of Newton, sh. pre 1775, storekeeper in Baltimore, Md. (SRA.CFI)

2

ALEXANDER, DAVID, res. Glasgow, d. Md, pro. 1757 PCC

ALEXANDER, DAVID, tr. 1775, fr. Greenock, Renfrewshire to Port Hampton, Va, .on *Rainbow*, arr. 3 May 1775. (SRO.JC27.10.3)

ALEXANDER, DAVID, res. Montrose, Angus, sett. Petersburg, Va, pre 1809. (SRO.SH.27.7.1809)

ALEXANDER, JOHN, sh. 1659, sett. Stafford Co, Va, fa. of Robert, Philip and John, d. 1677. (VG192)(GB.2.214)

ALEXANDER, JOHN, b. 1665, clergyman, edu. Balliol College, Oxford, sh. to Va. (CCVC5)

ALEXANDER, ROBERT, merchant, sett. Annapolis, Md pre 1732. (MSA.Md Deeds.20.576)

ALEXANDER, ROBERT, farmer, sett. Elk River, Cecil Co, Md, pre 1776, Loyalist. (PRO.AO13.1.90/106)

ALEXANDER, WILLIAM, purchasing agent, sett. Richmond, Va, 1784. (SA155)

ALEXANDER, WILLIAM, res. Galloway, merchant, sett. Cecil Co, Md, d. 17.. (MSA.Md Will.24.75)

ALGEE, JAMES, blockmaker, sh. pre 1830, m. Jane -, fa. of Mary, sett. Balt. (N.A.-M432/277-99)

ALISON, JOHN, merchant, res. Glasgow, sett. Va pre 1748. (SRO.CS16.1.80)

ALISON, WILLIAM, b. 16 Mar. 1712, s. of John Alison and Mary Maxwell, res. Glasgow, surgeon, sett. Va pre 1748, d. 1768 Port Royal, Va. (SRO.CS16.1.80)(SRO.B10.15.7345)(SRO.SH.12.10.1770)

ALLEN, ALEXANDER, nat. 22 Sep. 1818 Norfolk, Va.

ALLEN, GEORGE, res. Queensferry, West Lothian, d. Va, pro Jan. 1673 PCC.

ALLAN, HENRY, b. 1800, teacher, sett. Loudoun Co, Va. (N.A.-M932/982)

ALLAN, JAMES, Jacobite, tr. 24 May 1716, fr. Liverpool to Md, on *Friendship,* arr. Md Aug. 1716. (SPC.1716.311)(HM387)

ALLEN, JAMES, b. 1687, town caddy or laborer, Jacobite, tr. 24 Feb. 1747, fr. Liverpool to Va, on *Johnson*, arr. Port Oxford, Md, 5 Aug. 1747. (P.2.8)(MR210)(PRO.T1.328)

ALLAN, JAMES, b. 1715, cabinetmaker and joiner, res. Hamilton, Lanarkshire, sh. 1739, sett. Fredericksburg, Spotsylvania Co, Va, d. 30 Apr. 1779. (VMHB.13.429)(SRO.CS16.1.117)

ALLAN, JOHN, s. of James Allan, merchant, res. Hamilton, Lanarkshire, sett. Spotsylvania Co, Va, d. pre 1750, pro. 3 Apr. 1750 Spotsylvania Co.

ALLAN, JOHN, merchant, res. Ayrshire, sett. Richmond, Va, pre 1800.
(VMHB.87.326)

ALLASON, DAVID, b. 16 May 1736, s. of Zachariah Allason and Isabel Hall, Govan,
storekeeper, sh. 1757, sett. Falmouth and Winchester, Va, d. post 1815.
(SRA.CFI)(VMHB/1931)

ALLASON, JOHN. s. of John Allason, res. Glasgow, sett. Va pre 1772.
(SRO.CS16.1.151)

ALLASON, ROBERT, b. 19 Nov. 1721, s. of Zachariah Allason and Janet Grahame,
merchant, res. Gorbals, Glasgow, sh. 1761, sett. Va.   (SRA.CFI)

ALLASON, WILLIAM, s. of Zachariah Allason and Isobel Hall, merchant, res.
Gorbals, Glasgow, sh. 1737, sett. Norfolk and Falmouth, Va, m. Anne Hume, fa. of Polly,
d. Jan. 1800, bd. Falmouth.   (VMHB.85.45)(SRA.CFI)

ALLASON, WILLIAM, s. of John Allason, surgeon, res. Glasgow, sett. Port
Royal, Va, fa. of William, d. 1768.   (SRA.B10.15.7.7345)(SRO.SH.12.10.1770)

ANDERSON, AGNES, tr. Feb. 1667 to Barbados or Va.   (PC.2.263)

ANDERSON, ALEXANDER, b. 1735, sett. Augusta Co, Va, militiaman in Va Regt
1757.   (VMHB.1/2)(L)

ANDERSON, ANDREW, b. 1664, laborer, res. Selkirk, sh. 5 Aug. 1685, fr. London
to Md.   (CLRO/AIA)

ANDERSON, ANDREW, merchant, res. Glasgow, sett. Va pre 1747.
(SRO.CS16.1.79)

ANDERSON, ANDREW, merchant, res. Edinburgh, sh. pre 1755, sett. Jappahannock,
Rappahannock River, Va, d. 1760.   (SRO.RD4.198.558)

ANDERSON, CHARLES, clergyman, edu. King's College, Aberdeen, 1693,
sett. Va 1700, d. 7 Apr. 1718 Charles City, Va.   (Charles City g/s)

ANDERSON, DANIEL, b. 1748, sett. Va, m. (1) Maisy Beveridge 1774, (2) Mary
Reid Cameron 1797, d. 1813 Va.   (VSL28086)

ANDERSON, DAVID, b. 1760, merchant, sett. Petersburg, Va, d. 18 June 1812.
(Blandford g/s)

ANDERSON, ELEANOR, b. 1779, sett. Richmond, Henrico Co, Va.   (N.A.-M932/982)

ANDERSON, JAMES, Covenanter, tr. Sep. 1668, fr. Leith to Va, on *Convertin*.
(PC.2.534)

ANDERSON, JAMES, sh. 2 Nov. 1674, to St Mary's Co. Md, on *Bachelor of Bristol*.
(MSA.ESB.152)

ANDERSON, JAMES, b. 17 Nov. 1678, clergyman, edu. Edinburgh Uni. 1700,
sh. 1709, sett. Opecquon, Va, d. 16 July 1740 Pa.   (F.7.662)(SA102)

ANDERSON, JAMES, merchant, res. Leith, Midlothian, sett. Brooksbank, Essex Co, Va, d. 3 Mar 1788, pro 17 Sep. 1788 Edinburgh. (SRO.RD4.216.288)(SRO.RD3.231.708)(SRO.CC8.8.127)

ANDERSON, JAMES, b. 1745, m. Helen -, fa. of James, sett. Norfolk, Va 1790, d. 12 Mar. 1807. (New Kent Co g/s)

ANDERSON, JAMES, b. 1807, stonemason, arr. Baltimore 1829. (NA.M596)

ANDERSON, JOHN, b. 1703, scholar, res, Glasgow, sh. Oct. 1722, fr. London to Va. (CLRO/AIA)

ANDERSON, JOHN, b. 1724, sett. Fredericksburg, Va, militiaman in Va Regt 1756. (VMHB.1/2)(L)

ANDERSON, ROBERT, Jacobite, tr. 29 June 1716, fr. Liverpool to Va or Jamaica, *Elizabeth and Anne* , arr. Va. (SPC.1716.310)(CTB.31.208)(VSP.1.186)

ANDERSON, ROBERT, b. 1778, sett. Alexandria, Va, 1793, d. 1 Jan. 1833. (Nat.Int.9.7.1833)

ANDERSON WILLIAM, mariner, Va, m. Mary Gist, res. London, 24 Jan. 1768, Haddington, East Lothian. (Haddington Episc. Reg.)

ANDERSON, WILLIAM, b. 1700 Orkney Islands, sh. Aug. 1718, fr. London to Md, sett. Anne Arundel Co and Prince George Co pre 1731. (CLRO/AIA)

ANDERSON, WILLIAM, merchant, sett Va pre 1750. (SRO.CS16.1.84)

ANDERSON, WILLIAM HENRY, sh. pre 1830, sett. Va., fa. of Hezekiah. (CAG.1.419)

ANDREW, GEORGE, b. 1730, barber, sett. Prince George Co, Va, militiaman in Va Regt 1757. (L)

ANDREWS, JOHN, clergyman, sh. 1749, sett. King William Co and Fairfax Co, Va. (WMQ2.19.365)(EMA11)(SNQ.1.153)

ANDREWS, WILLIAM, clergyman, sett. Portsmouth, Va, pre 1776, Loyalist, sett. Scotland. (PRO.AO13.27.234/44)

ANNAN, ALEXANDER, b. 1728, butcher, res. Aberdeen, Jacobite, tr. 24 Feb.1747, fr. Liverpool to Va, on *Gildart* , arr. Port North Potomac, Md, 5 Aug 1747. (PRO.T1.328)(P.2.14)(JAB.2.419)(MR210)

ANNANDALE, WILLIAM, tailor, sett. King George Co, Va, pre 1744. (SRO.CS16.1.73)

ARBUTHNOTT, JOHN, b. 1684, tailor, res. Aberdeen, Jacobite, tr. 22 Apr. 1747, fr. Liverpool to Va, on *Johnson*, arr. Port North Potomac, Md, 5 Aug. 1747. (P.2.14)(MR69)(JAB.2.419)(PRO.T1.328)

ARBUTHNOTT, THOMAS, surgeon, res. Peterhead, Aberdeenshire, sett. Va, d. 10 Nov. 1742, pro.6 Feb. 1745 Edinburgh. (SRO.CC8.8.109)

ARCHER, WILLIAM, b. 1786, sh. fr. Greenwich, Kent, to N.Y. 25 Sep. 1815, nat. 3 May 1821 Washington, DC.

ARMOUR, JOHN, edu. Glasgow Uni 1747, sett. Va. (WMQ.2.22.194)

ARMSTRONG, EDWARD, drummer, thief, tr. 1772, fr. Port Glasgow to Md, on , *Matty* arr. Port Oxford, Md. 16 May 1772. (SRO.JC27.10.3)

ARNOLD, JANE, b. 1770, sh. to Va. pre 1800, mo. of Annie, sett. Prince William Co, Va. (NA.M932/982)

ARNOTT, DAVID, Jacobite, tr. 29 June 1716, fr. Liverpool to Va or Jamaica, on *Elizabeth and Anne*, arr. Va. 1716. (SPC.1716.310) (CTB.31.208)(VSP.1.186)

ARTHUR, JAMES, merchant, sett. James River, Va. pre 1751. (SRO.CS16.1.85)

ARTHUR, JAMES, b. 1801, cotton spinner sh. pre 1824 to N.Y., m. Jane -, fa. of `William, John, James, Isabel, David, Margaret, Emma, George, sett. Prince George Co, Md. (NA.M432/277-99)

ASHER, JOHN, b. 1745, gardener, res. Edinburgh, sh. Dec. 1773, fr. London to Va., on *Elizabeth*. (PRO.T47.9/11)

AULD, JAMES, b. 1665 Ayr, sett. Talbot Co, Md, m. Sarah -, fa. John, d. 1721, pro. 28 Feb. 1722 Md.

AULD, JOHN, merchant, res. Glasgow, sett. Va, pro 28 Oct. 1803 Edinburgh. (SRO.CC8.8.134)

AUSTIE, ROBERT, thief, res. Forres, Morayshire, tr. 1771, fr. Port Glasgow to Md., on *Crawford* , arr. Port Oxford, Md. 23 July 1771. (SRO.JC27.10.3)(AJ1167)

AVEN, ARCHIBALD, clergyman, res. Banff, sett. Norfolk, Va, pre 1774. (SRO.CS16.1.157)

AYRE, WILLIAM, Jacobite, tr. 24 May 1716, fr. Liverpool to Md, on *Friendship* , arr. Md Aug. 1716. (SPC.1716.311)(HM387)

AYSTON, JAMES, Jacobite, tr. 29 June 1716, fr. Liverpool to Va. or Jamaica, on *Elizabeth and Anne* . (SPC.1716.310)(CTB.31.208)

BAILLIE, ANDREW, merchant, res. Port Glasgow, sett. Va. pre 1790. (SRO.SH25.6.1790)

BAILLIE, GEILLIS, whore, thief, res. Edinburgh, tr. 28 Nov. 1704, fr Leith to Md. (SRO.PC2.28.307)

BAILLIE, GEORGE, b. 1703, bonnetmaker, res. Dundee, Angus, Jacobite, tr. 24 Feb. 1747, fr. Liverpool to Va., on *Gildart* , arr. Port North Potomac, Md, 5 Aug. 1747. (P.2.18)(PRO.T1.328)

BAILLIE, JEAN, tr. 1772, fr. Glasgow to Va., on *Brilliant*, arr. Port Hampton, Va., 7 Oct. 1772. (SRO.JC27.10.3)

BAINE, ALEXANDER, merchant, sett. Va. pre 1771. (SRO.CS16.1.143)

BAIN, ALEXANDER, b. 1747, sawyer, sh. Jan. 1774, fr. London to Md., on *Peggy*. (PRO.T47.9/11)

BAIN, ROBERT, merchant, sett. Richmond, Va., pre 1775. (SRO.CS16.1.165)

BAIN, WILLIAM, b. 1792, gardener, m. Elizabeth -, sett. Baltimore, Md. (NA.M432\277-99)

BAIRD, JAMES, shipmaster and merchant, res. Glasgow, sett. Va. pre 1764. (SRO.CS16.1.120)(SRO.CS17.1.1)(SRA.T.MJ.79)

BAIRD, JOHN, b. 1730, res. Ayrshire (?), sh. pre 1758, sett. Va., m. Catherine McClean, fa. of Absalom, d. 1760. (CAG.1.52\966)

BAIRD, JOHN, s. of John Baird, res. Glasgow, sett. Greencroft, Prince George Co, Va., fa. of John and William, d. 1738. (VSA.DB2.387)

BAIRD, PETER, s. of John Baird, merchant, res. Glasgow, sett. Petersburg, Va., pre 1740. (VSA.DB2.387)

BAIRD, PETER, mariner, res. Old Monklands, Lanarkshire, sett. Va., d. 21 Nov. 1800 .pro. 28 Mar. 1812 Edinburgh. (SRO.CC8.8.138)

BAIRD, WILLIAM, b. 6 June 1729 St Nicholas, Aberdeen, s. of William Baird and Janet Brown, wool-merchant and silkdyer, Jacobite, tr. 24 Feb. 1747, fr. Liverpool to Va., on *Gildart* , arr. Port North Potomac, Md 5 Aug. 1747. (P.2.20)(JAB.2.129)(MR219)(PRO.T1.328)

BAIRD, WILLIAM, s. of John Baird, merchant, sett. Va. pre 1807. (SRO.SH.18.4.1807)

BALFOUR, GEORGE, b. 1804, merchant, arr. Baltimore, Md 1824. (NA.M596)

BALFOUR, HELEN CATHERINE, da. of Charles Balfour, res. Peebles, m. John Tennant, physician, Port Royal, Va., in Canongate, Edinburgh, on 2 May 1794. (WMQ.2.1.142)(Canongate OPR)

BALFOUR, JAMES, s. of Andrew Balfour, res. Wick, Caithness, sh. pre 1743, sett. Charles City, Va. (SRO.RS21.2.341\2)

BALFOUR, WILLIAM, clergyman, edu. Marischal College, Aberdeen, 1730, sh. 1738, sett. Va. (EMA12)(WMQ2.20.131)

BALFOUR, WILLIAM, sett. Va., d. pre 1686, pro. 1686 PCC.

BALLENTYNE, ANDREW, b. 1767, weaver, sett. Monroe Co, Va. (NA.M932/982)

BALLENTYNE, HUGH, sett. Henrico Co, Va., d. pre 1736, pro Jan. 1736 PCC.

BALLENTYNE, JOHN, merchant, res. Ayr, sett. Va. pre 1763, m. Ann -, fa. of Ann and Elizabeth. (SRO.CS16.1.115)(SRO.RD2.242.500)

BALLENTYNE, PATRICK, tobacco merchant, res. Ayr, d. 1770 Va. (ACA.6.193)

BALMAINE, ALEXANDER, b. 1740 Edinburgh, clergyman, edu. Unis. of St Andrews and Edinburgh 1757-1760, sh. 1772, sett. Augusta ph. and Frederick ph, Va., m. Lucy Taylor, d. 1820. (VaJournal23.11.1786)(EMA12)(FPA310)

BALMAIN, WILLIAM, sett. Georgetown, Potomac River, Md, pro. Sep.1784 PCC.

BANKHEAD, JAMES, physician, edu. Edinburgh Uni. 1733, sett. Monroe Creek, Westmoreland Co, Va., m. (1) Ella Monroe (2) Christian Miller, fa. of William, James, John, Ellinor, Jane, d. 1788. (VG448)(WMQ.2.9.303)

BANKS, ALEXANDER, factor, sett. Manchester, Va. pre 1772. (UniVa/.John Smith pp)

BANKS, THOMAS, b. 1784, farmer, m. Margaret -, sett. Dinwiddie Co, Va. (NA.M932\982)

BANNATYNE, DUGALD, assistant storekeeper, sh. pre 1776, sett. Falmouth, Va., Loyalist, sh. June 1777 fr. N.Y. to Glasgow on *Betsey* . (SFV229)

BANNERMAN, BENJAMIN, sett. Portsmouth, Va. pre 1760, Loyalist, to Montrose, Angus, post 1776. (PRO.AO13.27.260\302)

BANNERMAN, WILLIAM, b. 1617, sh. 24 Oct. 1635, fr. London to Va., on *Constance*. (PRO.E157.20)

BARCLAY, ALEXANDER, b. 1711, res. Dundee, Angus, sh. 1726, sett. Amelia Co, Va, m. Amy Gamblin, d. 22 Oct. 1825. (VaGen.6.169)

BARCLAY, JOHN, s. of David and Christian Barclay, res. Kincardineshire, clergyman, sett. St Peter's, Talbot Co, Md. 17.. (MSA.MHR)

BARCLAY, JOHN, b. 1804, carpenter, arr. Baltimore Md. 1829. (NA.M596)

BARCLAY, PATRICK, s. of Andrew Barclay and Helen Lyon, merchant, res. Edinburgh, sh. pre 1745, sett. Va., m. Elizabeth -, fa. of George, d. London, pro. 19 July 1749 Essex Co, Va. (SRO.SH24.8.1745)(SRO.14.3.1749)(Essex Wills.8.296)

BARCLAY, WILLIAM, merchant, res. Lochwinnoch, Renfrewshire, sett. Md. pre 1814, pro.6 Apr. 1814 Baltimore.

BARON, ROBERT, clergyman, sh. 1700 to Bermuda, sett. Md. (EMA13)

BARR, JAMES, b. 1800, farmer, sett. Harford Co, Md, m. Elizabeth -, fa. of Elizabeth, Mary, William and Lewis. (NA.M432/277-99)

BARR, WILLIAM, sh. 2 Nov. 1674, on *Bachelor of Bristol* , to St Mary's Co, Md. (MSA.ESB.152)

BARRACK, JOHN, b. 1716, tailor, sett. Fort Cumberland, Md, militiaman in Va. Regt. 1756. (L)

BARRETT, NATHANIEL, planter, sh. pre 1754, sett. Northumberland Co, Va. (VMHB.2.149)

BARRY, THOMAS, Jacobite, tr. 28 July 1716, fr. Liverpool to Va., on *Godspeed,* arr. Md. Oct. 1716. (SPC.1716.310)(CTB31.209)(HM389)

BASSETT, JOHN, b. 1728, planter, sett. Stafford Co, Va., militiaman in Va Regt 1757. (VMHB.1/2)

BEALL, NINIAN, b. 1625, res. Largo, Fife, tr. 1650 to Barbados, sett. Calvert Co and Upper Marlboro, Md., m. Ruth Moore, fa. of John, Charles, Ninian, Sarah, Hester, Jane, Rachel, George, Mary, Thomas and Margery, d. 1717, Fife's Largo, Md., pro. 28 Feb 1717 Md. (CF.2.57)(ABG.2.2)

BEAMER, JANE, b. 1792, sh. 1828, sett. Monroe Co, Va. (NA.M423.982)

BEATS, MARY, b. 1781, arr. Norfolk, Va. Sep. 1823. (PA1821/3.299)

BEATTY, FRANCIS, Jacobite, tr. 29 June 1716, fr. Liverpool to Va. or Jamaica, on *Elizabeth and Anne* , arr. Va. (SPC.1716.310)(CTB.31.208) (VSP.1.185)

BEATTIE, WILLIAM, merchant, res. Dumfries, Dumfriesshire, sett. Va. pre 1749. (SRO.CS.1.81)

BECK, E., b. 1794, sett. Washington DC. (NA.M432/57)

BEGG, JOHN, merchant, sett. Norfolk, Va,1770, Loyalist. (PRO.AO12.100/141)

BEGG, MILES, Jacobite, tr. 28 July 1716, fr. Liverpool to Va., on *Godspeed,* arr. Md Oct. 1716. (SPC.1716.310)(CTB.31.209)(HM388)

BEITH, JOHN, res. Largs, Ayrshire, sh. 1815, sett. Lunenburg, Va., nat. 17 Oct. 1827. (US.DC.RB5.560)

BELL, ANDREW, b. 27 Mar. 1753 St Andrews, Fife, s. of Alexander Bell and Margaret Robertson, clergyman and tutor, edu. St Andrews Uni., sh. 1774 to Va., Loyalist, HEICS chaplain, d. 27 Jan. 1832. (Westminster Abbey g/s)

BELL, ALEXANDER, b. 1649 St Andrews, Fife, s. of Alexander Bell and Margaret Ramsay, d. 1744 Md. (SG.28.4.189)

BELL, DAVID, res. Glasgow, sh. pre 1745, merchant and planter, sett. Va. (SRA.B10.15.5959/60)

BELL of BELLMONT, DAVID, m. Judith Cary, sett. Albemarle Co, Va., 1755, d. pre 1781. (RAV8)

BELL, ROBERT, b. 1732 Glasgow, printer and publisher, sh. 1766, d. Richmond, Va, 23 Sep. 1784. (SOS67)

BELL, WILLIAM, sh. 2 Nov. 1674, on the *Bachelor of Bristol* , to St Mary's Co, Md. (MSA.ESB.152)

BELL, WILLIAM, b. 1780, farmer, sett. Jackson Co, Va. (NA.M932/982)

BELSCHES, JAMES, b. Perthshire, d. Invermay, Cabin Point, Va. 1798. (NH9.6.1798)

BERRY, JOHN, b. 1711, schoolmaster, res. Aberdeen, sh. Sep. 1735, fr. London to Md. (CLRO/AIA)

BEVERIDGE, MARY, da. of James Beveridge, res. Edinburgh, m. John Greenlees, merchant, Va., 1753. (SRO.GD90.2.236)

BEVERLEY, JOHN, Jacobite, res. Aberdeen, tr. 22 Apr. 1747, fr. Liverpool to Va., *Johnson*, arr. Port Oxford, Md, 5 Aug. 1747. (PRO.T1.328)(P.2.34)(MR210)

BEVERLEY, WILLIAM, Jacobite, res. Aberdeen, tr. 22 Apr. 1747, fr. Liverpool to Va., on *Johnson* , arr. Port Oxford, Md, 5 Aug. 1747, burgess of Glasgow 1781. (P.2.34)(MR210)(PRO.T1.328)

BIGGAR, JOHN, b. 1788, sett. Richmond, Va. (NA.M932/982)

BIGGS, JOHN, sett. Westmoreland Co, Va, pre 1773, m. Isabell Wilson 1782, fa. of Margaret, Jane, Alexander, Mary, Isabella,John, William and James. (TMR248)

BILL, Dr, physician, sh. pre 1705, sett. Va. (SPC.1705.431)

BISSETT, DAVID, s. of Thomas Bissett, storekeeper, res. Dunkeld, Perthshire, sett.Baltimore Co, Md pre 1753, m. Ann Atkinson 1755, sett. Bush River, Md, d. 6 Aug.1758. (MSA.Md.Wills.32.220/33.431)

BISSETT, JAMES, s. of Thomas Bissett, res. Glen Clova, Angus, attorney, sett. Baltimore, fa. of Thomas, d. 1760, pro. 10 Jan. 1760 Md. (MSA.Md Wills.33.220/431)

BISSETT, JAMES, s. of Thomas Bissett, res. Glen Albert, Little Dunkeld, Perthshire, sett. Baltimore Co, Md., d. 1760, pro. 10 Jan.1760 Md. (MSA.Wills.32.220/33.431)

BISSETT, JOHN, b. 1733, schoolmaster, sett. Stafford Co, Va, militiaman in Va Regt 1756. (VMHB1/2)(L)

BISSETT, JOHN, b. 19 Apr. 1761 Culsalmond, s. of Rev. John Bisset and Elizabeth Angus, clergyman, edu. Marischal College, Aberdeen, 1779, sett. Shrewsbury Md. 1792, d. 1810 London. (F.5.376)

BLACK, ALEXANDER, res. Edinburgh, sett. London Town, Anne Arundel Co, Md, d. 1760, pro 17 Dec. 1740 Md. (MSA.Md.Will.30.295)

BLACK, ALEXANDER, b. 14 Apr. 1750, s. of James Black, res. Abingdon Lanarkshire, tobacco merchant, sett. Va. (BOA28)

BLACK, DAVID, physician, sett. Blandford Va., d. 1772. (SA187)

BLACK, DAVID C., res. Arbroath, Angus, shipmaster, sett. Alexandria, Va. pre 1820. (UNC.Black pp2530)

BLACK, JAMES, b. 1729, laborer, Jacobite, tr. 24 Feb. 1747, fr. Liverpool to Va., on *Gildart*, arr. Port North Potomac Md. 5 Aug. 1747. (P.2.36)(PRO.T1.328)

BLACK, JANET, servant, res. Airth, Stirlingshire, tr. 1771, fr. Port Glasgow to Md., on *Crawford*, arr. Port Oxford, Md, 23 July 1771. (SRO.JC27.10.3)

BLACK, SAMUEL, b. 1727, sett. Augusta Co, Va, pre 1748, m. Nancy Jane Porter, fa. of John, William, Susan, James, Margaret, Mary, Martha, Nancy and Samuel, d. 1782. (TMR285)

BLACK, THOMAS, vagabond and robber, tr. 3 Sep. 1668, fr. Leith to Va, on *Convertin*. (PC.2.534)

BLACK, WILLIAM, b. 1679 , clergyman, res. Dumfries, Dumfriesshire, sh. 1706, sett. Accomack Co Va. (SCHR.14.149)

BLACKBURN, HUGH, sett. Md, d. 5 Jan. 1833, pro. 1836 Edinburgh. (SRO.SC70.1.53)

BLACKBURN, JOHN, merchant, res. Glasgow, sh. pre 1752, sett. Norfolk, Va. (SRO.B10.15.6183)

BLACKLOCK, DAVID, b. 1790, tanner, sh. pre 1830, m. Mary -, fa. of Sarah David Samuel, James, Jane, Josiah and William, sett. Baltimore Md. (NA.M432/277-99)

BLACKSTOCK, THOMAS, sett. Va., pro. 1822 Edinburgh. (SRO.SC70.1.26)

BLACKWOOD, JAMES, Jacobite, tr. 29 June 1716, fr. Liverpool to Va., on *Elizabeth and Anne*, arr. Va. 1716. (SPC.1716.310) (CTB.31.208)(VSP.1.185)

BLAIR, ARCHIBALD, physician, edu. Edinburgh Uni. 1685, sh. 1690, sett. Jamestown and Williamsburg, Va, fa. of John, burgess of Glasgow 1725, d. 1733. (SA187)

BLAIR, ARCHIBALD, burgess of Jamestown 1718, James City, Va, 1720, m. (1) Sarah Fowler (2) Mary Wilson, d. 1736. (RAV10)

BLAIR, ARCHIBALD, tr. 1728, fr. Glasgow to Md., on *Concord*, arr. Charles Co, Md, May 1728. (SRO.JC27.10.3)

BLAIR, ARCHIBALD, s. of James Blair, res. Edinburgh, sett. Richmond, Va, pre 1795. (SRO.RD4.259.410)(SRO.SH21.2.1800)

BLAIR, DAVID, b. 1737, merchant, sett. Fredericksburg, Va, 1762, Loyalist. (PRO.AO13.27.331/7)

BLAIR, GEORGE, merchant, sh. 1762, sett. Smithfield, Isle of Wight Co, Va., Loyalist. (PRO.AO12.56.184)(PRO.AO12.109.82) (PRO.AO13.27.338\77)

BLAIR, GEORGE, nat. 15 Jan. 1821 Norfolk, Va.

BLAIR, JAMES, b. 1656, s. of Rev. Robert Blair, clergyman, edu. King's College, Aberdeen, 1670, sh. 1685, Commissary of Va. 1689-1741, d. 1743. (SRO.RD2.59.439)(GM.13.443)(SM.5.343) (KCA.2.234)

BLAIR, JEAN, da. of Archibald Blair, m. John Blair jr, Councillor of Va. 26 Dec. 1756 Edinburgh. (Edinburgh OPR)

BLAIR, JOHN, s. of Peter Blair, merchant, res. Edinburgh, sett. Williamsburg, Va. pre 1746. (SRO.CS16.1.79)

BLAIR, JOHN, merchant, res. Edinburgh, sett. Richmond, Va, pre 1719. (SRO.22.8.1719)

BLAIR, JOHN, merchant, sett. Williamsburg, Va, pre 1725, burgess of Glasgow. (EBR.260.8000)(BGBG380)

BLAIR, JOHN, b. 1686, President of Council of Va., d. 5 Nov. 1771 Williamsburg, Va. (SM.34.109)

BLAIR, LILIAS, da. John Blair, res. Perthshire, sh. 1785, sett. Portsmouth, Va, m. (1) Dugald McPhail (2) Hugh McPherson, mo. of Elizabeth and John. (VMHB.66.423)

BLAIR, MARY, da. of M. Blair, res. Glasgow, sett. Charles Co, Md, m. - True, d. 4 Feb.. 1818 Md. (Frederick g\s)

BLAIR, MATTHEW, merchant, sett. Potomac River, Md. pre 1790. (SRO.CS238.misc26\1)

BLAIR, THOMAS, res. Glasgow, sett. Va., m. Anne -, d. 1739, pro. 25 Mar. 1740 Accomack Co.

BODY, WILLIAM, b. 1727, farmer, sett. Augusta Co, Va., militiaman in Va. Regt. 1756. (VMHB1\2)(L)

BOGLE, MATTHEW, s. of Robert Bogle, tobacco merchant, res. Glasgow, sett. Va. 1729, to Glasgow 1736. (SA52)

BOGLE, WILLIAM, merchant, sh. 9 Oct. 1685, fr. Port Glasgow to Va., on *Mayflower of Preston*. (SRO.E72.19.8)

BONTHRON, JOHN, b. 1789 Fife, sh. 22 Apr. 1817, fr. Fife to Philadelphia, nat. 2 June 1828 Washington, D.C.

BORTHWICK, JOHN, tr. 1720s, sett. Rappahannock River, Va. (SRO.GD24.1.464)

BOSTON, ..., sett. Accomack Co, Va, pre 1649. (CF.3.54)

BOSTON, HENRY, res. Ettrick , Selkirkshire, sh. 1640, m. Ann -, fa. of Isaac, sett. Somerset Co, Md, d. 1670. (BLG.2572)

BOTTOMLEY, JOSEPH, b. 1758, sett. Berkeley Co, Va. (VSA.24296)

BOURMAN, JAMES, b. 1754, surgeon, sh. Jan. 1775, fr. London to Md., on *Baltimore*. (PRO.T47.9/11)

BOW, JAMES, Jacobite, tr. 28 July 1716, fr. Liverpool to Va on *Godspeed*, arr. Md. Oct. 1716. (SPC.1716.310)(CTB31.209)(HM388)

BOWER, BARTHOLEMEW, res. Haddington, East Lothian, sett. Petersburg, Va, d. Apr. 1797. (VaGaz.2.5.1797)

BOWER, JOHN, tailor, res. Glasgow, Jacobite, tr. 24 Feb. 1747, fr. Liverpool to Va., on *Gildart*, arr. Port North Potomac, Md, 5 Aug. 1747. (P.2.44)(PRO.T1.328)

BOWIE, JOHN, b. 1688, sh. 1705, sett. Nottingham, Prince George Co , Va., m. Mary Mulliken 1707, fa. John , Eleanor, James, Allen, William, Thomas and Mary, d. Apr. 1759. (CF.7.91)(BLG2573)

BOWIE, JOHN, sh. 1740, sett. Caroline Co, Va. (WMQ2.22.345)

BOWIE, JOHN, clergyman, edu. Marischal College, Aberdeen, 1770, sh. 1771, sett. St George's, Md. (FPA.21.302)

BOWIE, ROBERT, b. 1733, servant, res. Strathbogie, Aberdeenshire, Jacobite, tr. 22 Apr. 1747, fr. Liverpool to Va., on *Johnson*, arr. Port Oxford, Md, 5 Aug. 1747. (P.2.46)(MR127)(PRO.T1.328)

BOWIE, ROBERT, b. 1700s, s. of Rev. Robert Bowie and Margaret Campbell, res. Rattray, Perthshire, surgeon, sett. Va. (F.4.171)

BOWLES, GEORGE, nat. 25 Sep. 1787 Norfolk, Va.

BOWMAN, DAVID, res. Kirkcaldy, Fife, m. Katherine -, planter, sett. Accomack Co, Va., d. 1785, pro. 28 Feb. 1786 Accomack Co, Va.

BOWMAN, JAMES OSWALD, s. of David Bowman, res. Kirkcaldy, Fife, sett. Georgetown, Md, pre 1796. (SRO.SH24.2.1796)

BOWMAN SAMUEL, b. 10 June 1681 Whitehaven, Cumberland, mariner, res. Glasgow, d. 18 June 1742 King George Co, Va. (King George g/s)

BOYD, ADAM, nat. 29 Aug. 1805 Norfolk, Va.

BOYD, ALEXANDER, sett. Northumberland Co, Va, d. 1755, pro. 9 Sep. 1755 Northumberland Co.

BOYD, ALEXANDER, s. of Robert Boyd, merchant and planter, res. Dunlop, Ayrshire, sett. Mecklenburg, Va. 1765, m. Anne Simpson. (VMHB.2)

BOYD, ANDREW, clergyman, sh. 1709 to Va. (EMA16)

BOYD, ANDREW, merchant, sett. Antigua and Va. pre 1765. (SRO.CS16.1.122)

BOYD, DAVID, res. Wigtown, sett. St Stephen's, Northumberland Co, Va., d. 1781, pro.10 Dec. 1781 Williamsburg, Va. (WMQ.7.126)

BOYD, JAMES, s. of John Boyd of Trochrig, Dailly, Ayrshire, m. Betty -, sett. King and Queen Co, Va, d. pre 1796. (SRO.RD5.239.415) (HAF.1.395)

BOYD, JOHN, s. of Rev. Boyd, res. Glasgow, merchant, sett. Richmond, Va. pre 1790. (DU.23g\11.5.33)

BOYD, JOHN, b. 1791, bottle porter, sett. Baltimore. (NA.M432/277-99)

BOYD, ROBERT, b. 27 Aug. 1745, s. of Rev. Andrew Boyd and Margaret Boyd, res. Twynholm, Kirkcudbrightshire, merchant, sett. Va., pro. Oct. 1783 Edinburgh. (SRO.CC8.8.126)(F.2.429)

BOYD, R., b. 1804, clerk, arr. Baltimore 1826. (NA.M596)

BOYD, ROBERT, b. 1801, sawyer, sett. Washington, DC, m. Jane -, fa. of John, Robert, Margaret, Sarah, Mary and Janet. (NA.M432\56.7)

BOYD, SPENCER, s. of James Boyd, physician and merchant, sett. West Point, King and Queen Co, Va, m. Lucy -, fa. James, Spencer, Robert, William and Julia, pro. 10 May 1779 Williamsburg Va .   (SRO.RD2.233\1.108)(SRO.GD1.26.60)(HAF.1.395) (SRO.CS16.1.168)

BOYLE, ALEXANDER, Jacobite, tr. 31 July 1716, fr. Liverpool to Va., on *Anne*. (SPC.1716.310)(CTB.31.209)

BRADEY, JOHN, b. 1752, sett. Westmoreland Co, Va. (VSA.23816)

BRAIDFOOT, WILLIAM JOHN, clergyman, m. - Mosely, sett. Portsmouth, Norfolk, Va. 1774, d. Portsmouth, Va. 1785. (EMA16)

BRAND, JAMES, Jacobite, tr. 24 Feb. 1747, fr. Liverpool to Va., on *Gildart*, arr. Port North Potomac, Md, 5 Aug. 1747. (PRO.T1.328)

BRAND, THOMAS, sett. Va. 1746, fa. of Thomas. (CAG.1.886)

BRANDER, ALEXANDER, b. 1800, merchant, fa. of Margaret, Isabella and Cara, sett. Petersburg, Va.   (NA.M932\982)

BRANDER, JAMES S., b. 31 Dec. 1795 , res. Inverness, sh. 1810, merchant, sett. Petersburg, Va, and N.Y., m. Harriet McCulloch 1820, d. 13 Feb. 1876 (ANY2.184)

BRANDER, JOHN, res. Elgin, Morayshire, sett. Bedford Co, Va., pro. 28 July 1778 Bedford Co.   (Bedford Wills1.309)

BRECHIN, JAMES, clergyman, sh. 1702, sett. Va. 1705-1719. (EMA16)(SNQ.1.153)

BRECKENRIDGE, HUGH HENRY, b. 1748, res, Campbelltown, Argyllshire, sh. 1753, sett. York Co, Pa, teacher, edu. Princeton Uni., sett. Md., d. Pa. 1816. (DAB.2.544)

BREEDING, ANDREW, b. 1664, s. of Thomas Breeding, sh. June 1684, fr. London to Md., on *Brothers Adventure*. (CLRO\AIA)

BRENDAN, JOHN, Jacobite, tr. 24 May 1716, fr. Liverpool to Md, on *Friendship*, arr. Md. Aug. 1716.   (SPC.1716.311)(CTB.31.207) (HM387)

BRIDEN, JOHN, res. Waumphrey, Moffat, Dumfriesshire, d. 1755 Va. (VaGaz26.9.1755)

BRISCOE, ELEANOR, da. of John Briscoe, res. Charles Co, Md, m. James Buchanan of Cattar, Dunbartonshire, pre 1769. (SRO.RS10.10.218)

BRITTEN, JOHN, b. 1805, sh. 1827, fr. Glasgow to Va., nat. 20 May 1833 Norfolk, Va.

BROADWATER, CHARLES, b. 1719, m. Ann Amelia Pierson, sett. Fairfax Co, Va pre 1767, d. 1806. (RAV14)

BROCKETT, ROBERT, s. of Robert Brockett, res. Lanarkshire, brickmaker, sh. 1785, sett. Alexandria, Va., fa. of Robert, d. 1829. (VMHB.

BRODIE, JOHN, b. 1727, servant, Jacobite, tr. 24 Feb. 1747, fr. Liverpool to Va., on *Gildart*, arr. Port North Potomac, Md, 5 Aug. 1747. (PRO.T1.328)

BRODY, ..., clergyman, sh. 1709 to Va. (EMA16)

BROWN, ABEL, sh. 1665, fr. Dumfries to Md, sett. Anne Arundel Co, Md, colonial official, fa. of Robert, d. 1702. (CF.1.46)

BROWN, ALEXANDER, s. of Thomas Brown, merchant, res. Md., burgess of Glasgow 1708. (BGBG280)

BROWN, ALEXANDER, b. 1781, res. Edinburgh, clerk, arr. Nov. 1799, sett. City Point, Petersburg, Va. (VSA. Aliens 1799)

BROWN, ALEXANDER, b. 1796, farmer, sett. Nelson Co, Va., m. Lucy -. (NA.M932\982)

BROWN, ANDREW, b. 1727, farmer, res. Dunnichen, Angus, Jacobite, tr. 24 Feb. 1747, fr. Liverpool to Va., on *Gildart*, arr. Port North Potomac, Md, 5 Aug. 1747. (P.2.52)(PRO.T1.328)

BROWN, CHARLES, tr. 1775, fr. Greenock to Va., on *Rainbow*, arr. Port Hampton, Va, 3 May 1775. (SRO.JC27.10.3)

BROWN, DAVID, edu. Glasgow Uni., sett. Somerset Co, Md, d. 1697, pro. 19 July 1697 Md. (MSA.MdWill.6.150)(SRO.RH1.2.488)

BROWN, DAVID, b. 1790, blacksmith, sett. Baltimore. (NA.M432\277-99)

BROWN, FRANCES, b. 1713, da. of Dr Gustavus Brown, res. Dalkeith, Midlothian, m. Rev. John Moncure, sett. Stafford Co, Va., d. 1792. (Aquia g\s)

BROWN, GEORGE, ship's surgeon, sett. Md. 1708, d. 1762. (SA178)

BROWN, GEORGE, merchant, sett. Norfolk, Va, pre 1766. (SRO.CS16.1.125)

BROWN, GEORGE, b. 1783, sh. pre 1810, sett. Baltimore, m. Jane -, fa. Ellen, George, John, James and Joseph. (NA.M432/277-99)

BROWN, GUSTAVUS, b. 10 Apr. 1689, s. of Gustavus Brown and Jane Mitchelson, physician, sett. Md. May 1708, m. (1) Frances Fowke 1710, (2) Margaret Boyd, fa. of Gustavus, Frances, Sarah, Mary, Christian, Gustavus, Elizabeth, Richard, Jane, Cecilia, Ann, and Margaret, d. Apr. 1762 Portobacco, Charles Co, Md.
(VG.147)(SRO.RD4.198.240)(MSA.MdWill.31.633)(SRO.SH.4.12.1792)

BROWN, JAMES, s. of James Brown, res.Dumfries, Dumfriesshire, sh. pre 1665, sett. Anne Arundel Co, Md. (CF.6.46)

BROWN, JAMES, res. Chapelton of Garioch, Aberdeenshire, sett. Va or Md 1763. (MdGaz.24.10.1771)

BROWN, JAMES, clergyman, edu. St Andrews Uni., sett. Va. 1769-74, .sett. Ga. 1779-81, Loyalist. (PRO.AO13.3486)

BROWN, JAMES MURRAY, b. 6 Apr. 1767, s. of Rev. Samuel Brown and Margaret Smith, res. Kilmabreck, Kirkcudbrightshire, sh. pre 1800, sett. Va., d. 23 Apr. 1824. (F.2.368)(BM.16.127)

BROWN, JOAN, res. Edinburgh, tr. 1696, fr. Newhaven, Midlothian, to Va. (SRO.RH15.14.58)

BROWN, JOHN, merchant, sett. Norfolk, Va., Loyalist, sett. N.S. 1783. (PRO.AO13.27.426)(LNS157)

BROWN, JOHN, Jacobite, tr. 29 June 1716, fr. Liverpool to Va or Jamaica, on *Elizabeth and Anne.* (SPC.1716.310)(CTB.31.208) (VSP.1.186)

BROWN, JOHN, res. Coldstream, Berwickshire, physician, sett. Williamsburg, Va., fa. of Charles and Robert, d. 1727, pro. 20 Aug. 1730 Edinburgh.
(SRO.CC8.8.93)(WMQ.6.253)(SRO.SH.5.10.1731)

BROWN, JOHN, b. 1703, res. Kirkbean, Galloway, sh. Aug. 1718, fr. London to Md. (CLRO/AIA)

BROWN, JOHN, merchant and shipwright, sett. Va. 1763, Loyalist, sett. Stenton, East Lothian. (PRO.AO12.100.213)(PRO.AO12.101.224) (PRO.AO13.27.436)

BROWN, JOHN, b. 1759, sett. Berkeley Co, Va, pre 1781. (VSA.24296)

BROWN, JOHN, res. Netherwood, Dumfriesshire, sett. Richmond, Va., d. 25 Dec. 1822. (EA.6182.95)

BROWNE, JOHN, Jacobite, tr. 31 July 1716, fr. Liverpool to Va, on *Anne.* (SPC.1716.310)(CTB.31.209)

BROWN, JOHN, (alias George Robertson), s. of James Brown and Margaret Burnie, Kirkcudbright, fa. of Irving and John, pro. 3 May 1824 Lynchburg, Va.

BROWN, JOHN, b. 1728, res. Leith, Midlothian, runaway fr *Berry*, Va, Mar. 1752. (Va.Gaz.3.1752)

BROWN, MARGARET, b. 1664, res. Coldstream, Berwickshire, m. Dr John Brown, sett. Williamsburg, Va., d. 22 Aug. 1720. (Bruton g/s)

BROWN, MARGARET, res. Glasgow, m. William Skirvin, sett. Somerset Co, Md., pro. 21 Feb. 1721 Md.

BROWNE, MARK, Jacobite, tr. 31 July 1716, fr. Liverpool to Va., on *Anne* (SPC.1716.310)(CTB.31.209)

BROWNE, NINIAN, Jacobite, tr. 28 July 1716, fr. Liverpool to Va, on *Godspeed*, arr. Md. Oct. 1716. (SPC.1716.310)(CTB.31.209) (HM389)

BROWN, ROBERT, b. 1786, stonecutter, sh. Sep. 1810, fr. Scotland to N.Y., nat. 13 Dec. 1823 Washington, D.C.

BROWN, ROBERT, physician, sett. Richmond, Va, pro. 1785 Edinburgh. (SRO.CC5.21.5)

BROWN, ROBERT, b. 1784, stonecutter, m. M. -, fa. of James etc., sh. Sept. 1810, sett. Washington D.C., nat. Washington 1823. (NA.M432/56-7)

BROWN, R., arr. Baltimore 1822. (NA.M596)

BROWN, Samuel, s. of James Brown, sh. pre 1665, fr. Dumfries, sett. Anne Arundel Co, Md, colonial official, m. Mary -, fa. of Thomas, Abel, Elizabeth and Mary, d. 1715. (CF.6.46)

BROWN, THOMAS, merchant, sh. 1770, sett. King and Queen Co, Va, Loyalist, sett. Fenwick, Ayrshire, 1782. (SRO.CS17.1.1) (SRO.RD2.233.108)

BROWN, WILLIAM, shoemaker, sh. 1714, fr. Glasgow to Potomac River, on *American Merchant*. (TM202)

BROWN, WILLIAM, s. of George Brown, sh. 1740, sett. Norfolk, Va., m. Janetta McAdam 1771, fa. Edwin etc., d. 1797. (BLG2582)

BROWN, WILLIAM, b. 1733, cooper, res. Edinburgh, sh. Apr. 1751, fr. London to Va. (CLRO/AIA)

BROWN, WILLIAM, soldier, fraudster, res. Aberdeen, tr. 1772, on *Betsy*, arr. Port of James River, Va, 29 Apr. 1772. (SRO.JC27.10.3) (AJ1238)

BROWN, WILLIAM, b. 1748, s. of Rev. Richard Brown, res. Haddington, East Lothian, physician, edu. Edinburgh Uni. 1770, sett. Alexandria, Va, d. 1792. (WMQ.2.20.257)

BROWN, WILLIAM, s. of James and Mary Brown, res. Kirkcudbright, d. 1811 Richmond, Va. (NGSL.65.210)

BRUCE, ALEXANDER, Jacobite, tr. 29 June 1716, fr. Liverpool to Va., on *Elizabeth and Anne*, arr. Va. (SPC.1716.310)(CTB.31.208) (VSP.1.185)

BRUCE, ALEXANDER, b. 1786, cooper, sett. Culpepper Co, Va. (NA.M932/982)

BRUCE, ANDREW, s. of Charles Bruce, res. Edinburgh, sett. Alleghany Co, Md, 1795. (SRO.RD3.276.1090)

BRUCE, CHARLES, b. 1733, sett. Frederick Co, Va, pre 1756, militiaman in Va. Regt. (VMHB.1/2)(L)

BRUCE, CHARLES, planter, sett. Albemarle Co, Va, pre 1756, militiaman in Va. Regt. (VMHB.1/2)(L)

BRUCE, CHARLES KEY, res. Edinburgh, sett. Richmond Co, N.Y., pro. 11 Mar. 1829 Baltimore.

BRUCE, GEORGE, sett. Northern Neck, Va, 1650, m. Elizabeth Pannill, fa. of Charles. (CAG.1.506)

BRUCE, JAMES, b. 1748, shoemaker, runaway Portsmouth, Va, 1772. (VaGaz.5.3.1772)

BRUCE, JAMES, seaman, runaway King and Queen Co, Va, 1772. (VaGaz.23.7.1772)

BRUCE, JOHN, res. Clackmannanshire, sh. 1665, sett. Md. (CAG.1.906)

BRUCE, JOHN, schoolmaster, edu. Marischal College, Aberdeen, sh. pre 1774, sett. Norfolk, Va. (EMA17)(LAM\FUL.23)

BRUCE, JOHN, b. 1793, farmer, sett. Winchester, Frederick, Co Va. (NA.M432\56-7)

BRUCE, MICHAEL, tr. July 1668, to Barbados or Va. (PC.2.478)

BRUCE, NORMAN, s. of Charles Bruce, res. Edinburgh, sh. pre 1785, sett. Washington Co, Md. (SRO.RD4.239.31)

BRUCE, PETER, b. 12 Mar. 1758, s. of William Bruce, res. Inverurie, Aberdeenshire, merchant, sh. 1770, sett. N.Y., m. Ann Langley, Va. 6 July 1786, d. 21 Dec. 1796. (ANY.I.228)

BRUCE, ROBERT, Jacobite, tr. 29 June 1716, fr. Liverpool to Va, on *Elizabeth and Anne*, arr. Va. (SPC.1716.310)(CTB.31.208)(VSP.1.185)

BRUCE, ROBERT, Jacobite, tr. 31 July 1716, fr. Liverpool to Va, on *Anne*. (SPC.1716.310)(CTB.31.209)

BRUCE, ROBERT, b. 13 Feb. 1749, s. of William Bruce, Inverurie, Aberdeenshire, merchant, sh. 1768, fr. Aberdeen to Va, sett. Norfolk, Va, m. Mary Langley, d. 28 Nov. 1796 N.Y. (ANY.I.160)

BRUCE, Mrs SELKRIG, wid. of Robert Dods of Prora, res. East .Lothian, d. 24 Apr. 1825 New Windsor, Md. (EA1825)

BRUCE, WILLIAM, s. of Charles Bruce, res. Edinburgh, sett. Washington Co, Md. pre 1785. (SRO.RD4.239.31)

BRUCE, WILLIAM, nat. 30 July 1823 Norfolk, Va.

BRYCE, ARCHIBALD, res. Glasgow, factor, sh. pre 1776, sett. Richmond, Va. (SRA.B10.12.4)

BRYCE, JOHN, res. Cambusnethan, Lanarkshire, mealmaker, Covenanter, tr. 18 June 1668, fr. Leith, Midlothian to Va, on *Convertin*. (PC.2.534)

BRYDEN, JAMES, b. 1751, innkeeper, sh. pre 1786, sett. Baltimore, coffee-house keeper N.Y. 1808, d. Apr. 1820 Baltimore. (ANY.2.8)

BRYDIE, CHARLES, s. of Charles Brydie, res. New Deer, Aberdeenshire, thief, tr. 22 May 1752, fr. Aberdeen to Va., on *Jean and Elizabeth of Aberdeen*. (AJ227)

BRYDIE, WILLIAM NAPIER, sett. Richmond, Va, pre 1816. (SRO.RD5.123.124)

BRYSON, ROBERT, b. 1750, coppersmith, sett. Frederick Co, Va, pre 1781. (VSL.Acc24296)

BUCHAN, JAMES, b. 1798, res. Perthshire, sh. 225 Dec. 1827, fr. Liverpool to Baltimore, sett. Va., nat. 30 May 1828 Eastern District, Va. (US D\C RB5.602)

BUCHAN, ROBERT, clergyman, edu. Edinburgh Uni. 1770, sh. 1772, sett. Va. (EMA17)(FPA310)

BUCHANAN, ALEXANDER, b. 1728, res. Auchleishie, Callander, Stirlingshire, Jacobite, tr. 22 Apr. 1747, fr. Liverpool to Va., on *Johnson*, arr. Port Oxford, Md, 5 Aug. 1747. (P.2.58)(MR67)(PRO.T1.328)

BUCHANAN, ALEXANDER, b. 1795, farmer, res, Glasgow, sett. Richmond, Va, nat. 2 Mar. 1811 Richmond. (US.D/C.1811)

BUCHANAN, ANDREW, b. 23 Nov. 1725, s. of George Buchanan and Christian Mitchell, merchant, res. Glasgow, sett. Va. pre 1776. (SRO.CS16.1.170)

BUCHANAN, ARCHIBALD, sett. Baltimore pre 1704, m. Mary Preble 9 Apr. 1705, d. 2 Mar. 1729.

BUCHANAN of DRUMHEAD, ARCHIBALD, merchant, res. Dunbartonshire, sh. pre 1751, sett. Williamsburg and Norfolk, Va. (SRO.RS10.8.250)

BUCHANAN, ARCHIBALD, s. of Archibald Buchanan of Drumhead and Janet Buchanan, merchant, res. Glasgow, sh. pre 1757, sett. Silverbank, Prince Edward Co, Va. (SRO.RS10.9.84)

BUCHANAN, ARCHIBALD, sett. Baltimore, Md, d. pre 1786, pro. 1786 PCC.

BUCHANAN, ARCHIBALD, b. 1790, res. Argyllshire, nat. 18 Mar 1823 Norfolk, Va.

BUCHANAN, DAVID, b. 10 Dec. 1760, s. of George Buchanan and Lilias Dunlop, merchant, edu. Glasgow Uni., sett. Va., d. 20 May 1827 Glasgow. (MAGU100)

BUCHANAN, GEORGE, b. 1697, physician, res. Dunbartonshire, sh. pre 1723, sett. Baltimore Co, Md, d. 1750. (SRO.RS10.7.275)(SA178)

BUCHANAN, GEORGE, merchant, res. Glasgow, sett. Va. pre 1773. (SRO.CS16.1.154)

BUCHANAN, JAMES, b. 1736, shoemaker, militiaman in Va. Regt. 1756. (VMHB.1/2)(L)

BUCHANAN, JAMES, s. of Archibald Buchanan of Drumhead, merchant, res. Dunbartonshire, sett. Falmouth, Rappahannock River, Va, pre 1759. (SRO.RS10.9.156)(SRO.SH16.3.1759)

BUCHANAN, JAMES, s. of James Buchanan of Gyleston, merchant, res. Dunbartonshire, sh. pre 1756, sett. Falmouth, Va. (SRO.RS10.9.40)

BUCHANAN, JAMES, assistant storekeeper, sett. Dumfries, Va, pre 1776, sh. 1777, fr. N.Y. to Glasgow, on *Betsey*. (SFV.229/233)

BUCHANAN, JOHN, b. 1725, servant, res, Auchterarder, Perthshire, Jacobite, tr. 24 Feb. 1747, fr. Liverpool to Va, on *Gildart*, arr. Port North Potomac, Md, 5 Aug. 1747. (P.2.60)(MR69)(PRO.T1.328)

BUCHANAN, JOHN, b. 1743, clergyman, edu. Edinburgh Uni. 1774, res. Dumfriesshire, sh. 1775 to Va., sett. Lexington ph. and Henrico ph, d. 1822 Richmond, Va. (FPA311)(EMA17)(OD20)

BUCHANAN, JOHN, b. 1744, sett. Caroline Co, Va. (VSL23816)

BUCHANAN, MARGARET, da. of John Buchanan of Glens, sh. pre 1768, sett. Va., m. Thomas Peters. (CPD540)

BUCHANAN, NEIL, merchant, sett. Va. pre 1778. (SRO.CS16.1.173)

BUCHANAN, ROBERT, merchant, res. Glasgow, sh. 1760, sett. Annapolis, Md, Loyalist. (ANY.I.262)

BUCHANAN, WILLIAM, res. Glasgow, sett. Petersburg, Va, pre 1776, Loyalist. (PRO.AO13.4.195)

BULLOCK, WILLIAM, sh. 2 Nov. 1674, to St Mary's Co, Md, on *Bachelor of Bristol*. (MSA.ESB.152)

BUNTINE, NICOL, merchant, res. Beith, Ayrshire, sett. Va., d. 1740 Beith. (HAF.1.294)

BURCH, RICHARD, Jacobite, tr. 28 July 1716, fr. Liverpool to Va. on *Godspeed,* arr. Md. Oct. 1716. (SPC.1716.310)(CTB.31.209) (HM389)

BURGESS, WILLIAM, b. 1795, sh. pre 1827, m. Elizabeth -, fa. of James, John and Amelia, sett. Braxton Co, Va. (NA.M932/982)

BURKE, THOMAS, b. 1801, nat. 27 July 1829 Norfolk City, Va.

BURN, JAMES, s. of William Burn, res. Edinburgh, sett. Baltimore pre 1782, m. Janet Scotland. (SRO.RD3.294.274)(SRO.SH12.8.1802)

BURNE, JOHN, Jacobite, tr. 29 June 1716, fr. Liverpool to Va. or Jamaica, on *Elizabeth and Anne*, arr. Va. 1716. (SPC.1716.310)(CTB.31.208)(VSP.1.186)

BURNET, ALEXANDER, b. 1749, clerk book-keeper, res. Edinburgh, sh. 26 Jan 1774, fr. London to Hampton, Va, on *Planter*, arr. 28 Apr. 1774. (PRO.T47.9/11)

BURNET, GEORGE, tr. Aug. 1751, fr. Aberdeen to Va. (AJ193)

BURNETT, JOHN, b. 1611, merchant, res. Aberdeen, sh. 24 Oct. 1635, fr. London to Va., on *Abraham of London*. (PRO.E157.20) (SPC.1638.277)

BURNETT, JOHN, b. 1719, miller, res. Ballandarg, Kirriemuir, Angus, Jacobite, tr. 22 Apr. 1747, fr. Liverpool to Va, on *Johnson*, arr. Port Oxford, Md, 5 Aug. 1747. (P.2.64)(PRO.T1.328)(MR96)

BURNETT, -, clergyman, sh. 1700 to Va. (EMA18)

BURNS, GEORGE, nat. 2 June 1794 Princess Anne Co, Va. (K3.369)

BURRIER, PETER, b. 1792, farmer, arr. Baltimore 1826. (NA.M596)

BURTON, ROBERT, b. 1758, res. Haddington, East Lothian, factor, sett. Richmond, Va. pre 1776, Loyalist, nat. 17 Dec. 1798 Washington, D.C., d. 16 May 1837. (PRO.AO13.33.153)(SRO.RD3.309.682) (US.D/C.1798.5)(SRO.SC70.1.58)

BURTON, WILLIAM, s. of William Burton, res. Port Glasgow, sett. James River, Va, pre 1756. (SRO.CS16.1.95)

BUTTER, THOMAS, Jacobite, tr. 24 May 1716, fr. Liverpool to Md, on *Friendship*, arr. Md Aug. 1716. (SPC.1716.311)(HM387)

CAIRNS, ROBERT, b. 1805, laborer, sh. pre 1828, fa. of Martha, sett. Petersburg, Dinwiddie Co, Va. (NA.M932/982)

CALDERHEAD, THOMAS, merchant, res. Glasgow, sett. Norfolk, Va, 1775, Loyalist. (PRO.AO13.2.355)

CALDERHEAD, WILLIAM, merchant, res. Glasgow, sett. Norfolk, Va, pro 1788 Edinburgh. (PRO.AO13.2.355)(SRO.CC8.8.127)

CALDWELL, DAVID, runaway fr. Prince William, Cumberland Town, Panmunkey River, Va, 1751. (VaGaz.4.1751)

CALLENDAR, JAMES THOMSON, b. 1758, sh. 1793, journalist, d. Richmond, Va, 17 Apr 1803. (VMHB.84.434)(GM.73.882)

CALLENDAR, WILLIAM, res. Edinburgh (?), gentleman's servant, sett. Va, fa. of Mary. (Edinburgh OPR/marriages1773)

CALLUM, ROBERT, merchant, sett. Raleigh, N.C., d. Petersburg, Va, 1817. (Raleigh Minerva 31.10.1817)

CAMERON, DONALD, Jacobite, tr. 22 Apr. 1747, fr. Liverpool to Va, on *Johnson,* arr. Port Oxford, Md, 5 Aug. 1747. (PRO.T1.328)

CAMERON, DOUGALL, res. Inverness, Jacobite, tr. 24 Feb. 1747, fr. Liverpool to Va., on *Gildart,* arr. Port North Potomac, Md, 5 Aug. 1747. (P.2.76)(MR34)(PRO.T1.328)

CAMERON, DUNCAN, Jacobite, tr. 22 Apr. 1747, fr. Liverpool to Va, on *Johnson,* arr. Port North Potomac, Md, 5 Aug. 1747. (PRO.T1.328)

CAMERON, EWEN, b. 23 Feb. 1768, s. of Duncan Cameron and Margaret Bain, res. Ferintosh, Ross and Cromarty, sett. Va 1785, m. Mary Bulford, fa. of Margaret, John, Duncan, Granville, William and Donald, d. 28 Feb. 1846 Tenn. (CCAI)

CAMERON, JOHN, Jacobite, tr. 22 Apr. 1747, fr. Liverpool to Va, on *Johnson,* arr. Port Oxford, Md, 5 Aug. 1747. (PRO.T1.328)

CAMERON, JOHN, Jacobite, tr. 28 July 1716, fr. Liverpool to Va, on *Godspeed,* arr. Md Oct. 1716. (SPC.1716.310)(HM388)

CAMERON, JOHN, res. Ferintosh, Ross and Cromarty, clergyman, edu. Aberdeen Uni. 1767, sh. 1770, sett. Va, m. Ann Owen Nash pre 1777, fa. of Duncan, d. Cumberland ph, Lunenburg Co, Va,1815. (CAG.1.534)

CAMERON, MALCOM, res. Fort William, Invernessshire, Jacobite, tr. 24 Feb. 1747, fr. Liverpool to Va, on *Gildart,* arr. Port North Potomac, Md, 5 Aug. 1747. (P.2.84)(MR35)(PRO.T1.328)

CAMERON, WILLIAM, clergyman, sett. Manchester, Chesterfield Co, Va, 1790. (ANQ

CAMPBELL, ABSOLOM, b. 1735, sett. Baltimore, militiaman in Va. Regt. 1756. (VMHB.1/2)(L)

CAMPBELL, AENEAS, b. 1730, res. Kilberry, Argyllshire, sh. pre 1757. sett. Md, m. (1) Margaret Hickman (2) Mrs Henrietta Cheney, fa. of James, Aeneas, Hester, Lydia, Ann, Mary and Elizabeth, contractor, pro. 21 Apr. 1812 Montgomery Co, Md.

CAMPBELL, ALEXANDER, tailor, sh. 1714, fr. Glasgow to Potomac River, on *American Merchant.* (TM202)

CAMPBELL, ALEXANDER, Jacobite, tr. 22 Apr. 1747, fr. Liverpool to Va, on *Johnson,* arr. Port Oxford, Md, 5 Aug. 1747. (PRO.T1.328)

CAMPBELL, ALEXANDER, res, Claddie, Aberdeenshire, laborer, Jacobite, tr. 22 Apr. 1747, fr. Liverpool to Va, on *Johnson,* arr. Port Oxford, Md, 5 Aug. 1747. (PRO.T1.328)(MR96)

CAMPBELL, ALEXANDER, res. Glasgow, m. Ann Arthur, sh. pre 1757, sett. Falmouth, Prince George Co, Md. (SRO.RD3.224.480) (Prince Wm Co Deeds R154)

CAMPBELL, ARCHIBALD, s. of Alexander Campbell and Margaret Stewart, res. Kirnan, Kilmichael, Argyllshire, clergyman, edu. Marischal College, Aberdeen 1739-45, to Va, sett. Wilmington Co. 1754-74. (EMA18)(SCM.12.9)(SEV20)

CAMPBELL, ARCHIBALD, res. Greenock, Renfrewshire, cooper, sh. pre 1770, sett. Va. (SRO.CS16.1.141)

CAMPBELL, ARCHIBALD, physician, sett. Norfolk, Va, 1760, Loyalist, sett. Bermuda 1782. (WMQ.2.16.40)

CAMPBELL, ARCHIBALD, factor, sett. Leonardstown, Potomac, Md, 1775. (MSA.11.41)(MdHist Mag.44.247)

CAMPBELL, CHARLES, merchant, res. Ayr, sett. Va. pre 1752. (SRO.CS16.1.99)

CAMPBELL, COLIN, factor, res. Glasgow, sett. Va. pre 1775, Loyalist, sett. Penobscot, N.B., 1786. (PRO.AO13.22.403)

CAMPBELL, DANIEL, b. 1702, res. Dunrobin, Sutherlandshire, sh. Aug. 1720, fr. London to Md. (CLRO/AIA)

CAMPBELL, DANIEL, merchant, res. Glasgow, sett. Falmouth, King George Co, Va, pre 1770. (Prince Wm Co Deeds R154)

CAMPBELL, DANIEL, s. of Alexander Campbell, res. Kilbride, sh. 1 Jan. 1770, fr. Glasgow to Md, sett. Portobacco, Md. (SRA.TD180.20)(MHS.MS1301)

CAMPBELL, DONALD, b. 23 July 1730, s. of Lachlan and Martha Campbell, res. Lorine, Islay, Argyllshire, sh. to N.Y., army officer, d. Washington D.C. Mar. 1803. (ANY.I.5)

CAMPBELL, DOUGAL, b. 1726, carpenter, sett. Fort Cumberland, Md., militiaman in Va. Regt. 1756. (VMHB.1/2)(L)

CAMPBELL, GILBERT, sh. pre 1768, customs controller, sett. Potomac, Va. (SRO.CS16.1.134)

CAMPBELL, HUGH, s. of Sir Hugh Campbell of Casnock, merchant burgess, res. Edinburgh, sh. 1677 to Bermuda, sett. Norfolk, Va, 1688. (BS.28)

CAMPBELL, HUGH, b. 1731, sailor, sett. King William Co, Va, pre 1756, militiaman in Va. Regt. (VMHB.1/2)(L)

CAMPBELL, ISAAC, b. 1720, clergyman, edu. Glasgow Uni. 1734, sh. pre 1747, sett. Trinity, Newport, Charles Co, Md, m. Jean Brown, fa. William, Jean, Gustavus, James, John and Cecilia, d. 30 July 1784 Newport. (EMA18)(VG165)

CAMPBELL, JAMES, clergyman, sh. 1721 to Va. (EMA18)

CAMPBELL, JAMES, merchant, sett. Va. pre 1769. (SRO.CC9/vol.64.21.4.1769)

CAMPBELL, JAMES, b. 1712, runaway, King George Co, Va, 1738. (VaGaz.26.1.1738)

CAMPBELL, JAMES, b. 1738, sett. Stafford Co, Va, militiaman in Va. Regt. 1757. (VMHB.1/2)(L)

CAMPBELL, JAMES, res. Ardesier, Nairn, merchant, edu. King's College, Aberdeen, 1794, sett. Baltimore.   (KCA263)

CAMPBELL, JOEL, b. 1739, s. of Joel Campbell, res. Glasgow, sett. Amherst Co, Va., m. Nancy E. Mills, d, 1832. (CCS/USA)

CAMPBELL, JOHN, sh. 2 Nov. 1674, to St Mary's Co, Md, on *Bachelor of Bristol.* (MSA.ESB.152)

CAMPBELL, JOHN, b. 1723, sett. Talbot Co, Md., militiaman in Va Regt. (VMHB.1/2)(L)

CAMPBELL, JOHN, b. 1726, planter, sett. Alexandria, Va, militiaman in Va Regt (VMHB.1/2)(L)

CAMPBELL, JOHN, merchant, sh. 1760, to Va., sett. Bladensburg, Va, 1790. (SRO.CS238.misc26/1)(Letterbook 1760-64/Alexandria Lib.Va.)

CAMPBELL, JOHN, Jacobite, tr. 24 Feb. 1747, fr. Liverpool to Va, on *Gildart*, arr. Port North Potomac, Md, 5 Aug. 1747.   (PRO.T1.328)

CAMPBELL, JOHN, clergyman, edu. King's College, Aberdeen, 1771, sh. 1773 to Va, Loyalist, sett. Jamaica.   (EMA18)

CAMPBELL, JOHN, merchant, sett. Va. pre 1798.   (SRO.SH.16.11.1798)

CAMPBELL, JOHN, b. 1753, farmer, m. Janet -, fa. of Margaret, Samuel, William, Mary, John, Andrew and James, arr. Baltimore 1821 on *Pallas.* (NA.M596)

CAMPBELL, JOHN, b. 23 Apr. 1766, s. of Rev. Peter Campbell and Margaret Scott, res. Glassary, Argyllshire, merchant, sh. pre 1790, sett. Va, d. Dec. 1796. (F.4.7)(SRO.SH.26.6.1792)

CAMPBELL, JOHN, b. 1795, sh. pre 1826, sett. Baltimore, Md, constable, m. Elizabeth - , fa. of Susan, Ann and Mary. (NA.M432/277-99)

CAMPBELL, LACHLAN, merchant, res. Glasgow, sh. 1764, fr. Glasgow to Va., sett. Fredericksburg, Va, Loyalist.   (PRO.AO13.28.81)

CAMPBELL, MURDOCH, servant, sett. Winchester, Frederick Co, Va. Sep. 1773.   (Rec. Indent.Philadelphia 1773)

CAMPBELL, NEILL, sh. 1758 to Va.   (SRO.NRAS.0396)

CAMPBELL, PATRICK, b. 25 May 1707, s. of John Campbell and Isabel Stewart, res. Glenlochy, Kenmore, Perthshire, sh. pre 1750 to Va. (SG.8/1.10)

CAMPBELL, PETER, coppersmith, sh. 1714, fr. Glasgow to Potomac River, on *American Merchant.*   (TM202)

CAMPBELL, PETER, b. 1755, merchant, res. Glasgow, sh. pre 1775, fr. Glasgow to Va., sett. Prince George Co, Va. (SRA.CFI)

CAMPBELL, QUINTIN, b. Nov. 1774, s. of Rev. Campbell, res. Glencairn, Galloway, banker and insurer, sh. 1790, fr. Liverpool to Baltimore, d. Philadelphia 6 Apr. 1863. (AP141)

CAMPBELL, ROBERT, b. 1778, farmer, sh. pre 1809 to Pa., fa. of Mary and Ann, sett. Wood Co, Va. (NA.M932/982)

CAMPBELL, SAMUEL, b. 1790, m. Margaret -, sett. Baltimore. (NA.M432/277-99)

CAMPBELL, SAUNDERS, Jacobite, tr. 22 Apr. 1747, fr. Liverpool to Va., on *Johnson*, arr. Port Oxford, Md, 5 Aug. 1747. (PRO.T1.328)

CAMPBELL, THOMAS, b. 1 Feb. 1763, s. of Alexander Campbell, clergyman and teacher, edu. Glasgow Uni., d. Bethany, WVa, 4 Nov. 1854. (WA162)

CAMPBELL, WALTER, res. Dunbartonshire, sett. Dorchester Co, Md, pro. 27 Aug. 1736 Md. (MSA.Wills.21.870)

CAMPBELL, WALTER, sett. Brunswick and Lunenburg, Va, m. Tabitha -, :pro. 24 Sep. 1751 Brunswick Co, Va. (Brunswick Wills.3.33)

CAMPBELL, WILLIAM, merchant, sett. Accomack Co, Va, pro. 5 Feb. 1716 Accomack Co.

CAMPBELL, WILLIAM, s. of ... Campbell and Elizabeth Adair, merchant, res. Glasgow, d. Va. 1718, pro. Sep.1718 PCC.

CAMPBELL, WILLIAM, storekeper, sett. Westmoreland Co, Va. pre 1731. (SRO.GD.1.455)

CAMPBELL, WILLIAM, s. of Gillian Campbell, res. Kilmichael, Argyllshire, horsethief, tr. 1775, fr. Greenock to Va., on *Rainbow,* arr. Port Hampton ,Va   3 May 1775. (SRO.JC27.10.3)

CAMPBELL, ZACHARIAH, b. 9 Oct. 1740, s. of James Campbell and Mary Murdoch, merchant, res. Glasgow, sh. pre 1763, sett. Vienna, Md and Frederickburg, Va. (SRO.B10.15.6863)

CANE, HUGH, Jacobite, tr. 29 June 1716, fr. Liverpool to Va or Jamaica, on *Elizabeth and Anne*, arr. Va. 1716.   (SPC.1716.310) (CTB.31.208)(VSP.1.186)

CAPERTON, JOHN, sh. 1725 to N.Y., sett. New River, Va, m. Polly Thompson, fa. of Adam. (CAG.1.299)

CARGILL, WILLIAM, b. 13 May 1726, s. of James Cargill and Elizabeth Ramsay, tobacconist, res. Montrose, Angus, Jacobite, tr. 24 Feb. 1747, fr. Liverpool to Md., on *Gildart,* arr. Port North Potomac, Md, 5 Aug. 1747. (P.2.324/98)(PRO.T1.328)

CARLYLE, ALEXANDER, s. of Adam Carlyle and Grizel Menzies, merchant, res. Limekilns, Dumfriesshire, sett. Hopewell, Somerset Co, Md. pre 1712, m. Margaret McAlister 1720, fa. of Adam and John, d. 1726. (WMQ.1.18.208)(MSA.Md.Prov.Ct.12.297)

CARLYLE, JOHN, b. 6 Feb. 1720, s. of Alexander Carlyle, merchant, res. Dumfries, Dumfriesshire, sett. Alexandria ,Va., m. (1) Sarah Fairfax (2) Sybil West, d. 1780. (SRO.SC36.63.1)(SRO.RS10.16.31)(RAV19)

CARMICHAEL, JAMES, b. 1737, joiner, sett. Prince George Co, Va., militiaman in Va Regt 1757. (VMHB.1/2)(L)

CARMICHAEL, JAMES, s. of William and Martha Carmichael, res. Lanarkshire, sh. 1760, sett. Baltimore, Md. (SG.28.3.147)

CARMICHAEL, JOHN, b. 5 May 1740, s. of William and Martha Carmichael, res. Lanarkshire, sh. 1760, sett. Baltimore, Md, m. Esther Carfield. (SG.28.3.147)

CARMICHAEL, MARION, res. Edinburgh, tr. 1696, fr. Newhaven, Midlothian to Va. (SRO.RH15.14.58)

CARMICHAEL, PETER, s. of William and Martha Carmichael, res. Lanarkshire, sh. 1760, sett. Baltimore, Md. (SG28.3.147)

CARMICHAEL, ROBERT, merchant, res. Dunbartonshire, sh. pre 1770, sett. Va. (SRO.RS10.10.295)(SRA.CFI)

CARMICHAEL, WALTER, merchant, Md., m. Mary Dick, 21 June 1767. (Edinburgh OPR)

CARMICHAEL, WILLIAM, res. Edinburgh, sett. Queen Anne Co, Md, pre 1768, fa. of William. (SRO.RD4.239.716)(MSA.MdWill.37.130)

CARMICHAEL, -, m. Katherine -, fa. of Katherine Elizabeth and Anne, sett. Queen Ane Co, Chester River, Md, pre 1786. (SRO.RD4.239.714)

CARMONT, JOHN, shopkeeper, sett. Norfolk, Va, pre 1770. (PRO.AO12.102.152)

CARNEGIE, ALEXANDER, b. 16 Oct. 1705, s. of Robert Carnegie and Janet Blair, laborer, res. Arbroath, Angus, Jacobite, tr. 22 Apr. 1747, fr. Liverpool to Va., on *Johnson*, arr. Port Oxford, Md, 5 Aug. 1747. (P.2.100)(MR96)(PRO.T1.328)

CARNEGIE, JOHN, b. 1673, s. of David Carnegie, clergyman, edu. Glasgow Uni., Balliol College, and Aberdeen Uni., res. Aberdeen, sh. Aug. 1698, fr. Liverpool to Va, on *Loyalty,,* sett. St Mary's, Whitechapel, Lancaster Co, Va, 1700-06. (LRO.HQ325.2Fre)(WMQ.2.19.365)

CARNEY, JAMES, b. 1751, res. Aberdeenshire, stonemason, nat. 7 Dec. 1798 Richmond, Va. (US.D/C.1798.4)

CARR, ALEXANDER, thief, tr. 1764, on *Boyd,* arr. Norfolk, Va, 24 Aug. 1764. (SRO.JC27.10.3)

CARR, THOMAS, b. 1701, barber, sett. Hampshire Co ,Va, pre 1756, 'militiaman in Va. Regt. (VMHB.1/2)(L)

CARR, THOMAS, b. 1716, piper, militiaman in Va. Regt. 1756. (VMHB1/2)(L)

CARRIE, JOHN, pedlar, res. Arbroath, Angus, Jacobite, tr. 24 Feb. 1747, fr. Liverpool to Va., on Gildart, arr. Port North Potomac, Md, 5 Aug. 1747. (P.2.102)(PRO.T1.328)(MR96)

CARRICK, HUGH, sett. Augusta Co, Va. pre 1775, fa. of Walter. (CAG.1.663)

CARRUTHERS, ANDREW, b. 1800, farmer, sh. pre 1825, sett. Baltimore, Md, m. Isabel -, fa. of Isabel, Laura, Bethia, Andrew and Sydney. (NA.M432/277-99)

CARRY, JOHN, b. 1749, stonemason, res. Fife, sh. Dec. 1773, fr. London to Va, on Elizabeth. (PRO.T47.9/11)

CARTER, Col. RICHARD, res. Rappahannock Va., burgess of Glasgow, 11 Aug. 1718. (BGBG 337)

CARUS, CHRISTOPHER, Jacobite, tr. 29 June 1716, fr. Liverpool to Va or Jamaica, on Elizabeth and Anne, arr. Va 1716. (SPC.1716.310)(CTB.31.208)(VSP.1.185)

CASKIE, JAMES, b. 1788, bank officer, sett. Richmond, Va, m. Elizabeth -, fa. of Mary and Nancy. (NA.M932/982)

CASKIE, JOHN, b. 17 Feb. 1790, res. Ayrshire, sh. 1807, sett. Manchester, Va., d. 13 Sep. 1867 Richmond, Va. (Shockaehill g/s)

CASSELL, JOHN, b. 1805. mason, sett. Wood Co, Va., m. Martha -, fa. Hugh, Alexander, Robert, Elizabeth, Martia, Margaret and William. (NA.M932/982)

CATER, MARY, b. 1796, arr. Baltimore 1823. (NA.M596)

CAVAN, HENRY, nat. 25 July 1804 Norfolk City, Va.

CAVAN, JOHN, b. 1783, d. Norfolk, Va, 27 Sep. 1802. (Raleigh Register 12.10.1802)

CHALMERS, DONALD, merchant, res. Glasgow, sett. Va pre 1765. (SRO.CS16.1.125)

CHALMERS, GEORGE, civil servant, sett. Baltimore 1765, Loyalist, sett. Britain 1786. (N.Y.L:GeoChalmers pp)

CHALMERS, JAMES. sett. Kent Co, Md. 1760, Loyalist, sett. N.S. 1783. (MdMag,II.33.135)(LNS158)

CHALMERS, JOHN, merchant, sh. pre 1795, nat. Richmond, Va, 13 Nov. 1802. (VSP.9.331)

CHALMERS, PATRICK, Jacobite, tr. 31 July 1716, fr. Liverpool to Va, on Anne. (SPC.1716.310)(CTB.31.209)

CHALMERS, ROBERT, res. Leith, Midlothian, sett. Md 1763 (MSA,Prov.Ct.DD3.165)

CHALMERS, WILLIAM, gardener, res. Mearns, Jacobite, tr. 22 Apr. 1747, fr. Liverpool to Va., on *Johnson*, arr. Port Oxford, Md, 5 Aug. 1747. (P.2.110)(MR70(PRO.T1.328)

CHAMBERLAIN, WILLIAM, b. 1810, clerk, arr. Baltimore 1826. (NA.M596)

CHAMBERS, JOHN, Jacobite, tr. 28 July 1716, fr. Liverpool to Va, on *Godspeed* arr. Md Oct. 1716. (SPC.1716.310)(CTB.31.209) (HM388)(MSA.25.347)

CHAPMAN, JAMES, gardener, res. Durn, Banffshire, Jacobite, tr. 22 Apr. 1747, fr. Liverpool to Va., on *Johnson*, arr. Port Oxford, Md, 5 Aug. 1747. (P.2.110)(MR122)(PRO.SP136.102)

CHAPP, JAMES, b. 1726, smith, res. St Marnoch's, Banffshire, Jacobite, tr. 24 Feb. 1747, fr. Liverpool to Va., on *Gildart*, arr. Port North Potomac, Md, 5 Aug. 1747. (P.2.110)(MR328) (PRO.T1.328)

CHISHOLM, ADAM, Jacobite, tr. 29 June 1716, fr. Liverpool to Va or Jamaica, on *Elizabeth and Anne*. (SPC.1716.310)(CTB.31.208) (VSP.1.186)

CHISHOLM, WILLIAM, farmer and merchant, sett. Pittenweem, Norfolk, Va, 1754, Loyalist, sett. Bahamas 1779. (PRO.AO13.2.259)

CHISHOLM, WILLIAM, b. 1747, res. Strathdean, Invernessshire, sh. 1822, sett. Preston Co, WVa. (NGSQ.72.2.83)

CHRISTALL, WILLIAM, merchant, res. Kippen, Stirlingshire, sett. Va, d. 1751, pro. 30 Oct. 1751 Accomack Co, Va.

CHRISTIAN, GILBERT, b. 1677, sh. Wigtown to Ireland 1702, m. Margaret Richardson, sh. 1726, sett. Staunton, Va. (GKF125)

CHRISTIE, ADAM, tr. Feb. 1721 to Va. (SRO.HH11)

CHRISTIE, CHARLES, s. of - Christie and Katherine MacNiece, merchant, sett. Joppa, Baltimore Co, Md, d. 1763. (MSA.Wills.30.279) (MSA.ProvCtDeeds.DD3.165)

CHRISTIE, JAMES, b. 14 Apr. 1695, s. of James Christie and Margaret Walker, merchant, res. Stirling, sett. Baltimore, d. 7 Aug. 1745. (SHC.20)

CHRISTIE, JAMES, farmer, s. 1714, fr. Glasgow to Potomac River, on *American Merchant*. (TM202)

CHRISTIE, JAMES, b. 1714, linenweaver, Jacobite, tr. 24 Feb. 1747, fr. Liverpool to Va, on *Gildart*, arr. Port North Potomac, Md, 5 Aug. 1747. (P.2.114)(PRO.T1.328)

CHRISTIE, JOHN, b. 1785, farmer, sh. pr 1825, sett. Alleghany Co, Md, m. Hannah -, fa. of Mary. (NA.M432/277-99)

CHRISTIE, PETER, nat. 24 Jan. 1814 Norfolk City, Va.

CHRISTIE, ROBERT, ex Lord Provost of Glasgow, d. Md 17 Jan. 1780. (SM.62.333)

CHRISTIE, THOMAS, b. 12 Apr. 1752, s. of John Christie and Janet Clarkson, res. Hailes, Edinburgh, surgeon and physician, edu. Edinburgh Uni. 1774, sh. Feb. 1775, to Philadelphia, m. Mrs Hannah McDonald 1780, sett. Hanover Co, Va., d. 22 Feb. 1812 Hanovertown, Va. (ANY.I.274)(SM.74.479)(Hanover g/s)

CHRISTIE, WILLIAM, b. 1749, clergyman, res. Kincardineshire, sh. 1795, sett. Philadelphia and Winchester, Va., d. 21 Nov. 1823 N.J. (GMC59)

CLAPERTON, THOMAS, weaver, Fochabers, Morayshire, Jacobite, tr. 22 Apr. 1747, fr. Liverpool to Va, on *Johnson*, arr. Port Oxford , Md, 5 Aug. 1747. (P.2.116)(MR122)(PRO.T1.328)

CLARK, ALEXANDER, runaway, Gloucester Co, Va, 1752. (VaGaz10.4.1752)

CLARK, ALEXANDER, m. Helen -, sett. Norfolk, Va, pre 1814. (SRO.RD5.70.586)

CLARK, ANDREW, b. 1781, grocer, m. Mary -, sett. Richmond, Henrico Co, Va. (NA.M932/982)

CLARKE, CHARLES, b. 1784, cabinetmaker, m. Dinah -, sett. Norfolk, Va, nat. 31 Oct. 1840 Norfolk City. (NA.M932/982)

CLARK, DUNCAN, Jacobite, tr. 29 June 1716, fr. Liverpool to Va or Jamaica, on *Elizabeth and Anne*, arr. York, Va, 1716. (SPC.1716.310)(CTB.31.208)(VSP.1.185)

CLARKE, GEORGE, b. 1784, ship's carpenter, sh. pre 1820, m. Ann -, fa. Tarleton, and Elizabeth, sett. Norfolk, Va, nat. 31 Oct. 1840. (NA.M932/982)

CLARK, HUGH, b. 1790, farmer, m. Mary -, sett. Ohio Co, Va. (NA.M932/982)

CLARK, JAMES, merchant, res. Glasgow, sh. pre 1754, sett. Va. (SRA.B10.15.6653)

CLARK, JAMES A., sh. pre 1818, sett. Washington, DC, 1826, nat. 29 Mar. 1829 Washington, DC.

CLARK, JOHN, woolcomber, res. Aberdeen, murderer, tr. 1772, fr. Glasgow to Va, on *Brilliant*, arr. Port Hampton, Va, 7 Oct. 1772. (AJ1272)(SRO.JC27.10.3)

CLARKE, JOHN, sett. Richmond, Va. pro. 10 June 1799 Richmond, Va.

CLARK, THOMAS, s. of Thomas Clark, res. Newcastle, Northumberland, thief, tr. 28 Nov. 1704, fr. Leith to Md. (SRO.PC2.28.307)

CLARK, WILLIAM, b. 1770, farmer, sett. Ohio Co, Va. (NA.M932/982)

CLEPHANE, DAVID, clergyman, edu. St Andrews Uni. 1694/1703, sh. 1710 to Va. (EMA20)

CLEPHANE, JAMES, b. 20 Oct. 1790, s. of Thomas Clephane, res. Fife, sh. July 1817, fr. Kirkcaldy, Fife, to Norfolk, Va, sett. Washington, D.C, m. Ann Ogilvie, fa. of Lewis, nat. 10 Dec. 1833 Washington D.C. (BLG2621)

CLERK, ALEXANDER, runaway, Gloucester Co, Va. 1752. (VaGaz10.4.1752)

CLEZY, GEORGE, b. 1786, machinist, sh. pre 1828, sett. Baltimore, m. Margaret -, fa. of Margaret, William and James. (NA.M432/277-99)

CLINDINNING, THOMAS, res. Glasgow, sett. Baltimore, d. pre 1762, pro. 5 Feb. 1762 Baltimore. (MSA.Will.31.570)

CLOSE, WILLIAM, b. 1795, miner, m. Sarah -, fa. of James, William, Alexander and Maria, sett. Alleghany Co, Md. (NA.M432/277-99)

COATS, JAMES, sh. pre 1791, sett. Port Royal, Va. (OD123)

COBB, JOSEPH, b. 1588, sh. 1613 to Va. (CAG.1.932)

COBIN, ROBERT, Jacobite, tr. 29 June 1716, fr. Liverpool to Va or Jamaica, on *Elizabeth and Anne*. (CTB.31.208)

COCHRANE, DAVID, merchant, res. Ayr, sh. 1777 to Va, on *Friendship of Ayr.* (SRO.AC7.56)(SRO.CS.GMB.56)

COCHRANE, DAVID, b. 27 Nov 1739, s. of David Cochrane and Helen Hamilton, merchant, res. Glasgow, sett. Richmond, Va, pre 1766. (SRO.RD3.242.127)(SRO.CS16.1.125)

COCKBURN, CHRISTINE, res. Edinburgh, tr. 1696, fr. Newhaven, Midlothian to Va. (SRO.RH15.14.58)

COFFIE, JAMES, tr. 1772, fr. Glasgow to Va., on *Brilliant*, arr. Port Hampton, Va, 7 Oct.1772. (SRO.JC27.10.3)

COLE, JOHN, b. 1736, planter, sett. Prince William Co, Va, militiaman in Va. Regt. 1756. (VMHB.1/2)(L)

COLQUHOUN, THOMAS. merchant, sh. pre 1795, nat. Richmond, Va, 13 Nov. 1802. (VSP.9.331)

COLQUHOUN, WALTER, s. of - Colquhoun and Margaret Williamson, merchant, sett. Va, Loyalist, sett. Jamaica 1783. (SRO.CS17.1.2)

COLTBERT, WILLIAM, b. 1734, smith and planter, sett. Westmoreland Co, Va, militiaman in Va. Regt. 1756. (VMHB.1/2)(L)

COLVIN, WILLIAM, cooper, sh. 1714, fr. Glasgow to Potomac River, on *American Merchant* (TM202)

COLVILLE, THOMAS, d. Alexandria, Fairfax Co, Va, 1768. (SM.30.334)

CONAHER, JOHN, Jacobite, tr. 24 May 1716, fr. Liverpool to Va, on *Friendship*, arr. Md Aug. 1716. (SPC.1716.311)(HM387)

CONN, HUGH, clergyman, d. Bladenburg, Prince George Co, Md, 28 June 1752. (SM.14.510)

CONNELL, WILLIAM, Jacobite, tr. 22 Apr. 1747, fr. Liverpool to Va, on *Johnson*, arr. Port Oxford, Md, 5 Aug. 1747. (P.2.124)(PRO.T1.328)

CONNOR, EDWARD, storekeeper, res. Greenock, Renfrewshire, sett. Loudoun Co, Potomac River, Va, d. pre June 1766. (Loudoun Co Deed Bk.F48)

COOKE, ROBERT, sett. Chaptico, Md, 1720, m. Sarah Fielding, fa. of John, d. 1728. (CAG.1.686)

COOK, THOMAS, farmer, Cushnie, Aberdeenshire, Jacobite, tr. 1716, fr. Liverpool to Va. (JAB.1.150)

COOLEY, JAMES, b. 1744, carpenter, sett. Frederick Co, Va. (VSA.24296)

COOPER, PATRICK, Jacobite, tr. 24 May 1716, fr. Liverpool to Va., on *Friendship*, arr. Md Aug. 1716. (SPC.1716.311)(HM386)

COPLAND, PETER, sett. Caroline Co, Va, 1743. (WMQ.2.22.345)

COPLAND, ROBERT, Jacobite, tr. 29 June 1716, fr. Liverpool to Va or Jamaica, on *Elizabeth and Anne*, arr. Va. (SPC.1716.310) (VSP.1.185)

CORDINER, JAMES, s. of James Cordiner, merchant, res. Paisley, Renfrewshire, sett. Rappahannock, Va., pro. 19 Mar. 1724 Edinburgh. (SRO.CC8.8.89)

CORRY, JAMES, sh. Dec. 1698, fr. Liverpool to Va. (LRO.HQ325.2Fre)

CORSTORPHEN, ROBERT, surgeon, sh. 1746, sett. James River, Va, fa. John, Robert and James. (UNC: Corstorphen pp)

COULTER, ALEXANDER, cabinetmaker, res. Glasgow, sett. Chestertown, Kent Co, Md, d. 1742, pro. 1 Mar. 1742 Md.

COULTER, HUGH, b. 8 Aug. 1717, s. of Michael Coulter and Janet Cumming, merchant, res. Glasgow, sett. Md, d. Oct.1763, pro 19 June 1766. (SRO.CC8.8.120)

COULTER, MICHAEL, sett. Warwick, Va, pre 1774. (SRO.RD3.238.391)

COUPAR, ROBERT, b. 2 Sep. 1750, s. of George Coupar, res. Balseir, Sorbie, Wigtownshire, schoolmaster, edu. Glasgow Uni. 1770, sh. pre 1776 to Va, d. Wigtown 18 Jan. 1818. (MAGU92)

COUPER, WILLIAM, b. 1774, sh. pre 1822 to Va, m. Elizabeth -, .fa. of John, sett. Norfolk, Va. (NA.M932/982)

COUTTS, HERCULES, b. 10 Aug. 1714, s. of James Coutts and Jean Van Der Hayden, merchant, res. Montrose, Angus, sett. Md pre 1751. (SRO.RD4.177.298)

COUTTS, JAMES, blackmailer, res. Aberdeen, tr. 25 May 1749, fr. Aberdeen to Va., on *Dispatch of Newcastle*. (AJ69)

COUTTS, JAMES, s. of James Coutts, clergyman, res. Aberdeen, sh. 1767, sett. Richmond Falls, James River, Va., d. 1787. (APB.4.106)

COUTTS, PATRICK, b. 7 Apr. 1726, s. of James Coutts and Marjory Gray, merchant, res. Aberdeen, sh. 1747 to Va., sett. Richmond Falls and Port Royal, Va, d. 27 Dec. 1777 Richmond. (APB.4.106)(SRO.RD4.212.846)

COWAN, ELIZABETH, b. 1723, runaway, Botetourt Co, Va, 1773. (VaGaz.2.12.1773)

COWAN, ROBERT, tobacco planter, sett. Bedford Co, Va, 1756, Loyalist. (PRO.AO13.28.130)

COWAN. ROBERT, b. 1746, sh. pre 1775, sett. Va., m. Susan Hood, fa. of Samuel, d. 1810. (TMR496)

COWAN. WILLIAM, b. 1695, tailor, res. Prestonpans, East Lothian, Jacobite, tr. 22 Apr. 1747, fr. Liverpool to Va, on *Johnson*, arr. Port Oxford, Md, 5 Aug. 1747. (P.2.130)(PRO.T1.328)(MT70)

CRAIG, GEORGE, b. 1740, gardener, runaway, Westmoreland Co, Va, 1775. (VaGaz.26.7.1775)

CRAIG, JAMES, b. 1 Nov. 1748, s. of Archibald Craig and Christian Innes, res. Elgin, Morayshire, clergyman, edu. Marischal College, Aberdeen 1763-67, sett. Cumberland ph, Lunenburg Co, and St John's, Baltimore Co, d. 1795. (FPA.21.302)

CRAIG, JAMES, mariner, d. Baltimore 1822, pro. 3 Mar. 1823 Baltimore.

CRAIG, JOHN, res. Aberdeen, thief, tr. Aug. 1753, fr. Aberdeen to Va, on *St Andrew* (AJ294)

CRAIG, JOHN, s. of James Craig of Braidland, Dalry, Ayrshire, store-keeper, sett. Va. 1769. (SRO.CS.C4.13)

CRAIG, JOHN, mariner, sett. Va. pre 1762. (SRO.CS16.1.114)

CRAIG, R., s. of - Craig, res. Cliffen, d. Bucks Co, Va, 1811. (EA.1811)

CRAIG, ROBERT, weaver, runaway, Dumfries, Prince William Co, Va, 1767. (VaGaz.10.12.1767)

CRAIG, THOMAS, b. 1768, merchant, sett. Baltimore. (NA.M432/277-99)

CRAIGDALLIE, HUGH, s. of Gilbert Craigdallie, surgeon, res. Perth, sett. Princess Anne Co, Va, pre 1776, fa. of Janet. (SRO.CS16.1.168)

CRAIGIN, ROBERT, b. 1726, tailor, Jacobite, tr. 22 Apr. 1747, fr. Liverpool to Va, on *Johnson*, arr. Port Oxford, Md, 5 Aug. 1747. (PRO.T1.328)(P.2.132)

CRAIGGS, THOMAS S., sh. to Md on *Mediterranean,* pro. 31 May 1740 Edinburgh. (SRO.MEP)

CRAIK, JAMES, s. of Robert Craik of Arbigland, surgeon and physician, res. Dumfriesshire, sett. Va. pre 1750, d. 6 Feb. 1814 Alexandria, Va. (DAI302)

CRAIK, ROBERT, physician, sett. Va., d. 1754. (SA187)

CRAM, PETER, b. 1732, planter, sett. Stafford Co, Va. pre 1756, militiaman in Va. Regt. (VMHB1/2)(L)

CRAMOND, JOHN, res. Glasgow, sett. Norfolk, Va, 1759, Loyalist, sett. Jamaica 1777. (SRO.CS16.1.170)(PRO.AO13.28.120) (VaGaz.4.4.1766)

CRAMPTON, JAMES, Jacobite, tr. 28 July 1716, fr. Liverpool to Va., on *Godspeed,* arr. Md Oct. 1716. (SPC.1716.310)(HM388) (CTB.31.209)

CRASTER, WILLIAM, Jacobite, tr. 29 June 1716, fr. Liverpool to Va or Jamaica, on *Elizabeth and Anne,* arr. Va 1716. (SPC.1716.310)(CTB.31.208)(VSP.1.186)

CRAWFORD, ANN, b. 1780, sett. Carroll Co, Md. (NA.M432/277-99)

CRAWFORD, DAVID, b. 1625, sett. New Kent Co, Va, pre 1692, d. 1710. (RAV27)

CRAWFORD, GEORGE, merchant, sett. Va pre 1769. (SRO.CS16.1.134)

CRAWFORD, JAMES, sh. 2 Nov. 1674, to St Mary's Co, Md, on *Bachelor of Bristol.* (MSA.ESB.152)

CRAWFORD, JAMES, clergyman, sh. 1711 to Md. (EMA22)

CRAWFORD, JAMES, merchant, sh. Sep. 1684, fr. Port Glasgow to Va on *Catherine of Glasgow.* (SRO.E72.19.9)

CRAWFORD, JOHN, b. 1600, res. Ayrshire, sett. New Kent Co ,Va pre 1675, fa. of David. (AGQ.7.15)

CRAWFORD, THOMAS, sett. Va 1643. (DAB.4.527)

CRAWFORD, THOMAS, clergyman, sh. 1703, sett. Md and Va. (EMA22)(SPG.11.153)

CRAWFORD, WILLIAM, sett. Elizabeth River, Va. pre 1689. (NEHGS.SCS.pp)

CREEL, CHARLES, sh. 1680, sett. Richmond, Va, fa. of Charles. (BAF

CRICHTON, JAMES, b. 1704, res. Glen Isla, Angus, sh. Aug. 1721, fr. London to Va. (CLRO/AIA)

CRICHTON, JOHN, res. Sanquhar, Dumfriesshire, d. Dumfries, Va, pro. 1728 PCC.

CRIGHTON, JAMES, Jacobite, res. Arbroath, Angus, tr. 24 Feb. 1747, fr. Liverpool to Va, on *Gildart,* arr. Port North Potomac, Md, 5 Aug. 1747. (P.2.134)(MR97)(PRO.T1.328)

CRIGHTON, JOHN, laborer, res. Cablen, Perthshire, Jacobite, tr. 24 Feb. 1747, fr. Liverpool to Va, on *Gildart,* arr. Port North Potomac, Md 5 Aug. 1747. (P.2.134)(PRO.T1.328)

CROMAR, JAMES, res. Aberdeenshire, sh. 1729, fr. Glasgow to Va., d. 1758, pro. 6 Apr. 1759 Chesterfield Co, Va. (APB.4.29)

CROOKBANE, JOHN, b. 1736, silvesmith, sett. Fredericksburg, Va., militiaman in Va. Regt. 1756. (VMHB1/2)(L)

CROOKS, THOMAS, b. 1793, nat. 22 Aug. 1820 Norfolk, Va.

CROOKSHANKS, CHARLES, sett. Baltimore, d. 1800, pro 29 July 1818 Edinburgh. (SRO.CC8.8.144)

CROSBIE, JAMES, res. Cambuslang, Lanarkshire, merchant, sett. Williamsburg, Va, d. pre 1753, pro 1 June 1753 Chesterfield Co, Va.

CROSS, JAMES, merchant, res. Glasgow, sett. Manchester, Prince Edward Co, Va. pre 1776, d. Norfolk, Va 10 Jan. 1787. (SRA.TD131.13)(SRO.SH.7.5.1788)(VaGaz.25.1.1787)

CRUDEN, ALEXANDER, b. 11 Dec. 1721, s. of Alexander Cruden and Giles Walker, res. Aberdeen, clergyman, edu. Marischal College, Aberdeen, sett. South Farnham, Va. 1752, Loyalist, d. Aberdeen, pro. June 1792 PCC. (KCA.2.312)(PRO.AO13.28.191)

CRUIKSHANKS, CHARLES, b. 28 Oct. 1746, s. of George Cruikshanks and Isobel Duncan, merchant, res. Glasgow, sett. Md pre 1775. (SRA.CFI)

CRUICKSHANK, ELIZABETH, res. Aberdeen, tr. Aug 1751, fr. Aberdeen to Va. (AJ193)

CUMMIN, ALEXANDER, Jacobite, tr. 31 July 1716, fr. Liverpool to Va, on *Anne*. (SPC.1716.310)(CTB.31.209)

CUMMING, ARCHIBALD, b. 1786, cotton spinner, fa. of Daniel, arr. Baltimore 1826. (NA.M596)

CUMMING, HELEN, b. 1790, cotton spinner, mo. of James and Jane, arr. Baltimore 1826. (NA.M596)

CUMMING, JANE, res. Alvie, Morayshire, Jacobite, tr. 22 Apr. 1747, fr. Liverpool to Va, on *Johnson*, arr. Port Oxford, Md, 5 Aug. 1747. (P.2.140)(PRO.T1.328)

CUMMING, JOHN, b. 1778, teacher, m. Margaret -, fa. of William, John, Samuel, Hugh and James, arr. Baltimore 1823. (NA.M596)

CUMMING, MARY, b. 1791, cotton spinner, arr. Baltimore 1826. (NA.M596)

CUMMING, ROBERT, merchant, res. Kilmarnock, Ayrshire, sett. Va. pre 1763. (SRO.CS16.1.115)

CUMMING, WILLIAM, b. 1725, s. of David Cumming, planter, sh. 1747, sett. Frederick Co, Va., m. Sarah Coppage, fa. of Thomas. (CAG.1.909)

CUMMINGS, WILLIAM, b. 1794, farmer, sh. pre 1822, sett. Md, m. Margaret -, fa. of John, Mary and Margaret, sett. Baltimore. (NA.M432\277-99)

CUMMINS, WILLIAM, b. 1690, s. of David Cummins, res. Forres, Morayshire, Jacobite, tr. 24 May 1716, fr. Liverpool to Va, on *Friendship*, arr. Md Aug. 1716. (SPC.1716.311)(HM386)

CUNNINGHAM, ADAM, physician in Va 1728-35.   (SA187)

CUNNINGHAM, ALEXANDER, cook, res. Glamis, Angus, fireraiser, tr. 10 Aug.1677, fr. Glasgow to Va, on *Swallow of Westchester*.   (PC.5.277)

CUNNINGHAM, ALEXANDER, sett. Va pre 1766, d. Dec. 1772 Glasgow. (PRO.AO13.29.1/501)(SRO.CS16.1.125)

CUNNINGHAM, ARCHIBALD, b. 1794, shoemaker, sh. pre 1830, m. Jeanette -, fa. of John, sett. Washington, D.C.   (NA.M432/56-7)

CUNNINGHAM, DAVID, s. of Sir John Cunningham of Robertland, sh. 1729 to Va. or Md. (MdGaz.16.10.1751)(WMQ.3.266)

CUNNINGHAM, GEORGE, s. of Cunningham of Bandalloch, assistant storekeeper, sh. pre 1776, sett. Falmouth, Va.   (SFV229)

CUNNINGHAM, JACK, merchant, sh. pre 1776, sett. Va.   (AHR.5.294)

CUNNINGHAM, JOHN, res. Goodlyburn, Perth, sh. pre 1823, sett. Baltimore. (SRO.B59.38.6269)

CUNNINGHAM, JOHN, sh. pre 1681, sett. Augusta Co ,Va, fa. of John, Robert, Patrick and David.   (AGB.1.156)

CUNNINGHAM, JOHN, res. Glasgow, sett. Md, pro. 16 Sep. 1676 Md.

CUNNINGHAM, JOHN, sh. pre 1776, merchant skipper, sett. Norfolk, Va, Loyalist. (PRO.AO13.28.118)

CUNNINGHAM, ROBERT, s. of Richard Cunningham and Ann Murray, res. Symington, Lanarkshire, sh. pre 1776, sett. Blandford, Va, m. Margaret Baird, fa. of Alexander and Richard, d. 1796.   (HAF.2.120)

CUNNINGHAM, WILLIAM, b. 1614, sh. 28 May 1635, fr. London to Va, on *Speedwell*. (PRO.E157/20)

CUNNINGHAM, WILLIAM, merchant, b. 1727, res. Kilmarnock, Ayrshire, sh. 1748, sett. Md and Va, fa. of William, Loyalist, sh. fr. James River to Glasgow Aug. 1776, sett. Ayrshire.   0(SRO.GD247.140)(SRO.CS16.1.133)(PRO.AO12.56.289) (PRO.AO13.29.1/501)(SFV.xi.232)

CURLY, JAMES, b. 1798, carpenter, sett. Richmond, Henrico Co, Va. (NA.M932/982)

CURLY, JOHN, b. 1796, engineer, m. Jane, sh. pre 1821, fa. of John and James, sett. Richmond, Henrico Co, Va.   (NA.M932/982)

CURRIE, DAVID, res. Edinburgh, clergyman, sh. 1730, sett. Va., d. Christchurch, Va, 1792.   (OD19)

CURRIE, JAMES, b. 1756, physician, res. Annandale, Dumfriesshire, sh. 1771, sett. Richmond, Va, m. Mrs Ingles 1789, d. 23 Apr. 1807.   (VMHB.67.176)

CURRIE, WILLIAM, clergyman and tutor, edu. Glasgow Uni., res. Glasgow, sh. pre 1734, sett. Va., m. Margaret Hackett, fa. of Ross, William and Richard, d. 26 Oct. 1803 Pa. (AP160)

CURRIE, WILLIAM, merchant, res. Glasgow and Greenock, Renfrewshire, m. Isabella -, fa. of Janetta, Andrew and John, sh. post 1784, sett. Richmond, Va., nat. 16 Sep. 1799. (US D/C.1799.7)

CURRY, WILLIAM, army deserter, Petersburg, Va, 1754. (VaGaz.19.7.1754)

CUTHBERT, ALEXANDER, b. 1745, bricklayer, res. Perth, sh. 1767, fr. London to Potomac River, runaway, Prince George Co, Va, 1767. (VaGaz.10.11.1767)

CUTHBERT, DAVID, b. 1755, brazier, sh. Jan. 1774, fr. London to Md, on *Jenny and Polly*. (PRO.T47.9/11)

CUTHBERT, MARION, da. of William Cuthbert, res. Newton Ayr, Ayrshire, m. William Thomson, sett. Va. pre 1798. (SRO.SH.13.2.1798)

CUTHBERT, WILLIAM, b. 1750, s. of Samuel Cuthbert and Agnes Reid, res. Cumnock, Ayrshire, d. Va. (HAF.1.366)

DAINGERFIELD, WILLIAM A., b. 13 Oct. 1769, physician, edu. Edinburgh Uni., sh. pre 1800, sett. Alexandria, Va, d. Prince George Co, Md 19 Oct. 1821. (WMQ.2.16.177)

DALGETTY, JOHN, Jacobite, tr. 24 May 1716, fr. Liverpool to Md, on *Friendship*. (SPC.1716.311)

DALLAS, WALTER, b. 1690s, s. of James Dallas of St Martins and Elizabeth Riddell, merchant, res. Edinburgh, sh. pre 1754, sett. Annapolis, Baltimore Co, Md, fa. of Nathan, Ann, Rachel, Katharine, Claire, Sarah and Elizabeth, d. pre 1722. (SRO.CS.GMB.282)(FD344)(SRO.CS16.1.95)

DALRYMPLE, CHARLES, s. of - Dalrymple of Orangefields, sh. 1 Sep. 1670, fr. Port Glasgow to Md. (MHS.76.1.15)

DALRYMPLE, JOHN, b. 1795, machinist, sh. pre 1824, m. Agnes -, fa. of George, Archibald and Robert, sett. Baltimore. (NA.M432/277-99)

DALRYMPLE, ROBERT, b. 1799, stonecutter, m. Mary, fa. of Ann, sett. Norfolk, Va., nat. 18 Aug 1831 Norfolk. (NA.M932/982)

DALYELL, JOHN, s. of James Dalyell, sh. pre 1765, sett. Frederick Co, Md. (SRO.RS23.19.339)(SRO.SC15.55.2)

DALZIEL, JOHN, Jacobite, tr. 1716 to Va or Carolina. (SPC.1716.128)

DALZIEL, JOHN, b. 1801, res. Shotts, Lanarkshire, sh. pre 1828, sett. Henrico Co, Va, nat. 12 May 1828 Eastern District, Va. (US.D/C.RB5.570)

DALZIEL, WALTER, b. 1804, res. Shotts, Lanarkshire, sh. pre 1828, sett. Richmond, Va, nat. 12 May 1828 Eastern District, Va. (US.D/C.RB5.571)

DARLING, ADAM, b. 1805, farmer, m. Jane -, sett. Wood Co, Va. (NA.M932/982)

DARLING, GEORGE, clergyman, edu. Edinburgh Uni., sh. 1735 to Va, sh. 1738 to London. (WMQ.2.20.130)

DARLING, JANE, b. 1776, sett. Wood Co, Va. (NA.M932/982)

DARLING, JOHN, b. 1663, s. of John Darling, cordiner, sh. Sep. 1684, fr. London to Md, on *Hound*. (CLRO/AIA)

DAVIDSON, ABRAHAM, b. 14 Feb. 1725, s,. of Alexander Davidson and Jean Strachan, res. Kincardine O'Neil, Aberdeenshire, sh. Apr. 1741, fr. Aberdeen or Peterhead to Va or Md, on *Charming Peggy*. (PMA86)

DAVIDSON, ALEXANDER, clergyman, edu. King's College, Aberdeen, 1693, sh. 1710 to Md. (EMA23)

DAVIDSON, ANDREW, Jacobite, tr. 24 May 1716, fr. Liverpool to Md, on *Friendship*. (SPC.1716.311)(HM387)

DAVIDSON, ANDREW, merchant, res. Paisley, Renfrewshire, sett. Va pre 1764. (SRO.CS16.1.120)

DAVIDSON, CHARLES, res. Edinburgh, thief, tr. 4 May 1666, fr. Leith, Midlothian to Va., on *Phoenix of Leith*. (ETR107)

DAVIDSON, CHARLES, servant, res. Aberzeldie, Jacobite, tr. 22 Apr 1747, fr. Liverpool to Va, on *Johnson*, arr. Port Oxford, Md, 5 Aug 1747. (P.2.144)(MR219)(PRO.T1.328)

DAVIDSON, JAMES, cooper, sh. 1765, sett. Nansemond Co, Va. (VaGaz.5.5.1768)

DAVIDSON, JAMES, b. 1743, physician, edu. Edinburgh Uni. 1768 and King's College, Aberdeen, 1769, sh. 1771 to Md, d. 1811. (SA178)

DAVIDSON, JAMES, s. of John Davidson, res. Ferryhill, sh. pre 1796, sett. Baltimore. (SRO.SH.30.6.1796)

DAVIDSON, JAMES, nat. 20 Aug. 1805 Norfolk, Va.

DAVIDSON, JOHN, accountant, res. Inverness, sh. Jan. 1755, fr. London to Md. (CLRO/AIA)

DAVIDSON, JOHN, cooper, sh. 1765, sett. Falmouth, Va. (VaGaz.5.5.1768)

DAVIDSON, JOHN, res. Aberdeenshire, sh. July 1741, fr. Aberdeen or Peterhead to Va or Md, on *Charming Peggy*. (PMA150)

DAVIDSON, PETER, b. 1662, s. of John Davidson, res. Dundee, Angus, sh. Aug. 1684, fr. London to Md, on *Assistance.* (LRO.MR.E.593)

DAVIDSON, WILLIAM, farmer, res. Cushnie, Aberdeenshire, Jacobite, tr. 24 May 1716, fr. Liverpool to Va., arr. Md. Aug. 1716. (SPC.1716.311)(JAB.1.151)(HM387)

DAVIDSON, WILLIAM, b. 1707, tailor, res. Perth, sh. Nov. 1727, fr. London to Va. (CLRO/AIA)

DAVIDSON, -, s. of - Davidson and Mary Grant, merchant, Pityoulish, Garten, Kincardineshire, sett. Washington, d. 1779. (Garten g/s)

DAVIE, ROBERT, Jacobite, tr. 22 Apr. 1747, fr. Liverpool to Va, on *Johnson,* arr. Port Oxford, Md, 5 Aug. 1747. (PRO.T1.328)

DAW, ANDREW, Jacobite, tr. 24 May 1716, fr. Liverpool to Va on *Friendship,* arr. Md 20 Aug. 1716. (SPC.1716.311)(HM387)

DAY, AUGUSTUS, b. 1773, sett. Fauquier Co, Va. (N.A.-M932/982)

DEACON, ABRAHAM, nat. 25 Mar. 1806 Norfolk City, Va.

DEAN, HUGH, sh. 1770, merchant, sett. Somerset Co, Md, Loyalist, sett. Bahamas 1783 and N.Y. 1790. (MdHistMag.2.33.134)(ANY.1.275)

DEANS, JAMES, merchant, sett. Chesterfield Co, Va, pro. 20 Apr. 1764 Chesterfield.

DEAN, JOHN, merchant, res. Glasgow, sh. pre 1757, sett. Tappahannock, Va. (SRO.B10.15.7036)

DENHAM, JAMES, Jacobite, tr. 24 May 1716, fr. Liverpool to Va, on *Friendship,* arr. Md Aug. 1716. (SPC.1716.311)(HM387)

DENISTOUN, ALISON, res. Edinburgh, tr. 1696, fr. Newhaven, Midlothian, to Va. (SRO.RH15.14.58)

DENNISON, JAMES, b. 1755, schoolmaster, res. Culreoch, Anwoth, Kirkcudbrightshire, sh. pre 1820, sett. Va, m. Nicolas Brown, fa. of William. (Anwoth g/s)

DENNISON, WILLIAM, b. 1813, s. of James Dennison and Nicolas Brown, res. Culreoch, Anwoth, Kirkcudbrightshire, sh. pre 1820, sett. Va. (Anwoth g/s)

DENNISTOUN, RICHARD, s. of James Dennistoun, merchant, res. Glasgow, sett. Hanover Co Va pre 1776, Loyalist, sett. Glasgow. (PRO.AO13.33.124)

DICK, ARCHIBALD. clergyman, sh. 1762 to Va. (EMA24)

DICK, DAVID, b. 1725, shoemaker, Jacobite, tr. 24 Feb. 1747, fr. Liverpool to Va, on *Gildart,* arr. Port North Potomac Md 5 Aug. 1747. (P.2.152)(PRO.T1.328)

DICK, GEORGE V., b. 1790, sh. 1819, sett. Richmond, Va, d. Oct. 1823 Alabama. (Cahawba Press 11.10.1823)

DICK, JAMES, b. 1706. s. of Thomas Dick and Jean Harvie, merchant, res. Edinburgh, sh. 1 June 1734, sett. London Town, South River, Md, m. Margaret -, fa. of Mary, d. 24 Sep. 1782 Lewistown, Md, bd. Anne Arundel Co, Md.(N.Y.Gaz.11.11.1782) (MSA.All Hallows OPR.56)

DICK, MARY, da. of Robert Dick, m. Walter Carmichael, merchant in Md, in Edinburgh 21 June 1767. (Edinburgh OPR)

DICK, THOMAS, s. of Robert Dick, merchant, res. Edinburgh, sett. Annapolis, Md, pre 1758. (SRO.SH.21.3.1758)

DICK, WILLIAM, nat. 21 May 1787 Norfolk City, Va.

DICKENS, LILIAS, b. 1790, sett. Washington, D.C. (N.A.M432/56-57)

DICKENSON, GEORGE, Jacobite, tr. 29 June 1716, fr. Liverpool to Va or Jamaica, on *Elizabeth and Anne*, arr. Va. (SPC.1716.310)(CTB.31.208)(VSP.1.185)

DICKSON, GILBERT, b. 28 Dec. 1774, s. of Rev. Jacob Dickson and Janet Richardson, Mousewald, Dumfries-shire, d. Sep. 1796 Norfolk, Va. (F.2.219)(EEC.12278)(Mousewald g/s)

DICKSON, JANE, b. 1788, sett. Baltimore. (N.A.M432/277-99)

DICKSON, ROBERT, nat. 29 Mar. 1787 Norfolk City, Va.

DIDIP, JOHN, tailor, res. Edinburgh, sett. Williamsburg, Va, pre 1752. (VaGaz5.3.1752)

DINWIDDIE, JOHN, b. 20 Dec. 1698, s. of Laurence Dinwiddie and Sarah Garshore, merchant, res. Glasgow, sett. Hanover, King George Co, Rappahannock River, Va, m. Rose Mason, fa. of Elizabeth and Jean, d. Glasgow 1726, pro. 29 June 1726 Glasgow. (SRO.CC9.7.52)(King George Will.1A.45)

DINWIDDIE, ROBERT, b. 2 Oct. 1692, s. of Robert Dinwiddie of Germiston and Elizabeth Cumming, res. Glasgow, edu. Glasgow Uni., sh. 1721 to Va, m. Rebecca Affleck pre 1738, fa. of Elizabeth and Rebecca, Customs Surveyor General of Va 1738-49, Lt. Gov. Va 1751-58, d. 28 July 1770 Bath, England, pro. Oct. 1770 PCC. (WMQ.2.21.411)(GM.40.493)(DAB.5.3.17)

DIXON, JAMES, Jacobite, tr. 28 July 1716, fr. Liverpool to Va, on Godspeed, arr. Md. (SPC.1716.310)(CTB.31.209)(HM387)

DIXON, JAMES, b. 1790, stonecutter, sett. Washington, D.C. (N.A.M432/56-57)

DOBBIE, GEORGE, assistant storekeeper, sett. Halifax Co, Va, 1770-76. (SFV.34)

DOBIE, THOMAS, b. 1785, res. Ayrshire, sh. 1808, sett. Richmond City, Va, nat. 5 Sep. 1825 Eastern District, Va. (US.D/C.RB5.493)

DODD, THOMAS, b. 1789, hostler, sett. Kent Co, Md. (N.A.M432/277-99)

DODDS, MARGARET, b. 1774, sett. Carroll Co, Md.   (N.A.M432/277-99)

DOMINGTON, GEORGE, b. 1804, cordiner, arr. Baltimore 1828.   (N.A.M596)

DONALD, ALEXANDER, s. of James Donald, res. Glasgow, sh. Mar. 1760 to Va.   (SRA.CFI)

DONALD, ALEXANDER jr, merchant, res. Greenock, Renfrewshire, sett. Va, d. pre 1806, pro. 1806 Edinburgh.   (SRO.CC8.8.136)

DONALD, ANDREW, attorney, res. Broom, Ayrshire, sett. Bedford Co, Va, 17.., fa. of Ann and Christian.   (SRA.CFI)

DONALD, J., b. 1795, mariner, arr. Baltimore Sep. 1820, on *William of Baltimore*. (N.A.-M596)

DONALD, ROBERT jr, merchant, res. Glasgow, sett. Petersburg, Va, pro. 22 Aug. 1806 Edinburgh.   (SRO.CC8.8.136)

DONALD, ROBERT, s. of Thomas Donald of Lyleston and Janet Cumming, merchant, res. Dunbartonshire, sh. pre 1757, sett. Va.   (SRO.RS10.9.97)

DONALD, ROBERT, s, of William Donald, merchant, res. Ayr, sett. Va pre 1788. (SRO.SH11.4.1788)

DONALD, ROBERT, merchant, sett. Warwick, Va, pre 1778.   (SRO.CS16.1.173)

DONALD, ROBERT, merchant, sett. Chesterfield Co, Va, pre 1775, m. Nancy Osborne. (VMHB.29.401)

DONALDSON, CHARLES, Jacobite, tr. 24 May 1716, fr. Liverpool to Va, on *Friendship*, arr. Md Aug. 1716.   (SPC.1716.311)(HM387)

DONALDSON, EBENEZER, runaway, Rufus Ferry, Pamunkey River, Va, Apr. 1770. (VaGaz26.4.1770)

DONALDSON, HENRY, b. 1610, sh. 15 May 1635, fr. London to Va, on *Plain Joan*. (PRO.E157.20)

DONALDSON, JAMES, s. of James Donaldson of Munoch, merchant, Bonnachra Mill, Dunbartonshire, sett. Annapolis, Md, m. Bridget Baillie, fa. of William, Henry and James, d. 1737, pro.15 Mar. 1737 Md.   (MSA.Will.21.891)(SRO.CS16.1.69)

DONALDSON, JAMES, b. 1697, wright, res. Edinburgh, Jacobite, tr. 24 Feb. 1747, fr. Liverpool to Va, on *Gildart*, arr. Port North Potomac, Md 5 Aug. 1747. (P.2.158)(MR98)(PRO.T1.328)

DONALDSON, JAMES, b. 1728, planter, sett. Stafford Co, Va, militiaman in Va Regt. 1756.   (VMHB1/2)(L)

DONALDSON, JAMES, sett. Norfolk, Va, d. 1803, pro. 24 Jan. 1803 Norfolk.

DONALDSON, JOHN, clergyman, edu. King's College, Aberdeen, 1700, sh. 1711, sett. King and Queen Co, Md, d. 1747 Md.   (EMA24)

DONALDSON, THOMA S, Jacobite, tr. 24 May 1716, fr. Liverpool to Va, on *Friendship*, arr. Md Aug. 1716. (SPC.1716.311)(HM387)

DONALDSON, WILLIAM, Jacobite, tr. 29 June 1716, fr. Liverpool to Va, on *Elizabeth and Anne*, arr. Va. (SPC.1716.310)(CTB.31.208)(VSP.1.185)

DONALDSON, WILLIAM, master cooper, sett. Portsmouth, Va, 1763. (PRO.AO12.55.115)

DONALDSON, WILLIAM, grocer, sett. Va, Loyalist, sett. Shelburne, N.S., 1783. (LNS154)

DONALSON, JAMES, farmer, m. Jemima -, fa. of Margaret, sett. Wood Co, Va. (N.A.-M932/982)

DORWAITE, JAMES, b. 1701, cordiner, res. Edinburgh, sh. Dec. 1721, fr. London to Md. (CLRO/AIA)

DOUGLAS, ARCHIBALD, b. 1695, runaway, Queen Anne Co, Md, 1720. (Amer.Wkly.Merc.21.7.1720)

DOUGLAS, GEORGE, b. 1703, scholar, res. Linton, Peeblesshire, sh. Feb. 1721, fr. London to Va. (CLRO/AIA)

DOUGLAS, GEORGE, m. Tabitha Drummond, sett. Accomack Co, Va, d. 1758. (RAV31)

DOUGLAS, HUGH, b. 1613, sh. 24 Oct. 1635, fr. London to Va, on *Constance*. (PRO.E157.20)

DOUGLAS, JAMES, sh. Dec. 1698, fr. Liverpool to Va, on *Globe*. (LRO.HQ325.2Fre)

DOUGLAS, JAMES, b. 1722, s. of James Douglas and - Wallace, res. Dunbarton, merchant, edu. Glasgow Uni. 1737, sh. pre 1754, sett. Dumfries, Prince William Co, Va, m. Catherine Brent, fa. of Archibald, Margaret, and Catherine, d. 18 Nov. 1766. (SRO.CS16.1.165)(SM.29.55)(VMHB.22.273)(MAGU19)(VMHB.19.94) (Frederick Deeds.25.357)

DOUGLAS, J. C., b. 1790, m. Ann -, overseer, sett. Prince Edward Co, Va. (N.A.-M932/982)

DOUGLAS, JOHN, b. 1633, sett. Blythwood Manor, Pickwixon, Md, pre 1645, m. Sarah Bonner, fa. of John, d. 1678. (CAG.1.256)

DOUGLAS, JOHN, sh. 2 Nov. 1674, to St Mary's Co, Md, on *Bachelor of Bristol*. (MSA.ESB.152)

DOUGLAS, JOHN, b. 1696, res. Castle Stewart, Wigtownshire, sett. Monacacy, Montgomery Co, Md, d. 2 Nov. 1732. (Monacacy g/s)

DOUGLAS, JOHN, b. 1776, gardener, m. Ann -, sett. Washington, D.C. (N.A.-M432/56-7)

DOUGLAS, JOHN, b. 1808, farmer, md. Mary -, fa. of Catherine, Susan, Abraham, William and George, sett. Ritchie Co, Va. (N.A.-M932/982)

DOUGLAS, THOMAS, b. 1732, baker, sett. Fredericksburg, Va, militiaman in Va Regt 1757. (VMHB.1/2)(L)

DOUGLAS, WILLIAM, b. 1609, sh. 1621 to Va, on *Margaret and John* , sett. Elizabeth City, Va pre 1624. (PRO.CO1.3.2)(PRO.CO1.3.14-172)

DOUGLAS, WILLIAM, s. of Hugh Douglas of Garallan and Katherine Home, res. Ayrshire, sh. pre 1760 to Va., sett. Loudoun Co, Va, m. (1) Elizabeth Lewis (2) - Chilton, fa. of Hugh, Bird, and Katherine, d. 1783. (TMR586)(HAW.2.337)(AGB.2.169)

DOUGLAS, WILLIAM, b. 3 Aug. 1708, s. of - Douglas and Griselda McKeand, res. Penningham, Galloway, clergyman and tutor, edu. Glasgow Uni., m. Nicola Hunter 1735, fa. of Margaret, sh. 6 Oct. 1750, sett. St James ph., Northam, Goochland Co, Va. (WMQ.2.1.158)(EMA25)(SNQ.1.154)

DOUGLAS, WILLIAM, b. 1792, farmer, sh. pre 1822, m. Eleanor -, fa. of Elizabeth, John, Mary, Jeremiah, William, Andrew and Eleanor, sett. Ritchie Co, Va. (N.A.-M932/982)

DOUGLAS, WILLIAM, b. 1798, carpenter, sh. pre 1830, m. Ann -, fa. of Albert and Mary, sett. Washington, D.C. (N.A.-M432/56-57)

DOULL, JAMES, s. of James Doull, surgeon, res. Edinburgh, sett. Md pre 1751. (SRO.RD4.172.158/525)

DOW, JOHN, b. 1717, servant, res. Stanley, Auchtergavin, Perthshire, Jacobite, tr. 24 Feb. 1747, fr. Liverpool to Va, on *Gildart*, arr. Port North Potomac, Md, 5 Aug. 1747. (P.2.162)(MR23)(PRO.T1.328)

DOWIE, WILLIAM, clergyman, sh. 1762 to Md. (EMA25)

DOWNEY, WILLIAM, b. 1799, farmer, m. Jane -, arr. Baltimore 1829. (N.A.-M596)

DREW, ROBERT, res. Glasgow, sett. Md pre 1776. (SRO.CS16.1.168)

DRISDELL, JAMES, nat. 17 Nov. 1794 Norfolk, Va.

DRUMMOND, JOHN, merchant, sett. Blandford, Va, and Md 1753-1776, Loyalist, sett. Glasgow. (SRO.CS16.1.89/115)(PRO.AO13.4.195)

DRUMMOND, JOHN, s. of Robert Drummond, res. Grangepans, West Lothian, sett. Brunswick, Va, pre 1807. (SRO.SH10.8.1807)

DRUMMOND, WILLIAM, sett. Jamestown, Va, pre 1648, m. Sarah -, fa. of Sarah and Elizabeth, Governor of Carolina 1664, d. 1677 Va, pro. 1677 PCC. (VMHB.18.2) (WMQ.2.20.484)

DRYSDALE, HUGH, m. Hester -, Lt. Governor of Va, d. 1726 Va, pro. Dec 1726 PCC.

DUFF, DAVID, tutor, sh. 1772, sett. Portobacco, Md. (SRO.GD248.564/3)

DUFF, ELEANOR, sett. Va 17.., m. William Green. (BD592)

DUFF, JOHN, laborer, res. Kirkton, Perthshire, Jacobite, tr. 22 Apr. 1747, fr. Liverpool to Va, on *Johnson,* arr. Port Oxford, Md, 5 Aug. 1747. (P.2.168)(MR206)(PRO.T1.328)

DUFF, ROBERT, b. 1722, painter, res. Glasgow, Jacobite, tr. 24 Apr. 1747, fr. Liverpool to Va, on *Gildart,* arr. Port North Potomac, Md, 5 Aug. 1747. (P.2.168)(PRO.T1.328)

DUFF, WILLIAM, sett. King George Co, Va, m. Elizabeth -, d. 1744, pro. 1745 King George Co. (BD592)

DUGUID, WILLIAM, b. 26 Feb. 1717, s. of William Duguid and Jean Henry, Aberdeenshire, sett. Va, m. Ann Moss. (ANE

DUN, JAMES, merchant, res. Edinburgh(?), sett. Md pre 1760.   (SRO.CS16.1.107)

DUNBAR, HANCOCK, clergyman, sh. 1725, sett. St Stephen's ph., King and Queen Co, Va, fa. of David, d. 1778.   (EMA25)(WMQ.2.22.532)(VaGaz4.12.78)

DUNBAR, JEREMY, farmer, res. Cushnie, Aberdeenshire, Jacobite, tr. 24 May 1716, fr. Liverpool to Va, on *Elizabeth and Anne,* arr. Sandy Point, James River, Va, sett. Newport, R.I.   (SPC.1716.310)(CTB.31.208)(VSP.1.185)(SRO.GD298)(SRO.GD103)

DUNBAR, JOHN, b. 1662, s. of John Dunbar, tailor, res. Glasgow, sh. fr. London to Md on *Benedict* .   (GM.15.404)

DUNBAR, JOHN, merchant, Jacobite, tr. June 1716, fr. Liverpool to Va, sett. Sandy Point, James River, Va, sett. Newport, R.I. 1720.   (SRO.GD298)

DUNBAR, JOHN, res. Glasgow, arr. Philadelphia 1772, sett. Va. (Rec.Ind.Phila.

DUNBAR, WILLIAM, res. Portsoy, Banffshire, arr. Va. 1784   (VaGaz12.7.1786)

DUNCAN, ANN L., b. 1785, sh. pre 1827, mo. of William, sett. Fluvanna Co, Va. (N.A.-M932/982)

DUNCAN, CHARLES, sett. Westerfield Co, Va, d. 29 Jan. 1808 London. (GM.78.175)(SM.70.159)

DUNCAN, DAVID, b. 1778, grocer, sett. Petersburg, Dinwiddie Co, Va.   (N.A.-M932/982)

DUNCAN, DAVID, b. 1793, nat. 1 Apr. 1820 Norfolk City, Va.

DUNCAN, GEORGE, b. 1797, gardener, sh. pre 1830, m. Sarah -, fa. of Adam and James, sett. Baltimore.   (N.A.-M432/277-99)

DUNCAN, JOHN, Jacobite, tr. 24 Feb. 1747, fr. Liverpool to Va, on *Gildart,* arr. Port North Potomac, Md, 5 Aug. 1747.   (PRO.T1.328)

DUNCAN, JOHN, brush manufacturer and merchant, res. Glasgow, sett. Md pre 1778. (SRO.CS16.1.173)

DUNCAN, PETER, b. 1624, res. Edinburgh, tr. 1650, sett. Nomini Creek, Va, 1655, m. Bessie Caldwell 1646, fa. of John, d. 1676. (BLG2665)

DUNCAN, PETER, b. 1715, laborer, res. Dundee, Angus, Jacobite, tr. 24 Feb. 1747, fr. Liverpool to Va, on *Gildart,* arr. Port North Potomac, Md, 5 Aug. 1747. (P.2.122)(MR99)(PRO.T1.328)

DUNCAN, ROBERT, Jacobite, tr. 29 June 1716, fr. Liverpool to Va or Jamaica, on *Elizabeth and Anne,* arr. Va. (SPC.1716.310)(CTB.31.208)(VSP.1.186)

DUNCAN, WILLIAM, painter, res. Glasgow, sett. Norfolk, Va, pre 1777. (SRO.CS16.1.171)

DUNCAN, WILLIAM, b. 1753, clerk and bookkeeper, sh. Dec. 1774, fr. London to Va, on *Caroline.* (PRO.T47.9/11)

DUNCAN, WILLIAM, clergyman, sett. Newport, Isle of Wight Co, Va, pre 1776, Loyalist. (PRO.AO13.27.38/45)

DUNCAN, Miss, b. 1790, arr. Norfolk, Va, June 1820. (PA139)

DUNCANSON, JAMES, b. 11 Feb. 1735, sh. July 1752, sett. St George's ph., Fredericksburg, Va, m. Mary -, d. 4 Mar. 1791 Fredericksburg. (Fredericksburg g/s)(VaHer.10.3.1791)

DUNCANSON, MATILDA, da. of John Duncanson, res. Inveraray, Argyllshire, d. 2 Aug. 1799 Washington, D.C. (GC1268)

DUNCANSON, ROBERT, merchant, res. Forres, Morayshire, sett. Fredericksburg, Va, d. 1764. (Spots.Deeds G266)

DUNDAS, WILLIAM, sh. Aug. 1679, via Barbados to Va, on *Young William.* (PRO.CO1.44.47)

DUNLOP, ALEXANDER, s. of John Dunlop, merchant, sh. pre 1751, sett. Va. (SRO.RD4.177.480)

DUNLOP, ARCHIBALD, merchant, res. Glasgow, sh. 1762, sett. Cabin Point, James River, Va. (SRO.CSGMB.51)(SRA.CFI)

DUNLOP, COLIN, merchant, res. Glasgow, sett. Va and Md pre 1776, fa. of James, Loyalist. (PRO.AO13.28.275)

DUNLOP, DAVID, b. 1803, merchant, m. Ann -, fa. of John, Sarah, David and James, sett. Petersburg, Va. (N.A.-M932/982)

DUNLOP, JAMES, b. 1754, s. of James Dunlop of Garnkirk, merchant and judge, edu. Glasgow Uni. 1768, storekeeper in Va and N.C. pre 1776, Loyalist, sett. Georgetown, Md. (SRO.RD3.282.551)(GUMA86)(PRO.AO13.33)(SRO.CS16.1.168) (SRA.Dunlop pp/LC1.1)

DUNLOP, JAMES, b. Nov. 1757, s. of David Dunlop, merchant, res. Glasgow, sh. 1773, sett. James River, Va, Loyalist, sett. Quebec 1779, d. 28 Aug. 1815 Montreal. (DCB. .284)(SRO.SH9.5.1799)

DUNLOP, JAMES, b. 1777, merchant, sett. Petersburg 1820, d. 13 July 1827 Petersburg, Va. (Raleigh Register 20.7.1827)(WMQ.2.17.13)

DUNLOP, JAMES jr, merchant, sett. pre 1795, nat. 13 Nov. 1802 Richmond, Va.

DUNLOP, JANET, tr. 1771, fr. Port Glasgow to Md, on *Polly*, arr. Port Oxford, Md, 16 Sep. 1771. (SRO.JC27.10.3)

DUNLOP, JOHN, merchant, res. Glasgow, sett. Va, fa. of Alexander, d. pre 1751. (SRO.RD4.177.480)

DUNLOP, WILLIAM, b. 29 Aug. 1708, s. of Alexander Dunlop, merchant, res. Glasgow, sett. Dumfries, Va, m. Mary Pope, fa. of Alexander, d. 21 Dec. 1739, bd. Dumfries. Prince William Co, Va. (WMQ.19.294)

DUNMORE, ROBERT, merchant, sett. Norfolk, Va, pre 1776, Loyalist, sett. Glasgow. (PRO.AO13.3.243)

DUNN, WILLIAM, Jacobite, tr. 29 June 1716, fr. Liverpool to Va or Jamaica, on *Elizabeth and Anne*, arr. Va. (SPC.1716.310)(CTB.31.208)(VSP.1.185)

DURWARD, ISABEL, b. 1786, sett. Wood Co, Va. (N.A.-M932/982)

DYCE, ANNE, b. 23 Sep. 1765, da. of Alexander Dyce and Fredericia Campbell, Aberdeenshire, m. Charles Davidson, Md, 14 Aug. 1802. (TOF681)

EAGLESON, WILLIAM, sh. 2 Nov. 1674, to St Mary's Co, Md, on *Bachelor of Bristol*. (MSA.ESB.152)

EASON, JOHN, b. 1717, gardener, res. Blairgowrie, Perthshire, sh. 1741, sett. Md. (SRO.RH9.17.308)

EASTON, THOMAS, b. 1700, baker, res. Canongate, Edinburgh, sh. Dec. 1719, fr. London to Md. (CLRO/AIA)

EASTOUN, AGNES, res. Edinburgh, tr. 1696, fr. Newhaven, Midlothian, to Va. (SRO.RH15.14.58)

EDMUNDSON, THOMAS, m. Martha Campbell, sett. Cecil Co, Md, pre 1724. (GKF288)

ELDER, DONALD, s. of William Elder, looter, res. Ifauld, Reay, Caithness, tr. 1772, fr. Glasgow to Va, on *Donald*, arr. Port James, Upper District, Va, 13 Mar. 1773, runaway, Richmond, Va, Apr. 1773. (VaGaz15.4.1773)(AJ1292)(SRO.JC27)

ELDER, WILLIAM, farmer, res. Ifauld, Reay, Caithness, looter, tr. 1772, arr. Port James, Upper District, Va, 30 Mar. 1773, runaway, Richmond, Va, Apr. 1773. (VaGaz15.4.1773)(AJ1292)(SRO.JC27.10.3)

ELGIN, GEORGE, sh. 1708, sett. Portobacco, Charles Co, Md, d. Sep. 1748. (SG.28.1.42)

ELGIN, JAMES, b, 1751, cook and bookkeeper, sh. Nov. 1774, fr. London to Va, on *Active*. (PRO.T47.9/11)

ELLIOT, ANDREW, b. 1725, sh. 1740s to Md. (SG

ESDALE, JOHN, merchant, res, Greenock, Renfrewshire, sett. Petersburg, Va, 1806. (SRO.CC8.8.136)

ESKBRIDGE, Captain GEORGE, Potomac River, burgess of Glasgow 17 Dec. 1718. (BGBG341)

ETBURN, WILLIAM, b. 1754, schoolmaster, sh. May 1774, fr. Whitehaven, Cumberland, to Va, on *Molly*. (PRO.T47.9/11)

EVANS, EDWARD, b. 1734, sett. Fredericksburg, Va, drummer in Va Regt 1757. (VMHB.1/2)(L)

EWART, JEAN, coal bearer, res. Edinburgh, infanticide, tr. Mar. 1771, fr. Port Glasgow to Md, on *Crawford*, arr. Port Oxford, Md, 23 July 1771. (SRO.JC27.10.3)

EWING, EBENEZER, res. Falkirk, Stirlingshire, m. Elizabeth Ashton, fa. of Thomas, sett. Bristol, York Co, Va, 1784, pro. 25 Oct. 1795 Williamsburg, Va.

EWING, JOHN, baker, sh. 1766, sett. Portsmouth, Va, Loyalist, sett. Shelborne, N.S. (LNS152)

EWING, ROBERT, sh. 1740, fr. Coleraine, Co Londonderry, to Va, sett. Bedford Co, Va, m. Mary Baker 1747, fa. of Robert, d. 1787. (BLG2676)

FAA, MARY, gypsy, res. Jedburgh, Roxburghshire, tr. 1 Jan. 1715, fr. Glasgow to Va. (GR530)

FAA, PETER, gypsy, res. Jedburgh, Roxburghshire, tr. 1 Jan. 1715, fr. Glasgow to Va. (GR530)

FAIRFAX of CAMERON, Lady CATHERINE, d. Va, pro. June 1719 PCC.

FAIRFAX, THOMAS, b. 1691, s. of Lord Thomas Fairfax and Catherine -, sh. 1747, sett. Northern Neck, Frederick Co, Va, d. Dec. 1782 Va. (Scot.Nat.11/186) (SM.44.165)(GM.52.149)

FAIRFAX, Colonel WILLIAM, President of the Council of Va, d. 2 Sep. 1757, Potomac River, Fairfax Co, Va. (SM.19.614)

FAIRLY, ALEXANDER, res. Kintyre, Argyllshire, d. Richmond, Va, 25 Oct. 1827. (RaleighReg.24.1.1828)

FAIRLEY, JAMES merchant, sett. Warwick Co, Va, pre 1776, Loyalist, sett. Pensacola, West Florida, 1781, sett. Kingston, Jamaica. (SRO.CS16.1.81)(PRO.AO13.34.478)

FALCONER, ALEXANDER, b. 1791, merchant, sett. Baltimore. (N.A.-M432/277-99)

FALCONER, JAMES, clergyman, res. Morayshire, sh. 1718, sett. Charles ph., York Co, Va, pro. 1728 York, Va.

FALCONER, THOMAS, farmer, sh. 1714, fr. Glasgow to Potomac River, on the *American Merchant*. (TM202)

FALLOW, JOHN, d. Ayr 1805, pro. 18 Jan. 1806 Baltimore.

FARQUHAR, THOMAS, merchant, res. Edinburgh, sett. Va. pre 1782. (SRO.CS17.1.1)

FARQUHAR, WILLIAM, res. Aberdeen, sh. 1700 to N.H., sett. Frederick Co, Md, fa. of Allen. (CAG.1.102)

FARQUHARSON, CHARLES, b. 1759, s. of James Farquharson and Ann Stuart, res. Ballitruan, Kirkmichael, Morayshire, property agent, m. Ann -, d. 2 June 1860, Baltimore, Md. (Kirkmichael g/s)(N.A.-M432/277-99)

FARQUHARSON, HARRY, s. of Arthur Farquharson of Cults, soldier, res. Glencairn, Aberdeenshire, Jacobite, tr. 1716, fr. Liverpool to Va, m. Elizabeth Morgan. (JAB.1.72)

FARQUHARSON, JOHN MICHAEL, res. Whitehouse, d. Petersburg, Sep. 1807 (SM.69.876)

FARQUHARSON, LAURENCE, s. of Donald Farquharson and Helen Gordon, res. Cobletoun of Tulloch, Aberdeenshire, Jacobite, tr. 28 July 1716, fr. Liverpool to Va, on *Godspeed*, arr. Md Oct. 1716. (SPC.1716.309)(JAB.1.73)(HM389)

FEGAN, JOHN, b. 1730, farmer, militiaman in Va Regt 1756. (VMHB.1/2)(L)

FENWICK, JOHN, gypsy, res. Jedburgh, Roxburghshire, tr. 1 Jan. 1715, fr. Glasgow to Va. (GR530)

FERGUSON, ALEXANDER, forger, tr. Feb. 1670, fr. Leith to Va, on *Ewe and Lamb*. (PC.3.650)

FERGUSON, ALEXANDER, Jacobite, tr. 29 June 1716, fr. Liverpool to Va, on *Elizabeth and Anne*, arr. Va. 1716. (SPC.1716.310)(CTB.31.208)(VSP.1.186)

FERGUSON, DONALD, Jacobite, tr. 29 June 1716, fr. Liverpool to Va or Jamaica, on *Elizabeth and Anne*. (SPC.1716.310)(CTB.31.208)

FERGUSON, DUNCAN, Jacobite, tr. 22 Apr. 1747, fr. Liverpool to Va, on *Johnson*, arr. Port Oxford, Md, 5 Aug. 1747. (PRO.T1.328)

FERGUSON, DUNCAN, b. 1713, farmer, res. Perthshire, Jacobite, tr, 22 Apr. 1747, fr. Liverpool to Va, on *Johnson*, arr. Port Oxford, Md, 5 Aug. 1747. (P.2.188)(MR71)(PRO.T1.328)

FERGUSON, DUNCAN, Jacobite, tr. 28 July 1716, fr. Liverpool to Va, on *Godspeed*, arr. Md Oct. 1716. (SPC.1716.310)(CTB.31.209)(HM388)

FERGUSON, DUNCAN, b. 1732, sett. Winchester Co, Va, drummer in Va Regt 1756. (VMHB.1/2)(L)

FERGUSON, DUNCAN, b. 1737, sett. Prince William Co, Va, militiaman in Va Regt 1756. (VMHB.1/2)(L)

FERGUSON, FINDLAY, plasterer, res. Edinburgh, m. Catherine Forbes, sett, Norfolk, Va, nat. 27 Oct. 1792 Norfolk, d.pre 1814. (SRO.RD2.262.549)(SRO.RD5.70.586)

FERGUSON, HALBERT, res. Edinburgh, tr. June 1673 to Va. (SRO.JC2.13)

FERGUSON, HENRY, Jacobite, tr. 24 May 1716, fr. Liverpool to Va, on *Friendship*, arr. Md Aug. 1716. (SPC.1716.311)(HM387)

FERGUSON, J., b. 1795, m. Anne -, sh. pre 1820 to N.Y., fa. of Robert, Bridget, Frances, Catherine, George and Rebecca, sett. Washington, D.C. (N.A.-M432/56-7)

FERGUSON, JAMES, Jacobite, tr. 29 June 1716, fr. Liverpool to Va or Jamaica, on *Elizabeth and Anne*, arr. Va. 1716. (SPC.1716.310)(CTB.31.208)(VSP.1.186)

FERGUSON, JAMES, res. Dungalston, sett. Baltimore pre 1821. (SRO.SH24.7.1821)

FERGUSON, JAMES, b. 1797, res. Perthshire, USN observatory astronomer, d. 1867 Washington, D.C. (TSA217)

FERGUSON, LAURENCE, Jacobite, tr. 29 June 1716, fr.Liverpool to Va or Jamaica, on *Elizabeth and Anne*, arr. Va. 1716. (SPC.1716.310)(VSP.1.186)

FERGUSON, PATRICK, Jacobite, tr. 29 June 1716, fr. Liverpool to Va or Jamaica, on *Elizabeth and Anne*, arr. Va 1716. (SPC.1716.310)(CTB.31.208)(VSP.1.185)

FERGUSON, PATRICK, Jacobite, res. Perthshire, tr, 22 Apr. 1747, fr. Liverpool to Va, on *Johnson*, arr. Port Oxford, Md, 5 Aug. 1747. (PRO.T1.328)

FERGUSON, ROBERT, Jacobite, tr. 31 July 1716, fr. Liverpool to Va, on *Anne*. (SPC.1716.310)

FERGUSON, ROBERT, merchant, sett. Jappahannock, Rappahannock River, Va, pre 1755. (SRO.RD4.198.558)

FERGUSON, ROBERT, storekeeper, res. Moniaive, Dumfriesshire, sett. Md pre 1774. (SRO.CS16.1.161)

FERGUSON, ROBERT, Chief Judge of the Orphans Court, d. 1 Sep. 1812 Mulberry Grove, Charles Co, Md. (MdGaz17.9.1812)

FERGUSON, THOMAS, b. 1725, sett. Williamsburg, Va, militiaman in Va Regt 1757. (VMHB.1/2)(L)

FERGUSON, WILLIAM, weaver, res. Lanark, Lanarkshire, Covenanter, tr. Sep. 1668, fr. Leith to Va, on *Convertin*. (PC.2.470)

FERGUSON, WILLIAM, Jacobite, tr. 28 July 1716, fr. Liverpool to Va, on*Godspeed*, arr. Md Oct. 1716.   (SPC.1716.310)(CTB.31.209)(HM389)

FIELD, ALEXANDER SCHAW, grandson of John Schaw, merchant in Edinburgh, and Margaret Borthwick, sett. Mecklenburg, Va, pre 1795.   (SRO.RD3.271.543) (SRO.RD4.279.377)

FIELD, JAMES, physician, m. Mary Schaw, fa. of William, Henrietta, Edmund, Hunce and Alexander, sett. Petersburg, Va, pre 1795.   (SRO.RD4.272.164)(RegEdinApp

FINLAY, ROBERT, s. of Rev. Robert Finlay, res. Glasgow, sh. pre 1772, sett. Md. (SRA.B10.15.7553)

FINLAY, WILLIAM, Jacobite, tr. 29 June 1716, fr. Liverpool to Va or Jamaica, on *Elizabeth and Anne*, arr. Va. 1716.   (SPC.1716.310)(CTB.31.208)(VSP.1.186)

FINNEY, ALEXANDER, s. of William Finney, res. Aberdeen, clergyman, edu. Marischal College, Aberdeen, 1714, sh. 1724, sett. Martin's ph.,and Brandon's ph., Va, 1724-1770. (SRO.SH1.2.1755)(EMA27)(OD16)

FINNEY, ROBERT, Jacobite, tr. 29 June 1716, fr. Liverpool to Va or Jamaica, on *Elizabeth and Anne*, arr. York, Va, 1716.   (SPC.1716.310)(VSP.1.185)

FINNEY, WILLIAM, clergyman, edu. King's College, Aberdeen, and Glasgow Uni., sh. 1710, sett. Henrico ph., Va, m. Mary -, fa. of William and Mary, burgess of Glasgow 1719, d. 1727 Va, pro. 5 June 1727 Henrico.   (SCHR.14.149)(OD15)

FINNIE, JOHN, farmer, res. Cushnie, Aberdeenshire, Jacobite, tr. 1716, fr. Liverpool to Va.   (JAB.1.151)(CTB.31.208)

FISHER, JOHN, merchant, sett. Va pre 1778.   (SRO.CS16.1.173)

FISHER, JOHN, b. 1806, m. Mary -, fa. of Mary, John, Robert, Elizabeth, Jane, Margaret and Isabella, arr. Baltimore 1824.   (N.A.-M596)

FISHER, MARGARET, whore and thief, res,. Edinburgh, tr. 28 Nov. 1704, fr. Leith to Md. (SRO.PC2.28.307)

FISHER, WILLIAM, b. 1807, blacksmith, m. Elizabeth -, fa. of Christian, Elizabeth, Mary, John, Sarah, William, James, Robert and Virginia, sett. Baltimore. (N.A.-M432/277-99)

FLEMING, ALEXANDER,   (?) s. of Earl of Wigton, sh. 1650, sett. Rappahannock, Va. (Americana.33.328)

FLEMING, ALEXANDER, b. 1727, horsehirer, res. Aberdeen, Jacobite, tr. 24 Feb. 1747, fr. Liverpool to Va, on *Gildart*, arr. Port North Potomac, Md, 5 Aug. 1747. (P.2.197)(JAB.2.425)(MR129)(PRO.T1.328)

FLEMING of FARM, Sir COLLINGWOOD, res. Rutherglen, Lanarkshire, d. 1764 Va. (SM.26.290)

FLEMING, GARDNER, merchant, sett. Suffolk, Va, pre 1764.   (SRO.CS16.1.120)

FLEMING, JOHN, s. of John Fleming and Lillias Graham, res. Wigtown, d. 27 Apr. 1686, New Kent Co, Va, bd. St Peter's ph.   (GKF125)

FLEMING, JOHN, b. 1738, planter, sett. Fredericksburg, Va, militiaman in Va Regt 1757.   (VMHB.1/2)(L)

FLEMING, PATRICK, s. of Robert Fleming, planter, res. Kirkintilloch, Dunbartonshire, sett. Accomack Co, Va, pre 1662.   (CBK147)

FLEMING, WILLIAM, b. 18 Feb. 1729, physician, res. Jedburgh, Roxburghshire, sh. 1755, sett. Staunton, Va, m. Ann Christian, sett. Kentucky 1779, d. Aug. 1795. (VMHB.85.372)(WMQ.6.158)

FORBES, ALEXANDER, sett. Talbot Co, Md, nat. 1695.   (MSA.19.281)

FORBES, ALEXANDER, clergyman, edu. King's College, Aberdeen, 1706, sh. 1709 to Va. (EMA27)

FORBES, ALEXANDER, b. 1795, weaver, sh. pre 1828 to Md, a. of Alexander, sett. Jefferson Co, Va.   (N.A.-M932/982)

FORBES, DAVID, physician, sett. Fredericksburg, va, 1774, m. Lady Margaret Stirling.   (OD44)

FORBES, GEORGE, s. of Thomas and Margaret Forbes, res, Deer, Aberdeenshire, sh. 1711, sett. St Mary's Co, Md, fa. of George, d. Oct. 1739, pro 31 Oct. 1739 Md, pro June 1742 PCC.   (MSA.Will.22.101)(APB.3.95)

FORBES, GEORGE, merchant, res. Aberdeen, sett. Good's Bridge, Va, pro. 7 June 1754 Chesterfield Va.

FORBES, HELEN, res. Edinburgh, m. A. Clark, sett. Norfolk, Va, pre 1815. (SRO.SH25.10.1815)

FORBES, JOHN, b. 1700, res. Aberdeenshire(?), sett. Dryden, Cheseldyne, Md, pre 1729, fa. of James, d. 26 Jan. 1737.   (BLG2688)

FORBES, JOHN, b. 1728, s. of William and Anna Forbes, merchant, res. Kintore, Aberdeenshire, sh. 1747, d. 1757 Va.   (HF412)

FORBES, MARGARET, res. Kirkton of Tough, Aberdeenshire, infanticide, tr. June 1755, fr. Aberdeen to Va on *Hope.*   (SM.17.266)(AJ388)

FORBES, THOMAS, farmer, res. Cushnie, Aberdeenshire, Jacobite, tr. 24 May 1716, fr. Liverpool to Va, on *Friendship,* arr. Md Aug. 1716. (SPC.1716.311)(JAB.1.151)(HM387)

FORBES, WILLIAM, plasterer, sett. King and Queen Co, Va, militiaman in Va Regt 1757. (VMHB.1/2)(L)

FORD, G., b. 1796, plasterer, arr. Baltimore on *Oryza* 1820.   (N.A.-M596)

FORD, WILLIAM, b. 1795, sh. pre 1825 to Massachusetts, m. Frances -, fa. of Frances and Catherine, sett. Baltimore. (N.A.-M432/982)

FORDYCE, CHARLES, res. Edinburgh, soldier, d. Va, pro. Nov. 1777 PCC.

FORSYTH, JAMES, sett. Va 1680. (DAB.6.533)

FORSYTH, WILLIAM, merchant, sett. Va pre 1778. (SRO.CS16.1.173)

FOSTER, JOHN, b. 1677, husbandman, Jacobite, tr. 24 Apr. 1747, fr. Liverpool to Va, on Johnson, arr. Port Oxford, Md, 5 Aug. 1747. (P.2.204)(PRO.T1.328)

FOSTER, THOMAS, Jacobite, tr. 29 June 1716, fr. Liverpool to Va or Jamaica, on Elizabeth and Anne, arr. Va 1716. (SPC.1716.310)(CTB.31.208)(VSP.1.185)

FOULIS, JAMES, s. of Andrew Foulis, res. Glasgow, clergyman, edu. Glasgow Uni. 1734, sh. 1750 to Va. (EMA28)(MAGU13)

FOWLER, ANDREW, b. 1735, farmer, sett. Fairfax Co, Va, militiaman in Va Regt 1756. (VMHB.1/2)(L)

FOWLER, JOHN, tr. 1775, fr. Greenock, Renfrewshire, to Va, on Rainbow, arr. Port Hampton, Va, 3 May 1775. (SRO.JC27.10.3)

FRAME, JAMES, b. 1766, s. of Rev. James Frame, res. Alloa, Clackmannanshire, d. 26 Oct. 1803 Petersburg, Va. (Blandford g/s)(DPCA74)

FRAZER, ALEXANDER, b. 1731, planter, sett. Culpepper Co, Va, militiaman in Va Regt 1757. (VMHB.1/2)(L)

FRASER, ALEXANDER, surgeon-apothecary, res. Freuchie, Fife, then Edinburgh, sett. Annapolis, Md, m. Elizabeth -, fa. of Stephen, Samuel, Alexander, and Anne, d. 25 June 1729, pro. 23 Oct. 1732 Md, pro. 1 June 1732 Edinburgh. (MSA.Will20.455)(SRO.CC8.8.95)

FRASER, ALLAN, shoemaker, sett. Norfolk, Va, pre 1776, Loyalist, d. N.Y. (PRO.AO13.24.169)

FRASER, ANNE, res. Freuchie, Fife, sett. Northampton Co, Va, m. Kendall Harmonson, mo. of John, d. pre 1776. (SRO.RD2.220.1267)

FRASER, DANIEL, officer in Fraser's Highlanders 1757-1763, merchant skipper in Va 1763 -1776, Loyalist. (PRO.AO13.4.195)

FRASER, DANIEL, d. Petersburg, Va, 8 Oct. 1803. (Raleigh Register17.10.1803)

FRASER, ELLEN, b. 1758, sett. Alleghany Co, Md. (N.A.-M432/277-99)

FRASER, JAMES, merchant, res. Inverness, sh. pre 1703, sett. Va. (SRO.CS96.3309)

FRASER, JAMES, b. 1730, waterman, militiaman in Va Regt 1756. (VMHB.1/2)(L)

FRASER, JAMES, b. 1733, planter, sett. King and Queen Co, militiaman in Va Regt 1757. (VMHB.1/2)(L)

FRASER, JAMES, shoemaker, sett. Norfolk, Va, pre 1776, Loyalist. (PRO.AO13.24.169)

FRASER, JAMES, b. 24 Aug. 1765, s. of Rev. George Fraser and Agnes Thomson, res. Moneydie, Perthshire, d. at sea between Va and Grenada. (F.4.225)

FRASER, JAMES, b. 1722, farmer, res. Highlands, militiaman in Va Regt 1757. (VMHB.1/2)

FRASER, JAMES, clergyman, sh. pre 1775, sett. Hartford, N.C., Loyalist, sett. Annapolis pre 1786. (PRO.AO13.24.172/182)

FRASER, JAMES, nat. 20 Mar. 1805 Norfolk, Va.

FRASER, JAMES, b. 1782, m. Caroline -, fa. of James, William, Charlotte, Mary and Sarah, sh. pre 1814, sett. Baltimore. (N.A.-M432/277-99)

FRASER, JOHN, clergyman, sh. 1701 to Va, d. Nov. 1742 Piscataway, Md. (EMA28)

FRASER, JOHN, b. 1737, laborer, sett. Cumberland Co, Va, militiaman in Va Regt 1757. (VMHB.1/2)(L)

FRASER, JOHN, clergyman, edu. Edinburgh Uni., sh. 1769 to Va, sett. East Florida. (EMA28)(FPA308)

FRASER, JOHN, b. 1785, iron dealer, sett. Baltimore. (N.A.-M432/277-99)

FRASER, THOMAS, s. of Simon Fraser of Fanallan, soldier, d. Norfolk, Va , pro. Jan. 1790 PCC.

FRASER, WILLIAM, sett. Henrico Co, Va, 1700, m. Hannah -, fa. of William. (CAG.1.562)

FRASER, WILLIAM, planter, res. Glasgow, sett. Va pre 1826. (SRO.SH4.10.1826)

FREEMAN, JAMES, b. 9 Dec. 1711, s. of James Freeman and Margaret Tennant, merchant and planter, res. Aberdeen, sh. Dec. 1729, fr. London to Md, m. - Wallace. (CLRO/AIA)(PMA/MS)

FRENCH, GEORGE, physician, sett. Frederick Co, Va, 17.. (OD44)

FROUD, JOHN, b. 1702, res. Blackshaw, Nithsdale, Dumfriesshire, sh. Aug. 1722, fr. London to Md. (CLRO/AIA)

FRUID, JAMES, s. of James Fruid, d. pre 1725 Md, pro. 1725 PCC.

FULLARTON, ALEXANDER, b. 1731, runaway, Augusta Co, Va, July 1751. (VaGaz18.7.1751)

FULTON,Mrs, b. 1802, mo. of Elizabeth and Janet, arr. Baltimore 1826. (N.A.-M596)

FYFFE, WILLIAM, clergyman, sh. 1729 to Va. (EMA29)

GALES, MARY, b. 1796, arr. Baltimore Sep. 1823. (PA303)

GALL, ALEXANDER, res. Peterhead, Aberdeenshire, sheepstealer, tr. June 1755, fr. Aberdeen to Va, on *Hope*. (AJ383/8)

GALLOWAY, CHRISTINE, m. John Ord 26 Dec. 1654, res. Aberdeen, adultress and thief, tr. 1668, fr. Aberdeen to Va. (ABR.JCB1.107)

GALLOWAY, JAMES, mariner, nat. Richmond Co, Va, 31 Aug. 1797. (VSP.8.446)

GALLOWAY, ROBERT, s. of Andrew Galloway, merchant, edu. Glasgow Uni. 1773, res. Glasgow, d. 1 Aug. 1794 Fredericksburg, Va. (EA3212/238)(MAGU105)

GALLOWAY, SAMUEL, b. 1645, res. Galloway, sett. Anne Arundel Co, Md, 1690, fa. of William, d, 17 Apr. 1719. (BLG2697)

GALT, JAMES, b. 1805, res. Irvine, Ayrshire, tsh. 1821, tobacco planter in City Point, Richmond, Va, nat. 1 Aug. 1826 Eastern District, Va. (US.D/C.RB5.520)(VMHB.87.326)

GALT, JOHN, res. Ayrshire, Covenanter, sh. 1684, sett. Hampton, Va. (WMQ.1.1.15)

GALT, JOHN, b. 1800, clerk, sett. Baltimore. (N.A.-M432/277-99)

GALT, WILLIAM, res. Ayrshire, Covenanter, sh. 1684, sett. Hampton, Va. (WMQ.1.1.15)

GALT, WILLIAM, b. 13 Apr. 1755, res. Dundonald, Ayrshire, sh. 1775, d. 26 Mar. 1825, Richmond, Va, pro. 1825 Richmond. (RaleighRegister.15.4.1825)

GALT, WILLIAM, b. 1801, merchant and farmer, sh. Sep. 1817, m. (1) Roxanna Dixon 1825 (2) Mary Bell Taylor, fa. of Frances, Thomas, Mary, Rosanna, Sally, Lucy, Jean, William and Anna, sett. Fluvanna Co, Va. (VMHB.87.326)(N.A.-M932/982)

GARDEN, ALEXANDER, b. 1808, tanner, m. Ruth -, fa. of Charles, Henry, Nicholas, and James, sett. Ohio Co, Va. (N.A.-M932/982)

GARDEN, DAVID, b. 1806, tanner, sh. pre 1828, m. Alice -, fa. of Alexander, sett. Ohio Co, Va. (N.A.-M932/982)

GARDEN, JAMES, s. of Alexander Garden, clergyman, edu. Marischal College, Aberdeen, sh. 1754 to Va. (EMA29)(FPA307)

GARDINER, JOHN, res. Dundee, Angus, d. Va, pro. Nov. 1816 PCC.

GARDNER, ARCHIBALD, Jacobite, tr. 5 May 1747, fr. Liverpool to Va, on *Gildart*, arr. Port North Potomac, Md, 5 Aug. 1747. (PRO.T1.328)

GARDNER, GEORGE, merchant, sett. Henrico Co, Va, nat. 7 Oct. 1793 Henrico Co.

GARDNER, JOB, b. 1704, escapee, Cecil Co, Md, 1729. (AmerWklyMerc7.8.1729)

GARDNER, PETER, b. 1729, tailor, Jacobite, tr. 5 May 1747, fr. Liverpool to Va, on *Johnson*, arr. Port North Potomac, Md, 5 Aug. 1747. (P.2.222)(PRO.T1.328)

GATT, WILLIAM, merchant, sh. 1775, d. 26 Mar. 1825 Richmond, Va. (DPCA1189)

GAULDIE, GEORGE, tr. 5 feb. 1752, fr. Aberdeen to Va, on *Planter*. (AJ265)

GAULL, GEORGE, schoolmaster, runaway, Mattawoman Creek, Charles Co, Md. (MdGaz20.7.1769)

GAY, WILLIAM, merchant, sett. Va pre 1772. (SRO.SH8.10.1772)

GEDDES, ALEXANDER, laborer, res Sanston, Aberdeenshire, Jacobite, tr. 5 May 1747, fr. Liverpool to Va, on *Gildart*, arr. Port North Potomac, Md, 5 Aug. 1747. (P.2.220)(JAB.2.427)(MR123)(PRO.T1.328)

GEDDES, ANDREW, schoolmaster, sh. 1695 to Md, sett. William and Mary College, Va, 1697. (WMQ.2.15.245)

GEDDES, GEORGE, b. 1805, gilder, sh. pre 1829 to Md, m. May -, fa. of William, Isabel, Sarah, George, James and Edward, sett. Baltimore. (N.A.-M432/277-99)

GEDDES, Captain JOHN, sett. James River, Va, burgess of Glasgow 1716, d. post 1719. (WMQ.2.20.556)

GEDDIE, JAMES, b. 1791, farmer, m. Harriet -, sett. Dorchester Co, Md. (N.A.-M432/277-99)

GEILLS, ANDREW, merchant and skipper, res. Glasgow, sett. Va pre 1744. (SRA.B10.15.5959)

GERMISTON, HARRY, res. Strichen, Orkney Islands, sett. Va pre 1741. (SRO.CS16.1.170)

GIBB, ALEXANDER, b. 1699, res. Linlithgow, West Lothian, sh. Nov. 1730, fr. London to Md. (CLRO/AIA)

GIBBON, ARTHUR, res. Aberdeenshire, sheepstealer, tr. 25 May 1749, fr. Aberdeen to Va, on *Dispatch of Newcastle*. (SM.11.252)(AJ68)

GIBBONS, JOHN, woolcomber, res. Aberdeen, conspirator, tr. 1772, fr. Glasgow to Va, on *Brilliant*, arr. Port Hampton, Va, 7 Oct. 1772. (SRO.JC27.10.3)

GIBSON, JAMES, merchant, res. Glasgow, sett. Pungataigue Creek, Accomack Co, Va, pre 1731. (SRO.AC

GIBSON, JAMES, merchant, res. Dumfriesshire, sh. pre 1771, sett. Suffolk, Va. (SRO.RS23.20.372/4)

GIBSON, JOHN, factor, res. Glasgow, sett. Colchester, Va, pre 1776. (SRA.779.21)

GIBSON, JOHN, s. of Robert Gibson, merchant, res. Kilmarnock, Ayrshire, sett. Va pre 1791. (SRO.SH.17.8.1791)

GIBSON, JOHN, b. 1784, s. of John Gibson, weaver, res. 10 Carnegie St., Edinburgh, sh. 1810, sett. Winchester, Va. (SRO.RD5.119.277)(1812/323)

GIBSON, ROBERT, sh. 2 Nov. 1674, to St Mary's Co, Md, on *Bachelor of Bristol.* (MSA.ESB.152)

GIBSON, ROBERT, Covenanter, tr. Oct. 1669 to Va. (PC.3.22)

GIBSON, ROBERT, s. of Matthew Gibson, merchant, res. Irvine, Ayrshire, sett. Norfolk, Va, pre 1793. (SRO.SH2.4.1793)

GIFFEN, DANIEL, b. 1768, farmer, sett. Ohio Co, Va, m. Nancy -. (N.A.-M932/982)

GILCHRIST, ANDREW, s. of George Gilchrist and Agnes Gibson, merchant, res. Glasgow, sh. pre 1733, sett. Accomack Co, Va. (SRO.CC9.7.62)

GILCHRIST, ISABEL, b. 1801, sett. Monroe Co, Va. (N.A.-M932/982)

GILCHRIST, JOHN, s. of George Gilchrist and Agnes Gibson, rs. Glasgow, m. Mary -, sett. Accomack Co, Va, d. 1751, pro. 26 Feb. 1751 Accomack.

GILCHRIST, JOHN, s. of Arthur Gilchrist and Lilias Barclay, merchant, res. Premnay, Aberdeenshire, d. 1762 Va. (APB.3.221)

GILCHRIST, JOHN, merchant, res. Galloway, sett. Norfolk, Va, m. Frances -, fa. of Elizabeth and Frances, pro. Nov. 1773 Norfolk, Va.

GILCHRIST, ROBERT, b. 1721, sh. 1739, sett. Caroline Co, Va, m. Catherine -, d. 16 July 1790 Port Royal, Va. (Port Royal g/s)(SM.52.517)(Va.Inde.21.7.1790) (WMQ.2.22.345)

GILCHRIST, ROBERT, s. of William Gilchrist, merchant, res. Kilmarnock, Ayrshire, sett. Md pre 1774. (SRO.RD3.246.375)

GILCHRIST, SAMUEL, b. 1794, farmer, arr. Baltimore Sep. 1823. (N.A.-M596)

GILCHRIST, THOMAS, s. of Thomas Gilchrist, merchant, res. Dumfries, Dumfriesshire, sett. Suffolk, Va, and Halifax, N.C., pre 1783. (SRO.RD4.235.686)

GILL. NATHAN W., nat. 27 May 1793 Norfolk City, Va.

GILLESPIE, GEORGE, merchant, res. Tynwald, Dumfriesshire, sett. St Mary's Co, Md, d. pre 1724, pro. Mar. 1724 PCC.

GILLESPIE, GEORGE LEWIS, sh. 1720, sett. Leesburg, Va, fa. of George. (BLG3001)

GILLIES, WILLIAM, assistant storekeeper, sett. James River, Va, Loyalist, sh. June 1777, fr. N.Y. to Glasgow, on *Betsey* . (SFV233)

GILLIES, WILLIAM, d. 14 Dec. 1813 Petersburg, Va. (RaleighRegister17.12.1813)

GILLIS, WILLIAM, b. 1799, carpenter, arr. Baltimore Sep. 1823. (N.A.-M596)

GILLISS, THOMAS, sett. Eastern Shore, Md, pre 1668. (DAB.7.292)

GILLOCH, LAWRENCE, sett. Orange Co and Culpepper Co, Va, pre 1763. (SG.23.170)

GILMER, Dr GEORGE E., b. 1700, s. of William Gilmer, res. Edinburgh, physician and pharmacist, edu. Edinburgh Uni., sett. Williamsburg, Va, 1731, d. 1757. (WMQ.15.225)(DAB.7.307)

GILMER, JOHN, m. Agnes -, sh. 1745, sett. Kerr's Creek, James River, Va, d. 10 Oct. 1759. (WMQ.2.17.118)

GILMER, THOMAS, physician, sett. Va. 1720. (CAG.1.586)

GILMORE, ROBERT, s. of William Gilmore, merchant, res. Kilmarnock, Ayrshire, sett. Lancaster, Va, fa. of John and Robert, pro. 23 May 1782 Williamsburg. (SRO.SH25.3.1795)(SRO.SH6.10.1794)

GILMOUR, GAVIN, merchant, sett. Md pre 1778. (SRO.CS16.1.173)

GILMOUR, ROBERT, storekeeper, sett. Northumberland Co, Va, pre 1776, Loyalist. (PRO.AO13.27.384/92)

GILMOUR, ROBERT, b. 10 Nov. 1748, s. of John Gilmour, merchant, res. Netherton, Kilmarnock, Ayrshire, sett. Oxford, Md, 1767, m. Louisa Airey 1771, fa. of Robert, William and John, sett. Baltimore, pro. 1782 Williamsburg, Va. (DAB.7.309)(SRO.CS16.1.151)(SRO.RS42.21.92)

GLASSELL, ANDREW, b. 8 Oct. 1738, s. of Robert Glassell and Mary Kelton, res. Galloway, sett. Madison Co, Va, 1756, m. Elizabeth Taylor 1776, fa. of Mildred, John, Mary, Helen, Jane, James, Andrew, Robert and William, d. 4 July 1827. (VMHB.10.202)(VG.5)(AGB.1.10)

GLASSELL, JOHN, b. 1734, s. of Robert Glassell and Mary Kelton, res. Dumfriesshire, sett. Fredericksburg, Va, m. Helen Buchan, fa. of Johanna, Loyalist, d. 1806 U.K. (AGB.1.10)

GLASSELL, WILLIAM, res. Haddington (?), East Lothian, sett. Fredericksburg, Spotsylvania Co, Va, pre 1792. (Spotsylvania DBN.3.4.1792)

GLASGOW, AGNES, sh. 1742 to Pa., sett. Buckingham Co, Va, m. John Snoddy. (AA.8.75)

GLASSFORD, JAMES, merchant, res. Glasgow, sh. 1760 to Quebec, sett. Norfolk, Va, 1765. (SRA.CFI)

GLASSFORD, JOHN, sh. 1758 to Va. (SA135)

GLEN, WILLIAM, clergyman, sh. 1707 to Va. (EMA30)

GLENN, JAMES ANDERSON, res. Paisley, Renfrewshire, tobacco merchant, sett. Petersburg, Va, pre 1822, m. Isabella Wilson. (UNC/Glenn pp)

GLENDINNING, DAVID, b. 1721, sett. Md, deserter Va Regt 1756.
(VMHB.1/2)(L)(VaGaz.27.8.1756)

GLENDINNING, JOHN, Jacobite, tr. 29 June 1716, fr. Liverpool to Va or Jamaica, on
Elizabeth and Anne, arr. Va 1716. (SPC.1716.310)(CTB.31.208)(VSP.1.185)

GLENDY, JOHN, Jacobite, tr. 24 May 1716, fr. Liverpool to Va, on *Friendship*,
arr. Md Aug. 1716. (SPC.1716.311)(HM386)

GLESSEN, JOHN, Jacobite, tr. 5 May 1747, fr. Liverpool to Va, on *Gildart*, arr. Port
North Potomac, Md, 5 Aug. 1747. (P.2.232)(PRO.T1.328)

GLOVER, JAMES, merchant, sh. 2 Dec. 1682, fr. Port Glasgow to Va, on
Supply of Chester. (SRO.E72.19.8)

GOLDIE, CATHERINE, da. of Thomas Goldie, m. Andrew Newton, Accomack Co, Va,
d. 22 May 1770, pro. 17 Oct. 1788 Edinburgh. (SRO.CC8.8.127)(VaGaz31.5.1770)

GOLDIE, GEORGE, b. 1741, clergyman, sh. 1766, sett. Frederick Co and St Mary's Co,
Md, m (1) ..... Eden, (2) Priscilla Barber, fa. of Jane and Margaret, d. 1791.
(VG.183)(EMA30)

GOLDIE, ROBERT, s. of ..... Goldie and Margaret Whiteman, res. Edinburgh, sett.
Chesterfield Co, Va, pro. 1757 Chesterfield.

GOLDIE, WILLIAM, b. 1736, husbandman, sh. Dec. 1774, fr. London to Va, on
Carolina . (PRO.T47.9/11)

GORDON, ADAM, sh. 1690, sett. Fredericksburg, Va, m. Sally Chapman, fa. of Charles.
(CAG.1.625)

GORDON, ALEXANDER, farmer, res. Cushnie, Aberdeenshire, Jacobite, tr. 24 May 1716,
fr. Liverpool to Va, on *Friendship*, arr. Md Aug. 1716.
(SPC.1716.311)(JAB.1.151)(HM386)

GORDON, ALEXANDER, merchant, res. Kirkcudbright, sett. Petersburg, Va, 17.., m.
Mary -, fa. of Peggy. (HBV

GORDON, ALEXANDER, clergyman, res, Glasserton, sett. Va and Md 1763-1775.
(SRO.CS16.1.143)

GORDON, ALEXANDER, surgeon and druggist, sett. Norfolk, Va, 1763, Loyalist,
d. London, pro. Mar. 1799 PCC. (PRO.AO13.29.672)

GORDON, ARCHIBALD, militiaman, Pittsylvania Co, Va, 1774, d. Franklin Co, Va.(HG

GORDON, BASIL, sett. Fredericksburg, Va, 1690. (CAG.1.625)

GORDON, BASIL, b. 15 May 1768, s. of Samuel Gordon, merchant,res. Kirkcudbright,
sh. 1784, sett. Windsor Lodge, Culpepper Co, Va, m. Anne Campbell Knox, fa. of
Basil and Douglas. (BLG2716)(WMQ.2.2.223)

GORDON, CHARLES, b. 1730, s. of Patrick Gordon, res. Binhall, Aberdeenshire, Jacobite, tr. 1747 to Md. (P.2.234)

GORDON, CHARLES, b. 11 Dec. 1764, res. Aberdeenshire, sett. Chestertown, Md, pre 1760, m. (1) Alice George (2) Elizabeth Nicolson, fa. of Mary, Hannah, Elizabeth Ann, John, Charles, Sarah, Alice and Joseph. (AA.3.23)

GORDON, DANIEL, sh. 2 Nov 1674, to St Mary's Co, Md, on *Bachelor of Bristol.* (MSA.ESB.152)

GORDON, ELIZABETH, res. Edinburgh, whore and thief, tr. 28 Nov. 1704, fr. Leith to Md. (SRO.PC2.28.307)

GORDON, ELIZABETH, res. Aberdeenshire, sett. Westover ph., Charles City Co, Va, m. (1) ... Brand (2) ... Hollinghurst, pro. 4 Dec. 1728 Charles City.

GORDON, ELIZABETH, da. of Professor Thomas Gordon, res. Aberdeen, m. Rev. John Scott, 1768, sett. Va, d. 15 Oct. 1802 Gordon's Vale, Va. (EA.4042.02)

GORDON, FRANCIS, s. of Sir Robert Gordon of Earlston, merchant, sett. Yecomico, Va, pre 1759, pro. 23 Apr. 1770 Edinburgh. (SRO.CC8.8.121)(SRO.CS16.1.103)

GORDON, GEORGE, s. of Adam Gordon and Elizabeth Cruickshank, merchant, sh. pre 1747, sett. Va. (Rathven g/s)

GORDON, GEORGE, res. Aberdeenshire, forger, tr. 5 Feb. 1752, fr. Aberdeen to Va, on *Planter.* (SM.14.509)(AJ265)

GORDON, GEORGE, s. of Rev. Charles Gordon, merchant and planter, res. Ashkirk, Roxburghshire, sett. Md, d. pre 1748. (APB.3.139)

GORDON, GEORGE, s. of James Gordon, res. Glasgow, edu. Glasgow Uni. 1781, d. Aug. 1794, Portobacco, Md. (MAGU131)(SM.56.734)

GORDON, JAMES, s. of Arthur Gordon of Carnousie, Banffshire, sett. King and Queen Co, Va, pre 1744. (SRO.RH15)

GORDON, JAMES, dyer, arr. Oxford, Md, Apr. 1774, on *Polly.* (VaGaz27.10.1774)

GORDON, JOAN, res. Edinburgh, tr. 1696, fr. Newhaven, Midlothian, to Va. (SRO.RH15.14.58)

GORDON, JOHN, clergyman, res. Aberdeenshire, sett. Wilmington, James City Co, Va, d. pre 1705. (SCM.5.366)(APB

GORDON, JOHN, s. of George Gordon, merchant, res. Aberdeen, sett. Va pre 1766. (SRO.CS16.1.125)

GORDON, JOHN, b. 28 Aug. 1717, s. of Dr John Gordon and Margaret Duell, clergyman, edu. King's College, Aberdeen, 1734, and Oxford Uni. 1737, sett. Anne Arundel Co, Md, d. 1790 St Michael's, Talbot Co, Md. (Talbot Wills VJ.P6/341)

GORDON, JOHN, b. 1748, runaway, Head of Elk, Cecil Co, Md, 10 Aug. 1766.
(NY Mercury25.8.1766)

GORDON, JOHN, merchant, sh. pre 1771, sett. Va and N.C. (SRO.B10.15.8270)

GORDON, JOHN, b. 1745, s. of George Gordon and Elizath Irvine, sett. Va pre 1800.
(St Nicholas, Aberdeen, g/s)

GORDON, PETER, s. of Rev. Algernon Gordon, millwright, res. Keith, Banffshire,
storekeeper in Vienna, Dorchester Co, Md, 1786, merchant in Baltimore, 1796.
(VG620)

GORDON, ROBERT, nat. 2 June 1794 Princess Anne Co, Va.

GORDON, ROBERT, b. 1787, clergyman, m. Mary ... , sh. pre 1823, sett. Norfolk, Va,
fa. of Cornelius, Robert, William, Mary, Sarah and Oramantha. (N.A.-M432/277-99)

GORDON, RODERICK, s. of .... Gordon of Carnousie, Banffshire, surgeon, sett. King and
Queen Co, Va, 1729-1744. (SRO.RH15)

GORDON, SAMUEL, b. 1717, s. of D. Gordon of Craig, res. Stewartry of Kirkcudbright,
sett. Petersburg, Va, d. 14 Apr. 1771, bd. Blandford, Va. (Old Blandford g/s)
(WMQ.6.22)(WMQ.2.2.223)

GORDON, SAMUEL, b. 1786, farmer, m. Agnes ... , sett. Stafford Co, Va. (N.A.-M932/982)

GORDON, THOMAS, b. 1751, bleacher, res. Edinburgh, sh. Mar. 1774, fr. London to Md,
on *Speedwell.* (PRO.T47.9/11)

GORDON, THOMAS, factor, sett. Halifax Co, Va, pre 1770. (SFV34)

GORDON, WILLIAM, b. 1702, runaway, North East Md, 1728. (NY Gaz.13.5.1728)

GORDON, WILLIAM, clergyman, sh. 1767 to West Florida, sett. Va and Exuma, Bahamas.
(EMA30)

GORDON, WILLIAM, res. Aberdeenshire, thief, tr. 5 Oct. 1754, fr. Aberdeen to Va, on
Fanny and Betty. (AJ300/23)

GOULD, ALEXANDER, b. 1777, m. Catherine ... , sh. pre 1824, fa. of Benjamin, Henry
and William, sett. Baltimore. (N.A.-M432/277-99)

GOURLAY, DAVID, nat. 1 May 1807 Norfolk City, Va.

GOVAN, ARCHIBALD, factor, sett. Hanovertown, King William Co, Va, 1758-1777,
Loyalist, sett. Glasgow. (PRO.AO13.30.378)

GOW, ALEXANDER, res. Perthshire, pro. 18 Oct. 1790 Norfolk, Va.

GOWIE, ALEXANDER, b. 1780, carpenter, m. Margaret Logan, sett. Washington, D.C.,
pre 1823. (SG.27.2.81)

GRACIE, ARCHIBALD, b. 25 June 1755, res. Dumfries, Dumfriesshire, sh. Apr. 1784, fr. Liverpool to N.Y., m. Esther Rogers, merchant, sett. Petersburg, Va, 1796, sett. N.Y., d. 12 Apr. 1829. (ANY.1.321)

GRACIE, MARY, res. Va, d. 11 June 1829 Edinburgh. (SRO.C237)

GRAEME, JANET, res. Aberfoyle, Stirlingshire, tr. May 1770, fr. Port Glasgow to Md, on *Crawford*, arr. Port Oxford, Md, 23 July 1771. (SRO.JC27.10.3)(AJ1170)

GRAEME, JOHN, b. 1795, m. Margaret ... , sh. pre 1825, fa. of Robert, John, Catherine, James, Charles and Thomas, sett. Richmond, Henrico Co, Va. (N.A.-M932/982)

GRAHAM, DAVID, Jacobite, tr. 28 July 1716, fr. Liverpool to Va, on *Godspeed*, arr. Md Oct. 1716. (SPC.1716.310)(CTB.31.209)(HM388)

GRAHAM, DUNCAN, merchant, res. Perthshire, sett. Ledard, Caroline Co, York River, Va, pre 1764. (SRO.RD2.197.470)

GRAHAM, FERGUS, Jacobite, tr. 29 June 1716, fr. Liverpool to Jamaica or Va, on *Elizabeth and Anne*, arr. York, Va, 1716. (SPC.1716.310)(CTB.31.208)(VSP.1.185)

GRAHAM, HARRY, res. Breckness, Orkney Islands, sh. 1668, fr. Leith(?) to Va. (SRO.GD217)

GRAHAM, JAMES, res. Orkney Islands, sh. 1668, fr. Leith (?) to Va. (SRO.GD217)

GRAHAM, JAMES, Jacobite, tr. 31 July 1716, fr. Liverpool to Va, on *Anne*. (SPC.1716.310)(CTB.31.209)

GRAHAM, JOHN, b. 30 Apr. 1711, s. of John Graham of Wackenston and Margaret Graham, merchant, res. Perthshire, sh. pre 1742, sett. Md, Stafford Co, Va, and Prince William Co, Va, m. (1) Christian Brown (2) Elizabeth C. Cocke, fa. of John, Duncan, Margaret, Robert, Mary, John, William, Walter, Elizabeth, Catherine, Catesby and Jean, d. Aug. 1787. (VG162)(NER.21.189)

GRAHAM, JOHN, s. of ... Graham and Jean Luke, tailor, res. Glasgow, sh. pre 1756, sett. Albemarle Co, Va. (SRA.B10.15.6950)

GRAHAM, JOHN, res. Glasgow (?), pro. Oct. 1820 Henrico Co, Va. (VSL.Acc28458)

GRAHAM, PETER, glover, sh. 1714, fr. Glasgow to the Potomac River, on the *American Merchant*. (TM202)

GRAHAM, RICHARD, merchant, res. Dumfries, Dumfriesshire, sett. Prince William Co, Va, m. Jane Brent 1757. (VMHB.19.94)

GRAHAM, ROBERT, b. 1730, res. Fintry, Stirlingshire, sh. Mar. 1750, fr. London to Md. (CLRO/AIA)

GRAHAM, ROBERT, b. 1779, res. Stirlingshire, sett. Chesterfield Co, Va, nat. 11 Sep. 1799. (US D/C.1799.6)

GRAHAME, SAMUEL, s. of Samuel Grahame, res. Dunsire, sett. Chaptico Co, Md, pre 1773, merchant, m. ... Pile, d. 1787. (MSA.Chancery.26.75)

GRAHAM, WILLIAM, sh. pre 1763, sett. Va, Loyalist, sett. London 1780. (PRO.AO13.29.701)

GRAHAM, WILLIAM, sett. Baltimore pre 1803. (SRO.SH.22.1.1803)

GRAHAM, ..., clergyman, sh. 1773 to Md. (EMA30)

GRAINGER, MARGARET, tr. 1771, fr. Port Glasgow to Md, on *Polly*, arr. Port Oxford, Md, 16 Sep. 1771. (SRO.JC27.10.3)

GRANT, ALEXANDER, b. 1734, planter, sett. Culpepper Co, Va, militiaman in Va Regt 1756. (VMHB.1/2)(L)

GRANT, ALLAN, b. 1687, laborer, res. Strathspey, Jacobite, tr. 5 May 1747, fr. Liverpool to Md, on *Johnson*, arr. Port Oxford, Md, 5 Aug. 1747. (P.2.250)(PRO.T1.328)(MR206)

GRANT, ALEXANDER, merchant, sett. Portsmouth, Va, pre 1781, Loyalist, sett. N.S. (PRO.AO13.25.190)

GRANT, ANGUS, b. 1725, laborer, Glengarry, Jacobite, tr. 5 May 1747, fr. Liverpool to Va, on *Johnson,* arr. Port Oxford, Md, 5 Aug. 1747. (P.2.250)(MR152) (PRO.T1.328)

GRANT, BETTY, tr. Mar. 1751, fr. Aberdeen to Va or the West Indies, on the *Adventure of Aberdeen.* (AJ170)

GRANT, CHARLES, land laborer, thief and housebreaker, tr. 1773, fr. Port Glasgow to Va, on the *Phoenix*, arr. Port Accomack, Va, 20 Dec. 1723. (SRO.JC27.10.3)

GRANT, JAMES, b. 1726, s. of John Grant of Glenmoriston, res. Invernessshire, sh. 1746, sett. Norfolk, Va, and Raleigh, N.C., m. Martha Buston 1767, fa. of James, d. 1786. (BLG2719)(CAG.1.302)

GRANT, JAMES, s. of Alexander Grant, res. Kinmuckley, sett. Vermont, Va, pre 1786. (SRO.SH.19.7.1786)

GRANT, JOHN, res. Forfar, Angus, tr. Aug. 1752, fr. Aberdeen to Va, on *St Andrew.* (AJ241)

GRANT, JOHN, b. 1713, weaver, res. Banff, Jacobite, tr. 5 May 1747, fr. Liverpool to Va, on *Johnson*, arr. Port Oxford, Md, 5 Aug. 1747. (P.2.262)(MR206)(PRO.T1.328)

GRANT, MARGARET, tr. Aug. 1756, fr. Aberdeen to Va, on *St Andrew.* (AJ451)

GRANT, MARGARET, fireraiser, tr. Mar. 1758, fr. Aberdeen to Va, on *Leathly.* (AJ507/533)

GRANT, MUNGO, coppersmith, res. Inverness, sh. May 1753, fr. London to Md. (CLRO/AIA)

GRANT, PATRICK, s. of John Grant, merchant, res. Castlehill, Edinburgh, sett. Baltimore, d. 20 Nov. 1812. (EA.1812)

GRANT, ROBERT, farmer, res. Cushnie, Aberdeenshire, Jacobite, tr. 29 June 1716, fr. Liverpool to Jamaica or Va, on *Elizabeth and Anne,* arr. Va 1716. (SPC.1716.310)(JAB.1.151)(CTB.31.208)(VSP.1.186)

GRANT, ROBERT, s. of Gregor Grant and Agnes Durward, res. Auchindoir, Aberdeenshire, sh. 1715, sett. Va, d. pre 1735. (APB.3.39)

GRANT, THOMAS, sett. Hanover Co, Va, pre 1724, fa. of Daniel, d. 1773. (CAG.1.143)

GRANT, WILLIAM, b. 1699, weaver, res. Aberdeen, Jacobite, tr. 5 May 1747, fr. Liverpool to Va, on *Gildart,* arr. Port North Potomac, Md, 5 Aug. 1747. (P.2.264)(PRO.T1.328)(MR127)

GRANT, WILLIAM, b. 1750, sett. Montgomery Co, Va, pre 1776. (VSL23816)

GRANT, WILLIAM, b. 1750, groom, sh. Mar. 1774, fr. London to Va, on *Brilliant.* (PRO.T47.9/11)

GRAY, ANDREW, s. of William Gray of Gartcraig, d. 21 Jan. 1802 Va. (SRO.CC8.8.128)

GRAY, ANDREW, b. 1805, cotton spinner, arr. Baltimore 1826. (N.A.-M596)

GRAY,EDWARD, dyer, d. Sep. 1795 Va. (Richmond and Manchester Adv.1.10.1795)

GRAY, GEORGE, res. Glasgow (?), tobacco factor, sett. Portobacco, Md, and post 1784 Dumfries, Va. (SRA.CFI)

GRAY, GEORGE, res. Edinburgh, pro. 1 Dec. 1828 Baltimore.

GRAY, HANNAH, da. of William Gray of Shirvadike, m. Jabez Pitt, sett. Va pre 1786. (SRO.SH.22.3.1786)

GRAY, JAMES, merchant, res. Aberdeen, sh. Feb. 1748, fr. Aberdeen to Va. (AJ2)

GRAY, JAMES, b. 1773, res. Lanarkshire, sett. Richmond City, Va, nat. 18 Sep. 1799. (US D/C.1799.13)

GRAY, JOHN, res. Keith, Banffshire, Jacobite, tr. 5 May 1747, fr. Liverpool to Va, on *Gildart,* arr. Port North Potomac, Md, 5 Aug. 1747. (P.2.266)(MR123)(JAB.2.430)(PRO.T1.328)

GRAY, JOHN, b. 1725, weaver, Liff, Dundee, Angus, Jacobite, tr. 5 May 1747, fr. Liverpool to Va, on *Johnson,* arr. Port North Potomac, Md, 5 Aug. 1747. (P.2.266)(MR102)(PRO.T1.328)

GRAY, JOHN, s. of John Gray, merchant, res. Glasgow, edu. Glagow Uni. 1736, sh. 1748, sett. Port Royal, Caroline Co, Va, Loyalist, d. 3 May 1787. (SM.50.362)(MAGU17) (SRO.CC8.8.128)(PRO.AO13.30.398/424)

GRAY, JOHN, b. 4 Mar. 1769, s. of William Gray of Gartcraig and Isabel Bowie, res. Glasgow, sh. 1784, sett. Port Royal, Va, and Stafford Co, Va, m. Lucy Robb, fa. of John etc, d. 18 July 1848. (CAG.1.628)(HFV

GRAY, L., b. 1719, res. Edinburgh, army deserter, Va, 3 July 1746. (VaGaz.7.1746)

GRAY, MARY, res. Edinburgh, whore and thief, tr. 28 Nov. 1704, fr. Leith to Md. (SRO.PC2.28.307)

GRAY, WILLIAM, soldier, thief and housebreaker, t. 1772, fr. Port Glasgow to Va, on Phoenix, arr. Port Accomack, Va, 20 Dec. 1772. (AJ193)(SRO.JC27.10.3)

GRAY, WILLIAM, b. 1755, res. Perth (?), sh. pre 1785 to Va, sett. Alabama. (TMR736)

GRAY, WILLIAM, res. Edinburgh, tr. 1696, fr. Newhaven, Midlothian, to Va. (SRO.RH15.14.58)

GRAY, WILLIAM, merchant, m. Lucy Miller, d. Port Royal, Va, 2 Jan. 1799. (EA3671/150)

GRAY, WILLIAM, s. of William Gray of Gartcraig, d, 21 Jan. 1802 Va. (EA.1802)

GRAYSON, BENJAMIN, merchant, sh. pre 1750, sett. Dumfries, Va, m. Susan Monroe. (VG303)

GREGG, ROBERT, s. of Matthew Gregg, storekeeper, res. Ochiltree, Ayrshire, sett. Hampton, Va, d. pre May 1762. (LC.Neil Jamieson pp)

GREEN, JOHN, merchant, sett. Petersburg, Va, d. 5 July 1797 Edinburgh. (EEC12318)(SRO.CC8.8.130)

GREENLEES, JOHN, merchant, Va, m.Mary Beveridge, res. Edinburgh, pre 1753. (SRO.GD90)

GREENLEES, PETER, robber, tr. Apr. 1754, fr. Leith, Midlothian, to Va. (AJ326)

GREGORY, ALEXANDER, s. of William Gregory, res. Kilmarnock, Ayrshire, sett. Alexandria, Va, 1830, d. 1835.

GREGORY, JAMES, merchant, sett. Urbanna, Va, 1758, Loyalist, sett. West Indies. (PRO.AO13.29.723/735)

GREGORY, PETER MALLARDY, b. 1798, s. of William Gregory, res. Kilmarnock, Ayrshire, d. 12 Mar. 1817 Alexandria, Va. (S.16.17)

GREGORY, WILLIAM, b. Nov. 1742, s. of William Gregory, merchant, res. Kilmarnock, Ayrshire, sett. Fredericksburg, Va, pre 1765. (WMQ.13.222)

GREGORY, WILLIAM, b. 3 Mar, 1789, s. of William Gregory, merchant and banker, res. Kilmarnock, Ayrshire, sh. 1807, sett. Alexandria, Va, m. (1) Margaret Bartleman (2) Mary Long, fa. of Douglas, William, Elizabeth, Margaret, Isabella, Julia, Boyd and Mary, d. 13 July 1875. (N.A.-M932/982)

GREIG, JAMES, b. 1785, d. 1823 Richmond, Va. (Family Visitor 6.9.1823)

GRIER, ROBERT, res. Lochenkitt, Covenanter, tr. Sep.1668, fr. Leith to Va, on *Convertin*. (PC.2.534)

GRIERSON, ANDREW, b. 1795, bricklayer, sett. Calvert Co, Md. (N.A.-M432/277-99)

GRIGG, JAMES, b. 1697, tailor, runaway, Queen Anne Co, Md, 1720. (Amer.Wkly.Merc.21.7.1720)

GRIMES, ANN, b. 1796, sh. pre 1822, mo. of Richard and Ellen, sett. Baltimore. (N.A.-M432/277-99)

GRINLY, DAVID, d. 24 Oct. 1783 Va. (VaGaz.25.10.1783)

GRINLY, JAMES, b. 1743, s. of Alexander Grinly, res. Dunbar, East Lothian, d. 10 July 1763 Bruton, Va. (Bruton g/s)

GROZAT, JOHN, nat. 19 May 1788 Norfolk City, Va.

GUNN, JOHN, tr. 12 Mar. 1754, fr. Aberdeen to Va, on *Fanny and Betty,* m. Agnes Taylor, fa. of Sarah. (AJ323)

GUSTIE, JONATHAN, b. 1794, m. Catherine ... , sh. pre 1828 to Pa., fa. of Jonathan and Jane, sett. Richmond, Henrico Co, Va. (N.A.-M932/982)

HACKETT, JANE, runaway, Cambridge, Md, Oct. 1736. (VaGaz.22.10.1736)

HADDEN, ... , tr. Feb. 1667, to Barbados or Va. (PC.2.263)

HAGAR, KATHERINE, res. Edinburgh, whore and thief, tr. 28 Nov. 1704, fr. Leith, Midlothian, to Md. (SRO.PC2.28.307)

HAGUE, JOHN, sett. Va pre 1783, m. Hannah Craddock, d. 1795 Richmond, Va. (WMQ.2.130)

HAGUE, RALPH, b. 1749, painter, res. Edinburgh, sh. Oct. 1774, fr. London to Md, on *Sophia*. (PRO.T47.9/11)

HAIG, JOHN, b. 1705, m. Sarah Syme, sett. Hanover Co, Va, d. 1770. (RAV46)

HAIG, WILLIAM, sh. Nov. 1677, fr. London to Va, on *Merchants Consent*. (PRO.E190.72/1-80/1)

HALIBURTON, DAVID, res. Edinburgh, sh. pre 1750 to Philadelphia, sett. Va, fa. of David. (AA.5.85)

HALIBURTON, ELIZABETH, res. Edinburgh, whore and thief, tr. 28 Nov. 1704, fr. Leith, Midlothian, to Md. (SRO.PC2.28.307)

HALYBURTON, WILLIAM, b. 7 Apr. 1762, surgeon, res. Haddington, East Lothian, sett. Va, m. Martha Dandridge, fa. of James, d. 1831 Va. (GHH.1.30)

HALYBURTON, WILLIAM, clergyman, sh. 1766 to Va, sett. N.Y.   (PCCol.4.819)(EMA32)

HALL, ISOBEL, b. 1784, sett. Ritchie Co, Va.   (N.A.-M932/982)

HALL, JOHN, b. 1787, farmer, sett. Ritchie Co, Va.   (N.A.-M932/982)

HALTON, JOHN, Jacobite, tr. 5 May 1747, f. Liverpool to Va, on *Gildart,* arr. Port North Potomac, Md, 5 Aug. 1747.   (P.2.272)(PRO.T1.328)

HAMILTON, ALEXANDER, merchant, res. Glasgow, sett. Piscataway, Md, 1760, d. 30 June 1799 Portobacco, Md.   (M.H.S.-MS1301)(SRA.CFI)(GC1263)

HAMILTON, ALEXANDER, b. 1712, s. of Dr William Hamilton and Mary Hamilton, physician, sh. 1738, sett. Annapolis, Md, m. Margaret Dulaney 1747, d. 11 May 1756. (NLS.6506)(DAB.8.170)(MHS1265)(GM.25.412)

HAMILTON, ALEXANDER, s. of John Hamilton of Kype, res. Mauchline, Ayrshire, sett. Prince George Co, Md, pre 1782.   (SRO.CS17.1.1)(Prince Geo.Co.Will.T1.430)

HAMILTON, ANDREW, res. Edinburgh, sh. 7 Oct. 1698, fr. Liverpool to Va, on *Submission.*   (LRO.HQ325.2FRE)

HAMILTON of OVERTON, ARCHIBALD, merchant, res. Glasgow, sett. Va pre 1778. (SRO.CS16.1.173)

HAMILTON, ARCHIBALD, merchant, res. Glasgow, sett. N.C. and Nansemond Co, Va, 1759-1776, Loyalist.   (PRO.AO13.95)

HAMILTON, DOUGLAS, sett. Suffolk, Va, pro. July 1783 PCC.

HAMILTON, GAVIN, merchant, res. Glasgow, sett. Norfolk, Va, pre 1750. (SRA.B10.15.6087)(SRO.CS16.1.170)

HAMILTON, GEORGE, b. 1667, s. of William, Duke of Hamilton, Earl of Orkney 1696, Governor of Va 1714.   (SN.3.266)

HAMILTON, GEORGE, b. 1751, carver and gilder, sh. May 1774, fr. Whitehaven, Cumberland, to Va, on *Molly.*   (PRO.T47/12)

HAMILTON, GEORGE, storekeeper, sett. Falmouth, Va, pre 1776, Loyalist. (PRO.AO13.27.384/92)

HAMILTON, JAMES, joiner, runaway, Bohemia Manor, Cecil Co, Md, 1735. (Amer.Wkly.Merc. 15.5.1735)

HAMILTON, JAMES, sett. Vienna, Md, pro. Feb. 1772 PCC.

HAMILTON, JAMES, s. of Robert Hamilton, cordwainer, res. Kilmarnock, Ayrshire, sett. Loudoun Co, Va, pre 1786.   (SRO.SH.3.10.1787)(SRO.RD3.246.950) (SRO.RD3.247.174)

HAMILTON, JANE, sh. 2 Nov. 1674, to St Mary's Co, Md, on *Bachelor of Bristol.* (MSA.ESB.152)

HAMILTON, JOHN, b. 1700, s. of Principal William Hamilton and Mary Robertson, physician, edu. Edinburgh Uni., res. Edinburgh, sett. Calvert Co, Md, pre 1750, d. 31 Mar. 1768. (SRO.CS16.1.114)(NLS6506)(SA178)(DAB.8.170)

HAMILTON, JOHN, res. Glasgow, sh. pre 1760, sett. Nansemond Co, Va, Loyalist, HM Consul in Richmond, Va, 1790-1812, d. 1816 England. (SRO.NRAS.0620) (PRO.AO13.95)

HAMILTON, JOHN, merchant, sett. Va pre 1778. (SRO.CS16.1.173)

HAMILTON, JOHN, tailor and habitmaker, sett. Baltimore 1773. (Md Journal4.9.1773)

HAMILTON, JOHN, b. 1725, sett. Bath Co, Va, pre 1750, fa. of Osborne. (GH

HAMILTON, JOHN, merchant, res. Glasgow, sh. pre 1770, sett. Norfolk, Va. (SRA.T79.18)

HAMILTON, ROBERT, gardener, res. Gorthie, Perthshire, Jacobite, tr. 5 May 1747, fr. Liverpool to Va, on *Johnson*, arr. Port Oxford, Md, 5 Aug. 1747. (P.2.274)(MR72)(PRO.T1.328)

HAMILTON, ROBERT, b. 1720, innkeeper and cordwainer, res. Kilmarnock, Ayrshire, sett. Loudoun Co, Va, pre 1740, m. Margaret McKee, fa. of James, d. pre 1786. (SRO.RD3.248.458)(SRO.RD3.246.950)(SRO.RD3.247.174)

HAMILTON, THOMAS, merchant, res. Leith, Midlothian, sett. Baltimore, nat. 15 Apr. 1805, pro. 9 Oct.1805 Baltimore. (MSA.Baltimore Wills.7.451)

HAMILTON, W., laborer, res. Dumfriesshire, deserter Suffolk Co, Va, 24 Sep. 1755. (VaGaz10.10.1755)

HAMILTON, WILLIAM, s. of John Hamilton of Dowar, storekeeper, sh. 1771, sett. Va and N.C., Loyalist. (PRO.AO12.101)

HAMILTON, WILLIAM, b. 1787, sh. pre 1809, sett. Baltimore, fa. of Caroline. (N.A.-M432/277-99)

HAMMER, MARTIN, sh. pre 1704, on *Pertuxan Merchant*, m. Anne Catherine Beren Martin, d. Va, pro. Aug. 1704 PCC.

HAMPTON, JOHN, sh. 1705, clergyman, sett. Md, d. Snow Hill, Md, Jan. 1722, pro. 2 Feb. 1722 Md.(CCMDG46)

HANNA, ANDREW, b. 1708, runaway, Annapolis, Md, 1729. (AmerWklyMerc28.9.1729)

HANNA, JOHN, s. of R. Hanna, res. Galloway, m. Mary Irvin, sett. Prince Edward Co, Va, d. pre 30 Aug. 1765. (VMHB.16.205)

HANNA, WILLIAM, s. of John Hanna, res. Galloway, clergyman, edu. Glasgow Uni. 1768, sh. 1772 to Va. (EMA32)(MAGU85)

HANNAH, ANDREW, nat. 23 Nov. 1803 Norfolk, Va.

HANNAH, PETER, merchant, res. Wigtownshire, sett. Petersburg, Va, pre 1829. (SRO.SH17.11.1829)

HANNAY, PATRICK, res. Caldons, Wigtownshire, sett. Va, pro. 1823 Edinburgh. (SRO.CC8.8.149)(SC70.1.28)

HARDIE, CATHERINE, da. of Robert Hardie, farmer, Va, m. Patrick MacDowall, block-maker, Leith, in Edinburgh 13 Jan. 1794.   (Edinburgh OPR)

HARDIE, THOMAS, res. Kelso, Roxburghshire (?), sett. Norfolk, Va, pre 1774. (SRO.RD3.224.347)

HARLETT, JANE, runaway, Cambridge, Md, 1736.   (VaGaz22.10.1736)

HARPER, ROBERT, Covenanter, tr. 10 June 1669, to Va.   (PC.3.22)

HARRET, Mrs F., b. 1781, arr. Baltimore 1823.   (P.A.303)

HARRIS, JOHN, Jacobite, tr. 29 June 1716, fr. Liverpool to Jamaica or Va, on *Elizabeth and Anne*, arr. Va 1716.   (SPC.1716.310)(CTB.31.208)(VSP.1.186)

HARROWER, JOHN, clerk and tutor, m. Anne Graeme, fa. of John, Elizabeth, George, and James, res. Lerwick, Shetland Islands, sh. 7 Feb. 1774, fr. London to Va, on *Planter,* d. Apr. 1777 Va.   (PRO.T47.9/11)

HARVEY, WILLIAM, b. 1727, sett. Elkton, Cecil Co, Md, 1763, m. Rebecca Carruuthers, fa. of Matthew, William and Robert, d. 1767.   (BGC

HARVIE, JOHN, b. Gargunnock, Stirlingshire, attorney, sett. Albemarle Co, Va, m. Martha Gaines 1747, d. 1767.   (VaHistColln.6.83)(DAB.8.375)(AA.9.54)

HARVEY, MUNGO, b. 1734, physician, d. 21 Mar. 1794 Westmoreland Co, Va. (VaHerald27.3.1794)

HARVIE, THOMAS, s. of James Harvie, res. Glasgow, thief, tr. 28 Nov. 1704, fr. Leith to Md.   (SRO.PC2.28.307)

HASTER, JOHN, b. 1663, s. of John Haster, laborer, res. Edinburgh, sh. June 1684, fr. London to Md, on *Brothers Adventures.*   (CLRO/AIA)

HASTIE, HENRY, merchant, res. Glasgow, sett. N.Y. 1800, d. 13 Jan. 1820 Norfolk, Va. (ANY.1.336)

HASTINGS, JOHN, shipmaster, res. Prestonpans, Midlothian, d. Va, pro. Sep. 1707PCC.

HAY, ALEXANDER, b. Aberdeen, tutor and clergyman, sh. pre 1789, sett. Antrim ph., Halifax Co, Va, 1790-1819, d. 1819.   (WMQ.2.19.406)

HAY, FRANCIS, storekeeper, sett. Dumfries, Va, 1772.   (SFV60)

HAY, JAMES, b. 1754, accountant, sh. June 1775, fr. London to Baltimore, on *Nancy.* (PRO.T47.9/11)

HAY, JAMES, nat. 24 Oct. 1808 Norfolk City, Va.

HAY, JOHN, runaway, Turkey Island, Henrico Co, Va, 1769.   (VaGaz13.4.1769)

HAY, JOHN, res. Aberdeen, thief, tr. 12 May 1754, fr. Aberdeen to Va, on *Fanny and Betty*.   (AJ300/323)(ABR.EB.1754)

HAY, JOHN, s. of James Hay, merchant, res. Kilsyth, Lanarkshire, sett. Va, pre 1775. (SRO.RD2.220.10)

HAY, JOHN, Jacobite, tr. 24 May 1716, fr. Liverpool to Md, on *Friendship*, arr. Md Aug. 1716.   (SPC.1716.311)(HM386)

HAY, PETER, storekeeper, sett. Surrey and Southampton Cos, Va, pre 1776, Loyalist. (PRO.AO13.33.297)

HAY, WILLIAM, b. 1692, sett. Prince Edward Co, Va, 1710, fa. of William. (CAG.1.740)

HAY, W., s. of James Hay, lawyer, edu. Glasgow Uni., res. Kilsyth, Lanarkshire, sh. 18 July 1768, fr. Greenock, Renfrewshire, to Va, arr. Norfolk, Va, 16 Sep. 1768, d. 1825 Va.   (WMQ.15.85)(MAGU79)

HAZEL, DAVID, b. 1731, planter, sett. Stafford Co, Va, militiaman in Va Regt 1757. (VMHB.1/2)(L)

HECTOR, JOHN, b. 30 Aug. 1705, s. of James Hector and Margaret Clerk, salmonfisher, res. Aberdeen, Jacobite, tr. 5 May 1747, fr. Liverpool to Va, on *Johnson,* arr. Port Oxford, Md, 5 Aug. 1747.(MR211)(P.2.282)(JAB.2.431)(PRO.T1.328)

HENDERSON, ALEXANDER, b. 1737, s. of Rev. Richard Henderson, res. Blantyre, Lanarkshire, merchant and tobacco factor, edu. Glasgow Uni. 1748, sh. 1756, sett. Colchester, Occoquan, and Dumfries, Va, m. Sarah -, d. 22 Nov. 1815 Dumfries, Va.   (MAGU39) (F.3.228)(SRA-T.MJ)(Lake Mont Clair g/s)(Alexandria Lib.Va:Letterbook)

HENDERSON, ARCHIBALD, res. Kilmarnock, Ayrshire, sett. Baltimore Co, Md, d. 1813, pro. 14 Oct.1813 Baltimore.

HENDERSON, ARCHIBALD, b. 2 Mar. 1733, s. of Rev. Richard Henderson and Janet Cleland, merchant, res. Blantyre, Lanarkshire, sett. Va, d. 9 Jan. 1816.   (F.3.228)

HENDERSON, CHARLES, Jacobite, tr. 29 June 1716, fr. Liverpool to Jamaica or Va, on *Elizabeth and Anne*, arr. Va 1716.   (SPC.1716.310)(CTB.31.208)(VSP.1.186)

HENDERSON, COLIN, smith, res. Torryburn, Fife, thief, tr. 1773, fr. Port Glasgow to Va, on *Phoenix,* arr. Port Accomack, Va, 20 Dec. 1773.   (AJ1293)(SRO.JC27.10.3)

HENDERSON, DAVID, sett. Fredericksburg, Va, pre 1783, fa. of David.   (ANY.2.19)

HENDERSON, JAMES, b. 1708, s. of William Henderson, res. Fife, sett. Augusta Co, Va pre 1760, d. 1784.   (RAV.46)

HENDERSON, JAMES, b. 1763, physician, sett. Va, d. 1829. (SA218)(VHS, Richmond - Letterbook 1783-1829)

HENDERSON, JOHN, b. 1749, planter, sett. Albemarle Co, Va. (VSL242296)

HENDERSON, JOHN, nat. 29 Mar. 1787 Norfolk City, Va.

HENDERSON, RICHARD, s. of Rev. Richard Henderson and Janet Cleland, merchant, res. Blantyre, Lanarkshire, sett. Bladensburg, Prince George Co, Md, m. Sarah Brice 19 Nov. 1761, d. 29 Aug. 1802, Springhill, Georgetown, Md. (EA.4051/02) (MHS-St John's, Piscataway, OPR)

HENDERSON, SAMUEL, b. 1755, sett. Rockbridge, Va, nat. 1800 Washington, D.C.

HENDERSON, THOMAS, res. Fife, sett. Yellow Springs, Jamestown, Va, 1607, fa. of Richard. (CAG.1.928)(CF.4.179)

HENDERSON, WILLIAM, planter, res. Newbigging, sh. pre 1743, sett. Churchill's Plantation, Rappahannock River, Va. (SRO.CH12.23.315/358)

HENDRY, DANIEL, res. Campbelltown, Argyllshire (?), sett. Va pre 1786. (SRO.SH22.5.1786)

HENDRY, JOHN, b. 1611, sh. 10 Aug. 1635, fr. London to Va, on *Safety*. (PRO.E157/20)

HENRY, DANIEL, sh. 2 Nov. 1674, to St Mary's Co, Md, on *Bachelor of Bristol*. (MSA.ESB.152)

HENRY, JOHN, clergyman, edu. Edinburgh Uni., sh. 1710, fr. Dublin to Philadelphia, sett. Rehobeth, Va. (AP164)

HENRY, JOHN, s. of Alexander Henry and Jean Robertson, surveyor, res. Aberdeen, sett. Richmond, Hanover Co, Va, pre 1730, m. Sarah Winston, fa. of William, Patrick, Jane, Sarah, Susanna, Mary, Anne, Elizabeth and Lucy, d. 1773. (VMHB.33.44)(CF.6.243)

HENRY, PATRICK, s. of Alexander Henry and Jean Robertson, clergyman, res. Aberdeenshire, sh. 1731, sett. St George'sph., Spotsylvania Co, Va, 1733/1734, Hanover Co, Va, 1737/1777, d. 11 Apr. 1777, pro. 7 Aug. 1777 Hanover Co, Va. (WMQ.2.21.64)(EMA33)

HENRY, ROBERT, sh. 1740 to N.J., clergyman, edu. Princeton Uni, sett. Charlotte Co, Va, m. Jean Caldwell, d. 8 May 1767 Cub Creek, Charlotte Co, Va. (CAG.1.335)

HEPBURN, MARY, res. Edinburgh, whore and thief, tr. 28 Nov. 1704, fr. Leith to Md. (SRO.PC2.28.307)

HEPBURN, WILLIAM, res. Dumfries, Dumfriesshire, tutor, sh. 1774 to Va. (NLS.McMurdo Maxwell pp)

HERCUS, GEORGE, b. 1792, pumpmaker, res. Haddington, East Lothian, sh. July 1817, fr. Leith, Midlothian, to Philadelphia, m. Margaret -, fa. of Helen, William, George and Alice, nat. 26 May 1828 Washington, D.C.   (N.A.-M432/277-99)

HERDMAN, JAMES, b. 12 May 1746, s. of William Herdman, res. Dunottar, Kincardineshire, clergyman, edu. King's College, Aberdeen, 1763, sett. Henrico Co, Va. (EMA33)(FPA309)

HERON, NATHANIEL, b. 1761, merchant, res. Wigtownshire, sh. 1792, sett. Norfolk, Va, d. 16 Aug. 1816 Petersburg, Va.   (GM.86.376)(1812)

HERON, PATRICK or PETER, b. 1785, merchant, sh. 1809, sett. Norfolk, Va, nat. 24 Feb. 1812 Norfolk City, Va.   (1812)

HERRING, JANET, washerwoman, res. East Lothian, Jacobite, tr. 5 May 1747, fr. Liverpool to Va, on *Johnson,* arr. Port Oxford, Md, 5 Aug. 1747. (P.2.286)(PRO.T1.328)

HEUGH, ANDREW, s. of Thomas Heugh, merchant and planter, res. Falkirk, Stirlingshire, sett. Leek Forest, Montgomery Co, Md, m. Sarah Needham, fa. of Elizabeth, Ann, Jean, Sarah, Mary, Andrew, Harriet, Christian, Martha, Margaret and John, d. 6 Jan. 1771, pro. 22 June 1791 Edinburgh.(SRO.CC8.8.128)(SRO.RD2.252.1227)(SRO.CS16.1.143)

HILL, ADAM, s. of ... Hill and Margaret Ramsay, res. Ayr, sett. Talbot Co, Md, fa. of Adam, pro. 14 Mar. 1768 PCC, pro. 2 Mar. 1769 Md.   (MdHistMag.3.184) (MSA.Will.35.253)

HILL, ELIZABETH, b. 1749, m. James Dunlop, sett. Port Royal, Va, d. 8 May 1780. (Port Royal g/s)

HILL, JAMES, Jacobite, tr. 24 May 1716, fr. Liverpool to Md, on *Friendship,* arr. Aug 1716 Md.   (SPC.1716.311)(HM387)(MSA.34.164)

HILL, JANET, res. Edinburgh, tr. 1696, fr. Newhaven, Midlothian, to Va. (SRO.RH15.14.58)

HITHERTON, ANDREW, b. 1780, sett. Richmond, Henrico Co, Va.   (N.A.-M932/982)

HODGE, ARCHIBALD, pedlar, tr. 9 Feb. 1721, fr. Leith, Midlothian, to Va. (SRO.HH.11)

HODGSON, GEORGE, Jacobite, tr. 28 July 1716, fr. Liverpool to Va, on *Godspeed,* arr. Oct. 1716 Md.   (SPC.1716.310)(CTB.31.209)(HM388)

HOGE, JOHN, s. of William Hoge, sh. to Perth Amboy, N.J., clergyman, edu. Princeton Uni., sett. Va and Pa., d. after 1795.   (CCVC25)

HOGE, WILLIAM, b. 1660, res. Musselburgh, Midlothian, sh. 1680, sett. Perth Amboy, N.J., m. Barbara Hume 1695, fa. of Joseph, Mary, George, John, William, Margaret, Alexander and James, sett. Kernstown, Va.   (CF.4.209)

HOGG, JAMES, s. of James Hogg, res. Edinburgh, sett. Augusta Co, Va, 1745. (SG.28.1.41)

HOGG, PETER, s. of James Hogg, res. Edinburgh, m. Elizabeth -, fa. of James, Peter, Ann, Elizabeth and Thomas, sett. Augusta Co, Va, 1745, and Kenawha, Va, 1775, d. 1782, pro. 22 Apr. 1782 Rockingham Co, Va.   (SG28.1.41)

HOGG, THOMAS, s. of James Hogg, res. Edinburgh, sett. Augusta Co, Va, 1745. (SG28.1.41)

HOGG, WILLIAM, b. 1660, res. Berwickshire (?), sh. 1687 to Perth Amboy, N.J., sett. Upper Opecquon, Frederick Co, Va, m. Barbara Hunter, fa. of John and James. (CAG.1.362)

HOGGAN, JAMES, tobacco factor, res. Glasgow, sh.pre 1774, sett. Bladensburg, Va. (SRA.CFI)

HOLLAND, THOMAS, Jacobite, tr. 29 June 1716, fr. Liverpool to Jamaica or Va, on *Elizabeth and Anne*.   (SPC.1716.310)(CTB.31.208)

HOME, FRANCIS, res. Wedderburn, Duns, Berwickshire, Jacobite, tr. 29 June 1716, fr. Liverpool to Jamaica or Va, on *Elizabeth and Anne,* arr. Va, sett. Rappahannock, Va. (SPC.1716.310)(CTB.31.208)(VSP.1.185)(VMHB.38.106)

HOME, GEORGE, b. 1698, s. of George Home of Wedderburn, res. Duns, Berwickshire, surveyor and merchant, Jacobite, tr. 1721, sett. Rappahannock, Culpepper Co, Va, m. Elizabeth Proctor 1727, d. 1760.   (VMHB.20.397)(OT91)

HONEY, JAMES, cabinetmaker, res. Perth, sett. Williamsburg, Va, d. Apr. 1787. (Williamsburg g/s)(VaGaz12.4.1787)

HONEYMAN, ROBERT. b. 13 Dec. 1747, s. of Rev. James Honeyman and Anne Allardyce, res. Kinneff, Kincardineshire, physician, edu. Marischal College, Aberdeen, and Edinburgh Uni. 1766, sh. 1773, m. Mary Pottle, sett. Louisa Co and Hanover Co, Va, d. 1824.   (OD48)(Kinneff g/s)(HF62)

HOOD, GEORGE, d. 1824 Nottoway Co, Va.   (Family Visitor24.1.1824)

HOOD, JOHN, merchant, res. Glasgow, sh. 1760 to Va, on *Joanna of Glasgow.* (SRO.CS.GMB50)(SRO.AC7/50)

HOOK, JOHN, b. 1745, s. of Henry Hook, merchant, res. Glasgow, sh.1758, sett. Blandford and New London, Bedford Co, Va, m. Elizabeth Smith 1772, d. 1808. (SRO.CS16.1.117)(VMHB.34.149)(VSA:John Hook pp)

HOPE, JOHN, merchant, res. Glasgow, sh. pre 1776, sett. Osborne and Halifax, Va. (SRA.T79.25)

HORSBURGH, ALEXANDER, merchant, res. Glasgow, sh. pre 1776, sett. Brunswick and Petersburg, Va, Loyalist, sh. July 1777, fr. N.Y. to Glasgow, on *Howe.* (SRA.T79.1)(SFV.233)

HOSIE, WILLIAM, woolcomber, res. Aberdeen, conspirator, tr. July 1772, fr. Glasgow to Va, on *Brilliant*, arr. Port Hampton, Va, 7 Oct. 1772.   (SRO.JC27.10.3)(AJ1278)

HOSSACK, JAMES, b. 1811, arr. Baltimore 1834 on *Lady Halsted.*   (N.A.-M596)

HOUSTOUN, ALEXANDER, merchant, sett. Norfolk, Va, pre 1776, Loyalist, sett. N.S. (PRO.AO13.24.274)

HOUSTOUN, JAMES, clergyman, sh. 1747, sett. Md. (EMA34)

HUGHES, MARY, b. 1760, servant, res. Glasgow, sh. Apr. 1775, fr. London to Md, on *Adventure.* (PRO.T47.9/11)

HUIE, JAMES, s. of James Huie, mariner, res. Glasgow, sett. Dumfries, Va, m. Helen Bullitt 1791, d. pre 1816. (VaHerald23.6.1791)(SRO.SC70.1.14)

HUME, THOMAS, Jacobite, tr. 28 July 1716, fr. Liverpool to Va, on *Godspeed,* arr. Md Oct. 1716. (SPC.1716.310)(CTB.31.209)(HM389)

HUNTER, ADAM, merchant, sett. Frederickburg, Va, pro. 16 May 1798 Stafford Co, Va. (Fred.Will.A3.94)

HUNTER, DAVID, merchant, res. Ayr, sh. pre 1769 to Va. (SRO.GMB53)(SRO.AC7.53)

HUNTER, HENRY, tailor, sh. 1714, fr. Glasgow to the Potomac River, on the *American Merchant.* (TM202)

HUNTER, ICHABOD, sett. Richmond, Va, m. Elizabeth -, pro. 14 May 1799 Richmond, Va.

HUNTER, JAMES, s. of James Hunter, merchant, res. Duns, Berwickshire, sh pre 1756, sett. Fredericksburg, King George Co, Va. (SRO.RS19.17.39)(SRO.SH.29.7.1756)

HUNTER, JAMES, s. of James Hunter, merchant, res. Edinburgh, sett. James River, Va, pre 1773. (SRO.RD2.256.112)

HUNTER, JAMES, merchant, Smithfield, Isle of Wight Co, and Southampton Co, Va, pre 1774, Loyalist, sett. Antigua. (PRO.AO13.30.616)

HUNTER, JAMES, d. 1784 Va, pro. 18 Nov. 1784 Baltimore, pro. Dec. 1784 Stafford Co.

HUNTER, JAMES, nat. 29 Apr. 1794 Norfolk City, Va.

HUNTER, JEAN, tailor's servant, res. Edinburgh, thief, tr. 1773, fr. Port Glasgow to Va, on *Phoenix,* arr. Port Accomack, Va, 20 Dec. 1773. (SRO.JC27.10.3)

HUNTER, JOHN, Jacobite, tr. 29 June 1716, fr. Liverpool to Va, on *Elizabeth and Anne.* (SPC.1716.310)(CTB.31.208)

HUNTER, JOHN sr, merchant, sett. Norfolk and Gosport, Va, Loyalist, d. Nov. 1778 N.Y., pro. Apr. 1783 PCC. (PRO.AO13.31.262)

HUNTER, JOHN jr, merchant, sett. Gosport, Va, 1769, Loyalist. (PRO.AO13.31.14)

HUNTER, JOHN, b. Mar. 1746, s. of James and Janet Hunter, res. Ayrshire, sett. Ayr Hill, Norfolk Co, Va, m. Janet Broadwater 1768, fa. of James, Robert, George Washington, John and Anne, d. post 1805. (HAF.1.204)

HUNTER, NICOLA, b. Sep. 1715, res. Glencairn, Nithsdale, Dumfriesshire, m. Rev. William Douglas 1735, mo. of Peggy, sh. 6 Oct. 1750, sett. Goochland, Va, d. 31 Dec. 1781. (DR)

HUNTER, PATRICK, Jacobite, tr. 24 May 1716, fr. Liverpool to Va, on *Friendship*, arr. Md Aug. 1716. (SPC.1716.311)(CTB.31.207)(HM387)

HUNTER, WILLIAM, s. of James Hunter, merchant, res. Duns, Berwickshire, sh. pre 1736, sett. Fredericksburg, Va, m. Martha Talliaferro 1743, fa. of James, William and Martha, d. 1754. (WMQ.2.19.118)

HUNTER, WILLIAM, printer and bookseller, sh. pre 1776, sett. Williamsburg, Va, fa. of William, Loyalist, sett. London. (PRO.AO13.30.551)

HUNTER, WILLIAM, joint postmaster general of North America, d. Va 1761. (SM.13.558)

HUNTER, WILLIAM, d. Alexandria, Va, 19 Nov. 1792. (1st Presb. g/s)

HUTCHESON, ALEXANDER, clergyman, edu. Glasgow Uni., sh. 1722, sett. Bohemia Manor, Cecil Co, Md 1723, d. Oct. 1766 Md. (CCMC50)(AP193)

HUTCHIN, ROBERT, sh. 2 Nov. 1674, to St Mary's Co, Md, on *Bachelor of Bristol*. (MSA.ESB.152)

HUTCHISON, WILLIAM, s. of John Hutchison, res. Sanquhar, Dumfriesshire, sett. Prince George Co, Md, d. 1711, pro. 23 Apr. 1711 Md. (Md.Will.13.317)

HUTTON, CHARLES, merchant, res. Glasgow, sett. Md pre 1767. (SRO.CS16.1.130)

HUTTON, THOMAS, b. 1663, s. of Thomas Hutton, res. Preston, Berwickshire (?), sh. July 1684, fr. London to Md, on *Golden Hynd*. (CLRO.MR.E593)

HYND, JAMES, b. 1790, nat. 31 Oct. 1840 Norfolk City, Va.

IMLAY, JEAN, res. Aberdeen, thief, tr. Aug. 1753, fr. Aberdeen to Va, on *St Andrew*. (AJ281/294)

INGLES, ANDREW, baker, runaway, Alexandria, Va, 1775. (VaGaz17.6.1775)

INGLIS, JAMES, s. of Thomas Inglis, res. Clackmannanshire, Lieutenant of the Md Loyalists, pro. 6 Dec. 1785 Edinburgh. (SRO.CC8.8.127)

INGLIS, MUNGO, b. 1657, schoolmaster, edu, Edinburgh Uni., tutor William and Mary College, Va, 1694-1705, d. 1719. (WMQ.6.87)

INGLIS, PETER, servant, res. Edinburgh, housebreaker, tr. 1772, fr. Port Glasgow to Va, on *Matty*, arr. Port Oxford, Md, 16 May 1772. (SRO.JC27.10.3)

INGRAM, JAMES, s. of Archibald Ingram of Cloberhill, merchant, res. East Kilpatrick, Dunbartonshire, sh. pre 1769, sett. Va. (SRA.CFI)

INNES, JAMES, b. 1726, runaway, Va, Feb. 1750. (VaGaz2.1750)

INNES, JOHN GEORGE, b. 1813, sh. 16 June 1826, sett. Richmond City, Va, nat. 15 July 1826, Eastern District, Va. (US.D/C.RB5.520)

INNES, ROBERT, s. of Robert Innes and Margaret Sproule, clergyman, edu. King's College, Aberdeen, sh. 1677 to Va. (F.6.259)

INNES, ROBERT, clergyman, sh. 1747, sett. Drysdale ph, Caroline Co, Va, 1754-1758, m. Catherine Richards, fa. of Robert, James and Harry. (DAB.9.486)

IRELAND, JAMES, b. 1748, res. Edinburgh, clergyman, d. 1806 Buckmarsh, Clarke Co, Va. (Berryville g/s)

IRVINE, ALEXANDER, lecturer, res. Drum, Aberdeenshire, sh. 1727 to Philadelphia, sett. William and Mary College, Williamsburg, Va, d. 1732. (WMQ.2.6.1/68)

IRVINE, FANNY, b. 1796, sett. Md and Wood Co, Va, mo. of Thereas, William, Maria, Melina, Frances and Tabitha. (N.A.-M432/277-299)

IRVINE, JAMES, b. 1713, shoemaker, res. Gribton, Nithsdale, Dumfriesshire, Jacobite, tr. 22 Apr. 1747, fr. Liverpool to Va, on Johnson, arr. Port Oxford, Md, 5 Aug. 1747. (P.2.298)(PRO.T1.328)

IRVING, ROBERT, res. Edinburgh, sett. Buckingham Co, Va, pre 1785. (WMQ.2.15.406)

IRVING, WILLIAM, farmer and merchant, sh. pre 1765, sett. Va. (SRA.T.MJ)

IRWIN, GEORGE, Jacobite, tr. 22 Apr. 1747, fr. Liverpool to Va, on Johnson, arr. Port Oxford, Md, 5 Aug. 1747. (PRO.T1.328)(P.2.298)

IRWIN, GEORGE, Md, d. 1745, Edinburgh. (MdGaz28.6.1745)

JACK, DAVID, s. of Dr Jack, physician, res. Hamilton, Lanarkshire, d. Portsmouth, Va, 3 May 1792. (EEC.11561)

JACK, THOMAS, merchant, sett. Nansemond Co, Va, and N.C. 1756-1776, Loyalist, sett. Airdrie, Lanarkshire. (PRO.AO13.30.632)

JACK, WILLIAM, b. 1749, smith, sh. Feb. 1774, fr. London to Md, on Speedwell. (PRO.T47.9/11)

JACKSON, DAVID, b. 1800, res. Kirkcaldy, Fife, sh. 1822, sett. Richmond Co, Va, nat. 7 July 1825 Eastern District, Va. (US.D/C.RB5/492)

JACKSON, PETER, b. 1785, m. Caroline -, fa. of John and Caroline, sh. pre 1827, sett. Cumberland Co, Va. (N.A.-M932/982)

JACKSON, WILLIAM, b. 1713, husbandman, res. Peebles, Peeblesshire, sh. Sep. 1735, fr. London to Md. (CLRO/AIA)

JAFFRAY, ALEXANDER, res. Stirling, Stirlingshire, pro. 5 Oct. 1822 Baltimore.

JAFFRAY, JAMES, res. Stirling, Stirlingshire, sh. 1768, sett. Baltimore. (see ref. in will of Alex Jaffray, above)

JAMIESON, AGNES, da. of Dr Samuel Jamieson, Va, m. James Neilson, merchant, Glasgow, 19 Oct. 1800. (GM.70.1286)

JAMIESON, ALEXANDER, weaver, murderer, Northumberland Co, Va, 1745. (VaGaz18.9.1745)

JAMIESON of BELLMOOR, ALEXANDER, physician, edu. King's College, Aberdeen, 1742, sett. Hampton, James River, Va. (SA187)

JAMIESON, ESTHER, b. 1772, sett. Brooke Co, Va. (N.A.-M932/982)

JAMIESON, JOHN, tinsmith, res. Glasgow, sh. pre 1765 to Va. (VaGaz30.10.1784)

JAMIESON, JOHN, b. 1780, baker, sett. Alexandria, Va. (N.A.-M932/982)

JAMIESON, NEIL, merchant, res. Glasgow, sett. Norfolk, Va, 1760, fa. of Neil, Loyalist, sett. London. (SRA.B10.15.7174)(PRO.AO13.6.72)(WMQ.2.22.532)

JAMIESON, PHILIP, bookkeeper, res. Edinburgh, sh. Dec. 1730, fr. London to Md. (CLRO/AIA)

JAMIESON, SAMUEL, sett. Accomack Co, Va, Loyalist, sh. 1778 to Glasgow. (PRO.AO13.31.136)

JAMIESON, WILLIAM, merchant, sett. Va pre 1778. (SRO.CS16.1.173)

JAMIESON, WILLIAM, b. 1745, m. Ann Read, d. Charlotte Co, Va, 1785. (TMR915)

JEFFREY, ALEXANDER, s. of Francis and Marion Jeffrey, merchant, res. Edinburgh, d. 1768, pro. 31 Jan. 1769 Accomack Co, Va.

JERDONE, FRANCIS, b. 30 Jan. 1720, s. of John Jerdone, factor and merchant, res. Jedburgh, Roxburghshire, sh. 1746, m. Sarah Macon 1753, sett. Hampton, Yorktown, and Louisa Co, Va, fa. of Mary, Francis, Sarah, Elizabeth, Isabella, Anne, John, William and Martha, d. 5 Aug. 1771. (Louisa g/s)(WMQ.2.11.10)

JOHNSON, AGNES, m. Robert White, sett. Fredericksburg, Va, pro 7 Dec. 1757 Spotsylvania Co, Va. (Spotsylvania WillB.336)

JOHNSON, JAMES, schoolmaster, sett. Dorchester Co, Md, pro. 16 Mar. 1749 Md.

JOHNSON, WILLIAM, Jacobite, tr. 28 July 1716, fr. Liverpool to Va, on *Godspeed*, arr. Oct. 1716 Md. (SPC.1716.310)(CTB.31.209)(HM388)

JOHNSTON, ANDREW, b. 1742, merchant, res. Glasgow, sett. Petersburg, Va, 1750, Loyalist, d. 5 May 1785. (SRO.CS16.1.84)(SRO.CC8.8.127)(PRO.AO13.33.153)

JOHNSTON, CHRISTOPHER, b. 28 Oct. 1750, s. of John Johnston and Janet Swan, banker and politician, res. Moffat, Dumfriesshire, sett. Northampton Co, Va, pre 1779, m. Susanna Stith, fa. of Maria, John and Janet, d. 6 Mar. 1819 Baltimore. (CF.4.270)

JOHNSTON, GEORGE, b. 1700, res. Aberdeen, sh. pre 1756 to Va, member of the House of Burgesses 1758-1766, d. 1766. (VSL.

JOHNSTON, JAMES, Jacobite, tr. 29 June 1716, fr. Liverpool to Jamaica or Va, on *Elizabeth and Anne,* arr. Va. 1716.   (SPC.1716.310)(CTB.31.208)(VSP.1.186)

JOHNSTON, JAMES, merchant, res. Glasgow, sh. 1760 to Va, on *Joanna of Glasgow.* (SRO.CS.GMB50)(SRO.AC.7.50)

JOHNSTON, JAMES, b. 1781, s. of James Johnston and Mary Bell, res. Sarkside, Gretna, Dumfriesshire, sett. Kempsvale, Va, pre 1820.   (Gretna g/s)

JOHNSTON, JEAN, thief, tr. Apr. 1754, fr. Leith, Midlothian, to Va.   (AJ326)

JOHNSTON, JOHN, b. 1800, farmer, arr. Baltimore 1826.   (N.A.-M596)

JOHNSTON, JOHN, b. Annandale, Dumfriesshire, sett. Eastern Shore, Md, pre 1657, m. Lucretia Massie, fa.of John, vestryman, St Peter's ph, New Kent Co, Va. (BLG2768)

JOHNSTON, JOHN, Jacobite, tr. 29 June 1716, fr. Liverpool to Jamaica or Va, on *Elizabeth and Anne,* arr. Va 1716.   (SPC.1716.310)(CTB.31.208)(VSP.1.186)

JOHNSTON, JOHN, s. of John Johnston, merchant, res. Glasgow, sett. Norfolk, Va, pre 1748.   (SRO.CS16.1.80)

JOHNSTON, JOHN, merchant, res. Glasgow (?), sett. Mecklenburg Co, Va, pre 1776. (SRA.779.1)

JOHNSTON, JOHN, b. 1778, s. of James Johnston and Mary Bell, res. Sarkside, Gretna, Dumfriesshire, sett. Kempsdale, Va, pre 1816.   (Gretna g/s)

JOHNSTON, JOHN, b. 1729, runaway, Va, 1752.   (VaGaz10.4.1752)

JOHNSTON, PETER, b. 1710, sh. pre 1763 m. Martha Butler or Rogers, sett. Osborne's Landing, James River, and Prince Edward Co, Va, fa. of Peter, d. 1786. (RAV51) (DAB.10.147)

JOHNSTON, ROBERT, Jacobite, tr. 29 June 1716, fr. Liverpool to Jamaica or Va, on *Elizabeth and Anne,* arr. Va 1716.   (SPC.1716.310)(CTB.31.208)(VSP.1.186)

JOHNSTON, ROBERT, b. 1731, physician, res. Dumfriesshire, d. 20 Oct. 1799, Isle of Wight Co, Va.   (NorfolkHerald5.9.1799)

JOHNSTON, STEPHEN, res. Dumfriesshire, sett. Nelson City, Va, 1760, fa. of Stephen.

JOHNSTON, THOMAS, b. 1637, sh. 4 Oct. 1677, fr. London to Va, on *Concord.* (NGSQ.64/2)

JOHNSTON, THOMAS, clergyman, sh. 1751 to Md.   (EMA37)

JOHNSTON, WILLIAM, b. 1807, farmer, arr. Baltimore 1826.   (NA.M596)

JORDAN, -, b. 1782, sett. Washington, D.C.   (N.A.-M432/56-57)

JUSTICE, WILLIAM, b. 1812, cabinetmaker, m. Mary -, fa. of Isabel, Ann, Margaret and Mary, sett. Richmond, Henrico Co, Va. (N.A.-M932/982)

KEDSLIE, JOHN, b. 1792, res. East Lothian, sh. Dec. 1807, fr. Liverpool to N.Y., sett. Washington, D.C., nat. Washington 1839, d. 14 Apr. 1847, pro. 1848 Edinburgh. (SRO.SC70.1.68)(SRO.F638)

KEITH, DUNCAN, b. 1745, carpenter, sh. June 1775, fr. London to Baltimore, on *Nancy.* (PRO.T47.9/11)

KEITH, GEORGE, b. 1584, clergyman, sh. 1612 to Bermuda on the *Plough,* sh. 1617 to Va on the *George,* sett. Elizabeth City, Va. (F.7.660)(PRO.CO1.3.114/72)

KEITH, GEORGE, b. 1638, res. Peterhead, Aberdeenshire, clergyman, edu. Marischal College, Aberdeen, 1658, sh. 1685 to Philadelphia, sett. N.J. and Md 1701, d. 1714 England. (SNQ.1.60)(Insh171)

KEITH, HENRY, sh. Aug. 1679, via Barbados to Va, on *Young William.* (PRO.CO1.44.47)

KEITH, JAMES, b. 6 Nov. 1696, s. of Robert Keith, res. Peterhead, Aberdeenshire, clergyman, edu. Marischal College, Aberdeen, Jacobite, sh. 1720, sett. Henrico Co and Fauquier Co, Va, m. Mary Isham Randolph 1733, d. Hamilton ph, Va, 1758. (VMHB.31.327)(CAG.1.665)(CCVC29)

KEITH, JAMES, b. 1727, servant, Glenbervie, Kincardineshire, Jacobite, tr. 24 Feb. 1747, fr. Liverpool to Va, on *Gildart,* arr. Port North Potomac, Md, 5 Aug. 1747. (P.2.310)(PRO.T1.328)

KEITH, JOHN, b. 1614, s. of George Keith, sh. 1617, fr. Bermuda to Va, on the *George,* sett. Elizabeth City, Va. (PRO.CO1.31.114/172)

KEITH, Sir WILLIAM, b. 1680, s. of Sir William Keith and Jean Smith, res. Inverugie, Aberdeenshire, sh. 1714 to Va, Surgeon General. (DAB.10.292)(SNQ.9/3.118)

KEITH, WILLIAM. thief and vagrant, tr. 1775, on *Aeolis,* arr. Port North Potomac, Md, 17 Oct. 1775. (SRO.JC27.10.3)

KELVIE, WILLIAM, b. 1714, husbandman, res. Kilabright, sh. May 1739, fr. London to Md. (CLRO/AIA)

KEMLO, JOSEPH, blacksmith, res. Hardgate, Old Machar, Aberdeenshire, Jacobite, tr. 24 Feb. 1747, fr. Liverpool to Va, on *Gildart,* arr. Port North Potomac, Md, 5 Aug. 1747. (P.2.310)(MR211)(JAB.2.432)(PRO.T1.328)

KEMP, JAMES, b. 1764, res. Keith Hall, Kinkell, Aberdeenshire, clergyman, edu. Marischal College, Aberdeen, 1786, sh. 1787, sett. Dorchester Co, Md, d. 28 Oct. 1827, Baltimore. (MHS:obit.)(HKK12)

KENNON, ROBERT, merchant, res. Dumfries, Dumfriesshire, sett. Va 1769, d. 15 July 1807 Petersburg, Va. (SRO.CS16.1.134)(RaleighReg.23.7.1807)

KENNON, WILLIAM, attorney, res. Dumfriesshire, sett. Richmond Co, Va, d. pre 1765, pro. 30 Dec. 1768 Edinburgh, pro. Feb. 1765 PCC.

KENNEDY, Captain ALEXANDER, b. 1729, d. Oct. 1789 Va. (VaHerald 15.10.1789)

KENNEDY, ALEXANDER, b. 1736, s. of Alexander Kennedy, cooper, res. Edinburgh, sh. 26 Feb. 1774, fr. London to Hampton, Va, on the *Planter*, arr. Fredericksburg, Va, 28 Apr. 1774, fa. of James. (PRO.T47.9/11)(OD60)(RegEdinAppr1798)

KENNEDY, ARCHIBALD, b. 5 May 1764, s. of Daniel Kennedy and Mary Brodie, res. Glasgow, d. Norfolk, Va, 1803. (GM..73.86)(EA.4042/02)

KENNEDY, DANIEL, Jacobite, tr. 28 July 1716, fr. Liverpool to Va, on *Godspeed*, arr. Md Oct. 1716. (SPC.1716.310)(CTB.31.209)(HM389)

KENNEDY, DAVID, b. 1733, merchant, militiaman in Va Regt 1756. (VMHB1/2)(L)

KENNEDY, DAVID, m. Maria McKessan, sett. Va, d. 1783. (RAV53)

KENNEDY, DAVID, b. 1800, plasterer, sh. pre 1830, m. Susan -, fa. of Janet, William, Susan and Charles, sett. Ohio Co, Va. (N.A.-M932/982)

KENNEDY, GEORGE SCOTT, b. 1700, res. Maline, sh. 1730, sett. Md, High Sheriff of Frederick Co. (HWC.2.1189)

KENNEDY, JAMES, sh. pre 1786, sett. Baltimore, m. Rachel Jennings, fa. of John. (CAG.1.910)

KENNEDY, JOHN, wright, sh. 1714, fr. Glasgow to the Potomac River, on the *American Merchant*. (TM202)

KENNEDY, JOHN, Jacobite, tr. 29 June 1716, fr. Liverpool to Jamaica or Va, on the *Elizabeth and Anne*, arr. Va 1716. (SPC.1716.310)(CTB.31.208)(VSP.1.185)

KENNEDY, MARY, b. 1753, spinner, sh. May 1774, fr. London to Md, on the *Joseph and Mary*. (PRO.T47.9/11)

KENNEDY, MATTHEW, b. 1738, s. of Walter Kennedy, m. Jane Buchanan 1770, sh. pre 1776, sett. Augusta Co, Va, 1780, fa. of John, Walter and Matthew, d. 1784. (CF.7.279)

KENNEDY, MATTHEW, b. 1766, sett. Georgetown, D.C., pre 1802, m. Christina Hines, fa. of William, John, Mary and Napoleon, d. 1847 Ohio. (OVG70)

KENNISS, ANDREW, b. 1734, carpenter, sett. Spotsylvania Co, Va, militiaman in Va Regt 1757. (VMHB.1/2)(L)

KENNY, JOHN, Jacobite, tr. 28 July 1716, fr. Liverpool to Va, on the *Godspeed*, arr. Md Oct. 1716. (SPC.1716.310)(HM388)

KERR, ALEXANDER, merchant, sh. 1794, sett. Manchester, Va. (1812)

KERR, ANNA, res. Edinburgh, tr. 1696, fr. Newhaven, Midlothian, to Va. (SRO.RH15.14.5

KERR, CHARLES, b. 1803, farmer, arr. Baltimore 1824. (N.A.-M596)

KERR, DAVID, b. 1726, s. of Professor John Kerr, lawyer, res. Edinburgh, sh. 1744, sett. Middlesex Co, Va, m. - Tucker, d. 10 July 1771 Urbanna, Va. (SM.34.517)

KERR, DAVID, b. 3 Feb. 1749, res. Monteith, Stirlingshire, sh. 1769, sett. Falmouth, Va, and Annapolis, Md, m. (1) Miss Hammond (2) Rachel Leeds Bozman, fa. of John etc, d. 2 Nov. 1814. (BLG2781)

KERR, EDWARD, s. of Edward Kerr and Jean Munro, merchant, res. Irvine, Ayrshire, sett. Va pre 1759. (SRO.CS16.1.103)

KERR, GEORGE, s. of Edward Kerr and Jean Munro, merchant, res. Irvine, Ayrshire, sett. Va pre 1759. (SRO.CS16.1.103)

KERR, GEORGE BROWN, merchant in Norfolk, Va, d. pre 1816. (SRO.RD5.85.713) (SRO.SH.6.9.1810)

KERR, JOHN, Jacobite, tr. 29 June 1716, fr. Liverpool to Jamaica or Va, on the Elizabeth and Anne, arr.Va 1716. (SPC.1716.310)(CTB.31.208)(VSP.1.185)

KERR, JOHN, shipmaster, sett. va pre 1776, Loyalist, sett. Ecclefechan, Dumfriesshire, 1783. (PRO.AO13.32.114)

KERR, JOHN, s. of Ninian Kerr, merchant, res. Beith, Ayrshire, sett. Henrico Co, Va, pro. 20 June 1776 Glasgow. (SRO.CC9.7.70)

KERR, JOHN R., b. 1799, tobacconist, sett. Richmond, Henrico Co, Va, m. Martha -. (N.A.-M932/982)

KERR, MARGARET STEWART, sett. Va, m. W.B.Lamb pre 1816. (SRO.SH8.4.1816) (SRO.RD5.85.713)

KERR, MARY, res. Kenmuir (?), sett. Norfolk, Va, pre 1816. (SRO.SH8.4.1816)(SRO.SH1.6.1830)

KERR, WILLIAM, sett. Manchester, Va, d. 1812 Ayr, pro. 6 Jan. 1813 Glasgow. (SRO.CC9.7.81)

KIDD, ALEXANDER, Jacobite, tr. 29 June 1716, fr. Liverpool to Jamaica or Va, on the Elizabeth and Anne, arr. Va. 1716. (SPC.1716.310)(CTB.31.208)(VSP.1.186)

KIDD, WILLIAM CAMPBELL, b. 4 Oct. 1795, s. of Professor James Kidd and Ann Boyd, res. Aberdeen, clergyman, edu. King's College, Aberdeen, 1813, d. 31 Aug. 1825 Richmond, Va. (KCA.2.406)(BM.18.780)

KILMAN, WILLIAM, b. 1750, blacksmith, sh. Dec. 1773, fr. London to Va, on the Elizabeth. (PRO.T47.9/11)

KILPATRICK, AGNES, res. Edinburgh, whore and thief, tr. 28 Nov. 1704, fr. Leith to Md. (SRO.PC2.28.307)

KINCAID, DAVID, s. of James Kincaid of Kincaid, sett. Spotsylvania Co, Va, 1716, fa. of David. (KFR.8)

KINCAID, GEORGE, s. of Alexander Kincaid, res. Edinburgh, sett. Augusta Co, Va, 1746, fa. of Samuel, d. 1756. (KFR.9)

KINCAID, JAMES, s. of Alexander Kincaid, res. Edinburgh, sett. Augusta Co, Va, 1746. (KFR.9)

KINCAID, JAMES, b. 1789, s. of John Kincaid of Kincaid, tallow chandler, sh. 1807, to Alexandria, Va, on the William and John, sett. Richmond, Va, 1812, and Georgetown, D.C. 1820. (SRO.RD5.185.294)(SRA.TL.X10/11)(1812)

KINCAID, JOHN, burgess of Edinburgh, sett. Va pre 1743. (BGBE113)

KINCAID, ROBERT, s. of Alexander Kincaid, res. Edinburgh, sett. Augusta Co, Va, 1746, and Alleghany Co, m. Anna -, fa. of Archibald, Andrew, John, Robert, William and Matthew. (KFR.13)

KINCAID, SAMUEL, s. of Alexander Kincaid, res, Edinburgh, sett. Augusta Co, Va, 1746. (KFR.13)

KING, ANN, b. 1777, sett. Alleghany Co, Md. (N.A.-M432-277/299)

KING, JAMES, b. 1726, laborer, res. Darrow, Aberdeenshire, Jacobite, tr. 22 Apr. 1747, fr. Liverpool to Va, on the *Johnson,* arr. Port Oxford, Md, 5 Aug. 1747. (P.2.322)(PRO.T1.328)

KING, JAMES, s. of James and Elizabeth King, sett. Va, to Glasgow by 1788, pro. Nov 1788 PCC.

KINNAIRD, JAMES, b. 1792, res. Leith, Midlothian, m. Mary -, sh. 1816, fr. Leith, sett. Richmond City, Va, nat. 12 Oct. 1826 Eastern District, Va. (US.D/C.RB5/520)

KINNAIRD, SAMUEL, b. 1795, m. Mary -, sett. Richmond, Va. (N.A.-M532/582)

KINNINGBURGH, JOHN, wright, res. Glasgow, sett. Va pre 1751. (SRO.SH8.6.1751)(SRO.CS16.1.89)

KIRK, MARGARET, res. Edinburgh, tr. 1696, fr. Newhaven, Midlothian, to Va. (SRO.RH15.14.58)

KIRK, WILLIAM, res. Orr(?), m. Elizabeth -, sett. Fauquier Co, Va, d. 1779, pro. 27 Nov. 1780 Fauquier Co.

KIRKLAND, JOHN, b. 1735, planter, sett. Northumberland Co, Va, militiaman in Va Regt 1756. (VMHB.1/2)(L)

KIRKPATRICK, JAMES, merchant, sett. Alexandria, Va, pre 1779. (SRO.CS16.1.179)

KIRKPATRICK, JOHN, b. 1811, s. of Robert Kirkpatrick and Margaret Young, res. Torthorwald, Dumfriesshire, d. 1853 Md. (Torthorwald g/s)

KIRKPATRICK, THOMAS, merchant, sett. Alexandria, Va, pre 1779. (SRO.CS16.1.175)

KIRKWOOD, ADAM, sh. 2 Nov. 1674, to St Mary's Co, Md, on *Bachelor of Bristol*. (MSA.ESB.152)

KIRKWOOD, ELIZABETH, sh. 2 Nov. 1674, to St Mary's Co, Md, on *Bachelor of Bristol*. (MSA.ESB.152)

KNOBLOCK, JANET, b. 1779, sh. pre 1820 to Md, mo. of Frances, sett. Washington, D.C. (N.A.-M432/56-57)

KNOWLES, WILLIAM, b. 16 July 1713, s. of John Knowles and Barbara Malcolm, salmon fisher, res. Nether Banchory, Aberdeenshire, Jacobite, tr. 24 Feb. 1747, fr. Liverpool to Va, on *Gildart*, arr. Port North Potomac, Md, 5 Aug. 1747.   (P.2.326)(PRO.T1.328)

KNOX, ALEXANDER, merchant, sett. Va pre 1781.   (SRO.CS16.1.183)

KNOX, ROBERT, s. of John Knox, merchant, res. Port Glasgow, m. Rose Townsend, fa. of John, Robert, Elizabeth and Janet, sett. Va and Md, d. 1782, pro. 30 Oct. 1782 Fauquier Co, Va, pro. 14 Dec. 1782 Charles Co, Md (SRO.CS17.1.1)(SRO.RD5.398.456)(SRO.SH8.3.1819)

KNOX, THOMAS, servant, res. Cruden, Aberdeenshire, thief, tr. Oct. 1774, fr. Greenock, Renfrewshire, to Va, on *Rainbow*, arr. Port Hampton, Va, 3 May 1775. (SRO.JC27.10.3)(AJ1396)

KNOX, WILLIAM, merchant, sett. Va pre 1781.   (SRO.CS16.1.183)

KYD, JOHN, s. of George Kyd, weaver, res. Arbroath, Angus, sett. Washington, D.C. pre 1831. (SRO.SH17.10.1851)

KYLE, FORBES, b. 1755, coach wheeler, sh. May 1774, fr. London to Md, on *Union*. (PRO.T47.9/11)

LAIDLAY, THOMAS, b. 1 Jan. 1756, s. of James Laidlaw and Jane Stewart, res. Ayrshire, sh. 1774 to Philadelphia, m. Sarah Osborn 1778, sett. Morgantown, Monnongahala Co, Va, fa. of Thomas, James and John, d. 17 Mar. 1838 Cabell Co, Va. (CF.4.327)(AA.6.86)

LAING, DAVID, b. 1731, s. of W. Laing, shipmaster, res. Inverkip, Renfrewshire, d. 21 May 1762 Va, bd.Blandford, Va.   (Old Blandford g/s)(WMQ.5.235)

LAING, JOHN, merchant, res.Cromarty, Ross and Cromarty, sett. Md pre 1740. (SRO.AC7.45.666)

LAING, THOMAS, leadminer, res. Aberdeen, Jacobite, tr. 24 Feb. 1747, fr. Liverpool to Va, on *Gildart,* arr. Port North Potomac, Md, 5 Aug. 1747, runaway, Va, Feb. 1751. (P.2.328)(JAB.2.432)(MR206)(PRO.T1.328)(VaGaz.2.1751)

LAIRD, KATHERINE, res. Edinburgh, whore and thief, tr. May 1666, fr. Leith to Va, on *Phoenix of Leith*.   (ETR107)

LAIRD, JOHN, s. of William Laird, merchant, res. Port Glasgow, sett. Georgetown, Md, pre 1794.   (SRO.RD3.269.640)

LAIRD, THOMAS, b. 1757, sett. Kanasha Co, Va. (N.A.-M932/982)

LAMOND, JOHN JOSEPH, b. 1721, groom, res. Aberdeen, Jacobite, tr. 24 Feb. 1747, fr. Liverpool to Va, on *Gildart,* arr. Port North Potomac, Md, 5 Aug. 1747, arr. Port North Potomac, Md, 5 Aug. 1747. (P.2.330)(JAB.2.432)(MR8)(PRO.T1.328)

LAMONT, JOHN, res. Argyllshire, sh. 1764, sett. Bedford Co, Va, d. 1823. (LC311)

LAMONT, LAUCHLAN, s. of James Lamont and Isobel McAllister, res. Auchagoyl, Argyllshire, sh. 1765, sett. Norfolk, Va, d. 30 Apr. 1773 Norfolk, Va. (LC469)

LANDRETH, JOHN, s. of William Landreth and Margaret Brown, res. Stichill, Berwickshire, m. Mrs Margaret Gillis, 25 Mar. 1765, Stephen ph, Wicomico Co, Md. (Stephen OPR)

LANG, GEORGE, s. of George Lang, barber, res. Glasgow, sett. Va pre 1763. (CS16.1.117)

LANG, THOMAS, s. of Thomas Lang, shipmaster, res. Greenock, Renfrewshire, sett. Va, m. Mary Lewis, d. 1826 Va. (Inverkip g/s)

LANG, WILLIAM, seaman, runaway, Va, Apr. 1752. (VaHerald10.4.1752)

LANGSTON, WILLIAM, nat. 20 Feb. 1786 Norfolk City, Va.

LAUDER, DAVID, Jacobite, tr. 28 July 1716, fr. Liverpool to Va, on *Godspeed,* arr. Md Oct. 1716. (SPC.1716.310)(CTB.31.209)(HM388)

LAUDER, FRANCIS, b. 22 Oct. 1729, res. Auldearn, Nairnshire, schoolmaster and clergyman, edu.Marischal College, Aberdeen, 1751, sh. 1761 to Md. (FPA301)

LAUDER, GEORGE, Jacobite, tr. 29 June 1716, fr. Liverpool to Jamaica or Va, on *Elizabeth and Anne,* arr. Va 1716. (SPC.1716.310)(CTB.31.208)(VSP.1.186)

LAURIE, JAMES, b. 1716, tailor, res. Selkirk, Selkirkshire, sh. Jan. 1736, fr. London to Md. (CLRO/AIA)

LAURIE, JAMES, b. 1782, clergyman, sh. 1802, fa. of Blair, nat. Washington, D.C. 1813. (N.A.-M432/56-57)

LAWRENCE, JOHN, b. 24 July 1754, s. of William Lawrence and Margaret Mitchell, res. Rathen, Aberdeenshire, postmaster, sett. Va. (WMQ.26.66)(VMHB.22.83)

LAWRY, ALEXANDER, laborer, res. Dumfries, Dumfriesshire, sh. Sep. 1658, fr. Bristol to Va. (BRO.04220)

LAWRY, THOMAS, Jacobite, tr. 24 May 1716, fr. Liverpool to Md, on the *Friendship,* arr. Md Aug. 1716. (SPC.1716.311)(HM386)

LAWSON, GAVIN, merchant, res. Lanarkshire, sh. pre 1776, sett. Culpepper Co, Va, Loyalist. (PRO.AO13.27.384/92)(SRO.RS42.21.92)

LAWSON, JAMES, merchant, res. Glasgow, sett. Charles Co, md, pre 1769, fa. of Robert, Mary and Agnes, Loyalist. (MSA.Chancery.46.161)(PRO.AO13.33.367)

LAWSON, JOHN,b. 1754, d. Dumfries, Va, 1823. (FamilyVisitor23.8.1823)

LAWSON, PETER, weaver, Torryburn, Fife, thief, tr. 1773, fr. Port Glasgow to Va, on Phoenix, arr. Port Accomack. Va, 20 Dec. 1773. (SRO.JC27.10.3)(AJ1293)

LAWSON, ROBERT, b. Dumfries, Dumfriesshire, clergyman, sett. Md 1713. (CCMC52)

LAWSON, ROBERT, merchant, Va, d. Oct. 1787 Glasgow, pro. 1 Oct. 1788 Glasgow. (SRO.CC9.7.73)

LAWSON, ROBERT, planter, res. Glasgow, sett. Charles Co, Md, pro. 26 June 1798 Md. (MSA.Wills.46.161/228)

LAWSON, THOMAS, s. of James Lawson, res. Glasgow, m. Catherine -, sett. Norfolk, Va, pro. 17 May 1790 Norfolk, Va.

LAWSON, WILLIAM, res. Durham, Jacobite, tr. 24 Feb. 1747, fr. Liverpool to Va, on Gildart, arr. Port North Potomac, Md, 5 Aug. 1747. (P.2.335)(PRO.T1.328)

LEES, JOHN, tr. 1773, fr. Glasgow to Va, on Thomas of Glasgow, arr. James River, Va, 3 July 1773. (SRO.JC27.10.3)

LEIPER, THOMAS, b. 15 Dec. 1745, s. of Thomas Leiper and Helen Hamilton, res. Strathavon, Lanarkshire, tobacco merchant and banker, sett. Md June 1763, d. 6 July 1825 Pa. (CAG.1.660)(DAB.11.154)

LENDRUM, THOMAS, burgess of Aberdeen, sh. 1765, sett. Port Royal, Va, fa. of Thomas, d. pre 1784. (EMA40)(SRO.SH3.1.1784)(ROA.1.288)

LENOX, CHARLES, b. 1754, res. Glasgow, sett. Prince William Co, Va, pre 1776. (VSL.23816)

LENNOX, JOHN, burgess of Glasgow, sett. Rappahannock River, Va, pre 1718. (BGBG337)

LEONARD, M., b. 1789, mechanic, arr. Baltimore 1824. (N.A.-M596)

LESLIE, ALEXANDER, b. 1767, farmer, res. Fife, sett. Richmond City, Va, nat. 28 Nov. 1799 Eastern District, Va. (US.D/C.1799.34)

LESLIE, ANDREW, b. 1793, stonecutter, m. Mary -, sett. Petersburg, Va. (N.A.-M932/982)

LESLIE, DANIEL, b. 1728, planter, militiaman in Va Regt 1755. (VMHB.1/2)(L)

LESLIE, JOHN, sett. Richmond, Va, pro. Nov. 1820.

LESLIE, JOHN, b. 1791, sh. 1811, cabinetmaker, sett. Baltimore. (N.A.-M432/277-299)(1812)

LESLIE, ROBERT, farmer, sh. 1745, sett. Cecil Co, Md. (DAB.11.185)

LESLIE, ROBERT, b. 1794, res. Ayrshire, sh. 1817, tobacco manufacturer, sett. Petersburg, Va, 1818, m. Nancy Duncan, d. Oct. 1878. (WMQ.2.17.13) (N.A.-M932/982)

LESTER, FRANCIS, b. 1756, hairdresser, res. Edinburgh, sh. Sep. 1774, fr. London to Md, on *Neptune*. (PRO.T47.9/11)

LEVEN, ABRAHAM, b. 1721, tailor, res. Linlithgow, West Lothian, sh. May 1739, fr. London to Md. (CLRO/AIA)

LEYBURN, PETER, merchant, sett. Md 1771, Loyalist. (PRO.AO13.6.231)

LIDDLE, ADAM, b. 1757, runaway, Va, 1776. (VaGaz4.10.1776)

LIKELY, JOHN, storekeeper, sett. Fauquier Co, Va, 1771, Loyalist, sh. Aug. 1776, fr. James River, Va, to Glasgow. (SFV232)

LILBURN, WILLIAM, factor, sett. St Inigo's, St Mary's Co, Md, pre 1775. (MdHistMag.44.247)(MdArch.11.41/44)(MSA.Prov.Pet.1775)

LINDSAY, BENJAMIN, woolcomber, res. Aberdeen, conspirator, tr. July 1772, fr. Glasgow to Va, on *Brilliant*, arr. Port Hampton, Va, 7 Oct. 1772. (SRO.JC27.10.3)(AJ1272)

LINDSAY, DAVID, b. 2 Jan. 1603, s. of Sir Jeremy Lindsay and Jane Ramsay, res. Leith, Midlothian, clergyman, sett. Wicomico ph, Northumberland Co, Va, 1655, m. Susanna -, fa. of Robert, d. 3 Apr. 1677. (CCVC32)(Northumerland g/s)

LINDSAY, ELIZABETH, gypsy, Jedburgh, Roxburghshire, tr. 1 Jan. 1715, fr. Glasgow to Va. (GR530)

LINDSAY, EUPHEMIA, sett. Bridge St., Old Town, Baltimore, pre 1798. (SRO.RD3.282.51)

LINDSAY, JAMES, s. of Sir Jeremy Lindsay of Annatland, sett. Gloucester Co, Va, 1635, fa. of Caleb. (WMQ.2.6.348)

LINDSAY, JAMES, Jacobite, tr. 29 June 1716, fr. Liverpool to Jamaica or Va, on *Elizabeth and Anne*, arr. Va. 1716. (SPC.1716.310)(CTB.31.208)(VSP.1.186)

LINDSAY, JAMES, sh. 1795, sett. Rockbridge Co, Va, fa. of Andrew. (DAB.11.277)

LINDSAY, WILLIAM, clergyman, edu. Glasgow Uni., sh. 1735, sett. Bristol, Va. (SCHR.14.149)

LISTON, ROBERT RAMAGE, m. Janet -, sett. Md, d. 6 Jan. 1825 Queensferry, West Lothian, pro. 30 June 1825 Edinburgh. (SRO.CC8.8.150)

LITHGOW, ALEXANDER, res. Douglas, Lanarkshire, sett. Va pre 1793. (SRO.SH3.5.1793)

LITHGOW, JOHN, sh. 2 Nov. 1674, to St Mary's Co, Md, on *Bachelor of Bristol*. (MSA.ESB.152)

LITTLE, CHARLES, s. of Andrew Little and Christine Murray, res. Annandale, Dumfriesshire, sh. 1769, sett. Alexandria, Va, m. Mary Marley. (SG.15.46)

LITTLE, JOHN, b. 1744, husbandman, sh. Dec. 1774, fr. London to Va, on *Carolina*. (PRO.T47.9/11)

LITTLE, MARGARET, res. Edinburgh, tr. 1696, fr. Newhaven, Midlothian, to Va. (SRO.RH15.14.58)

LITTLE, WILLIAM, s. of Andrew Little and Christine Murray, res. Annandale, Dumfriesshire, sett. Jefferson Co, Va, 1768, fa. of Robert, William, Charles, John and Thomas. (WMQ.2.22.216)

LITTLEPAGE, RICHARD, res. Port Glasgow, sett. Pamunkey River, Va, burgess of Glasgow 1716. (BGBG335)

LIVINGSTON, JOHN, b. 27 Jan. 1684, s. of William Livingston and Bessie Guidall, merchant, res. Aberdeen, sett. Va. (LVC405)

LIVINGSTON, JOHN, s. of John Livingston, sh. pre 1735, sett. Stratton Major ph, King and Queen Co, Va, m. Frances Muscoe. (LVC409)

LIVINGSTON, KATHERINE, res. Edinburgh, whore and thief, tr. 28 Nov. 1704, fr. Leith to Md. (SRO.PC2.28.307)

LIVINGSTON, WILLIAM, b. 18 Nov. 1682, s. of William Livingston and Bessie Guidall, res. Aberdeen, sh. pre 1716, sett. Va, m. Sarah -, theatre owner in Williamsburg, Va, d. pre 1729 Spotsylvania Co, Va. (WMQ.3.5.361)(LVC405)

LIVINGSTON, WILLIAM, Governor of Md, d. Elizabethtown, Md, 28 July 1790. (SM.52.464)

LOCHEAD, HENRY, b. 16 Aug. 1741, s. of Henry Lochead and Jean Park, merchant, res. Glasgow, sh. pre 1766, sett. Petersburg, Va. (SRO.CS16.1.125)(SRA.B10.12.4) (SRA.B10.15.7488)

LOCKHART, ARCHIBALD, b. 1736, carpenter, sett. Prince William Co, Va, militiaman in Va Regt 1756. (VMHB.1/2)(L)

LOCKARD, HENRY, merchant, res. Glasgow, sett. Alexandria, Va, pre 1777. (SRO.CS16.1.171)

LOGAN, GEORGE, merchant, res. Glasgow, sett. Kemp's Landing, Princess Anne Co, Va, 1746, m. Isabel Campbell, Loyalist, d. 15 June 1781 Glasgow, pro. Aug. 1781 PCC. (SRO.RD3.211.295)(PRO.AO13.30.71/2)(SRO.SH.20.12.1799)

LOGAN, MICHAEL, merchant, sh. 1774, sett. Petersburg, Va, Loyalist. (PRO.AO13.31.169)

LOGAN, THOMAS, merchant, set. Westmoreland Co, Va, pre 1767. (SRO.CS16.1.130)

LOGAN, THOMAS, res. Aberdeen, m. Susanna Daly 13 Feb. 1774 St Paul's, Baltimore. (St Paul's OPR)

LOMAX, JOHN, merchant, res. Glasgow, sett. Md pre 1754, pro 22 Nov 1757 PCC.

LONG, HENRY, b. 1714, butcher, sett. Norfolk, Va, militiaman in Va Regt 1757. (VMHB.1/2)(L)

LOTHIAN, ALEXANDER, res. Edinburgh, sett. St Mary's Co, Md, d. 2 Dec. 1768. (MSA.Wills.37.254)

LOTHIAN, ELIZABETH, da. of John Lothian, res. Burntisland, Fife, sh. 1765 to Va. (VaGaz1774)

LOURIE, JOHN, b. 1735, joiner, sett. Essex Co, Va, militiaman in Va Regt 1757. (VMHB.1/2)(L)

LOUTIT, WILLIAM, b. 1804, res. Orkney Islands, sh. 1817, nat. 20 June 1831 Norfolk, Va.

LOVE, ALLAN, merchant, sh. pre 1771, sett. Va and N.C.   (SRA.B10.15.8270)

LOVE, WILLIAM, merchant, sett Va pre 1778.   (SRO.CS16.1.173)(SFV182)

LOW, DAVID, s. of - Low and Isabel Richard, tailor, res. Forfar, Angus, sett. Md pre 1763.   (SRO.RS35.20.79)

LOW, JOHN, res. Kincardineshire, tr. 5 Feb. 1752, fr. Aberdeen to Va, on the *Planter*. (AJ265)

LOWE, ABRAHAM, Jacobite, tr. 24 May 1716, fr. Liverpool to Md, on *Friendship*, arr. Aug. 1716 Md.   (SPC.1716.311)(HM386)(MdArch.34.164)

LOWE, JAMES, Jacobite, tr. 24 May 1716, fr. Liverpool to Md, on *Friendship*, arr. Md Aug. 1716.   (SPC.1716.311)(HM387)

LOWE, JOHN, b. 1750, res. Kenmore, Galloway, tutor and clergyman, sh. 1773, sett. St George, Hanover Co, Va, d. 1798 Kentucky.   (VMHB.67.174)

LOWERY, WILLIAM, m. Janet Anderson, d. 1687, pro. 14 Mar. 1687 Norfolk, Va.

LUCKY, JOHN, b. 20 Oct. 1728, s. of William Lucky and Helen Black, servant,res. St Nicholas, Aberdeen, Jacobite, tr. 24 Feb. 1747, fr. Liverpool to Va, on *Gildart*, arr. Port North Potomac, Md, 5 Aug. 1747.   (P.2.352)(MR211)(JAB.2.433) (PRO.T1.328)

LUMSDEN, HENRY, Jacobite, tr. 24 May 1716, fr. Liverpool to Md, on *Friendship*, arr. Aug. 1747 Md.   (SPC.1716.311)(HM387)

LUMSDEN, JAMES, b. 1752, baker, sh. Mar. 1774, fr. London to Va, on *Brilliant*. (PRO.T47.9/11)

LUNAN, PATRICK, s. of Rev. Alexander Lunan and - Elphinstone, clergyman, res. Daviot, Fyvie, Aberdeenshire, sh. 1760 to Va. (EMA41)

LUNDIE, JAMES, res. Buchan, Aberdeenshire, clergyman, edu. King's College, Aberdeen, 1741, sh. 1767 to Va. (EMA41)

LUSKIE, JOHN, fa. Charles, sett. Charles Co, Md, pro. 29 Mar. 1769 Md. (MSA.Wills.38.446)

LYLE, JAMES, b. 1724, facctor and merchant, sett. Manchester, Chesterfield Co, Va, d. 1812. (VSA:Jas Lyle PP)

LYLE, JAMES, b, 1733, carpenter, sett. Williamsburg, Va, militiaman in Va Regt 1757. (VMHB.1/2)(L)

LYLE, JAMES, merchant, sett. Va, d. 18 Feb. 1813 Meadowhead of Strathblane, Stirlingshire, pro. 29 Mar. 1813. (SRO.CC9.7.81)

LYLE, JAMES, res. Port Glasgow (?), sett. Va pre 1758. (SRO.CS16.1.100)

LYNN, MARGARET, res. Argyllshire, sh. pre 1718 to Va, m. John Lewis, mo. of Thomas. (CAG.1.906)

LYON, CHARLES, sett. Princess Anne Co, Va, pre 1776, Loyalist, sett. Halifax, N.S. (PRO.AO13.25.336)

LYON, JANE, sh. 2 Nov. 1674, to St Mary's Co, Md, on *Bachelor of Bristol,* (MSA.ESB.152)

LYON, JOHN, res. Forfar, Angus, tr. Aug. 1752, fr. Aberdeen to Va, on *St Andrew.* (AJ241)

LYON, THOMAS, b. 1793, machinist, m. Harriet, sh. pre 1827 to Md, fa. of Margaret, Sarah and Rebecca, sett. Baltimore. (N.A.-M432/277-99)

LYON, WALTER, student of divinity and tutor, sh. 1754, fr. Glasgow to Va, sett. Princess Anne Co, Va. (PAL34)

LYON, WILLIAM, Jacobite, tr. 29 June 1716, fr. Liverpool to Jamaica or Va, on *Elizabeth and Anne,* arr. Va. 1716. (SPC.1716.310)(CTB.31.208)(VSP.1.186)

LYON, WILLIAM, b. 1715, physician, d. 1794 Baltimore. (OD187)

MacALLISTER, ARCHIBALD, s. of James MacAllister, sh. 1760, sett. Norfolk, Va. (UNC/MacAllister PP.3774)

MacALLISTER, HECTOR, s. of James MacAllister, merchant, sh. 1760, sett. Norfolk, Va, Loyalist. UNC/MacAllister PP.3774)(SRO.CS16.1.174)(PRO.AO13.31.205) (PRO.AO.T79.21.29)

MacALLISTER, HENRY, merchant, sett. Md 1750, d. 1768. (MdMag.6.213)

MacALLISTER, WILLIAM, merchant, sett. Va pre 1769. (SRO.CS16.1.107)

McALLISTER, WILLIAM, nat. 2 Apr. 1814 Norfolk City, Va.

McALPIN, JAMES, b. Aug. 1761, merchant, res. Glasgow, sh. pre 1776 to Va, sett. Philadelphia, d. 20 July 1847   (AP236)

McALPINE, ROBERT, physician and surgeon, res. Lanarkshire, sett. Norfolk, Va, fa. of Jane and Margaret, nat. Princess Anne Co, Va, 2 June 1823.   (SRO.SH7.11.1827)

McARTHUR, DUNCAN, s. of Charles McArthur, workman, res. Inveraray, Argyllshire, tr. 1772, fr. Port Glasgow to Va, on *Phoenix*, arr. Port Accomack, Va, 20 Dec. 1772. (SRO.JC27.10.3)(AJ1290)

McARTHUR, JAMES, sr, b. 1731, weaver, res. Glasgow, sett. Hampshire Co, Va. (VSA.24296)

MacAULAY, ALEXANDER, b. Nov. 1754, merchant, res. Glasgow, sh. 1775, sett. Yorktown, Va, m. Elizabeth Jerdone 1782, fa. of Alexander, Patrick, Helen, Sarah, John, Francis and Patrick, d. 17 July 1798 Yorktown, Va.   (WMQ.11.180)(WMQ.2.22.235) (WMQ.2.23.235)(WMQ.2.23.509)

MacAUSLAND, HUMPHREY, res. Greenock, Renfrewshire, d. 12 Oct. 1792 Philadelphia, pro. 6 Nov. 1792 Spotsylvania Co, Va.   (Spotsylvania Wills.E1191)

McBEAN, ANGUS, res. Leipick, Fort William, (Invernessshire?), d. 1815, pro. 6 Dec. 1815 Baltimore.

McBEAN, ANGUS, Jacobite, tr. 31 July 1716, fr. Liverpool to Va, on *Anne*. (SPC.1716.310)(CTB.31.209)

McBEAN, DANIEL, Jacobite, tr. 7 May 1716, fr. Liverpool to Va, on *Anne*. (SPC.1716.310)(CTB.31.209)

McBEAN, FRANCIS, Jacobite, tr. 28 July 1716, fr. Liverpool to Va, on *Godspeed,* arr. Oct. 1716 Md.   (SPC.1716.310)(CTB.31.209)(HM388)

McBEAN, JOHN, Jacobite, tr. 24 May 1716, fr. Liverpool to Md, on *Friendship*, arr. Md Aug. 1716.   (SPC.1716.311)(HM387)(MdArch.34.164)

McBEAN, WILLIAM, Jacobite, tr. 24 May 1716, fr. Liverpool to Va, on *Friendship*, arr. 20 Aug. 1716 Md.   (SPC.1716.311)(HM386)

McBRYDE, HUGH, merchant, res. Irvine, Ayrshire, sett. Dorchester Co, Md, pre 1775. (SRO.RD2.232.642)

McBRYDE, WILLIAM, merchant, res. Irvine, Ayrshire, sett. Dorchester Co, Md, pre 1775. (SRO.RD2.232.642)

McCAA, WILLIAM, merchant, sett. va pre 1771.   (SRO.CS16.1.143)

McCAI, CHARLES JOHN, s. of William McCai, res. Glasgow, sh. Nov. 1711, fr. Glasgow to Va, sett. Essex Co, Va. (Essex Deeds 14.39)

McCALL, ARCHIBALD, b. 28 Apr. 1734, s. of Samuel McCall and Margaret Adams, merchant, res. Glasgow, sh. 1752, sett. Tappanannock, Essex Co, Va, m. Catherine Flood, Loyalist, d. Oct. 1814.   (VMHB.73.313)(PRO.AO13.31.210)

McCALL, JAMES, storekeeper, res. Glasgow, sh. pre 1765, sett. New Glasgow, Essex Co, Va. (SRA.T79.41)

McCALL, SAMUEL, schoolmaster and planter, res. Glasgow, sett. Va pre 1765. (SRO.CS16.1.120)

McCALLUM, GILBERT, Jacobite, tr. 22 Apr. 1747, fr. Liverpool to Va, on *Johnson*, arr. Port Oxford, Md, 5 Aug. 1747.   (P.3.22)(PRO.T1.328)

McCALLUM, JOHN, Jacobite, tr. 28 July 1716, fr. Liverpool to Va, on *Godspeed,* arr. Md Oct. 1716.   (SPC.1716.310)(HM389)

McCALLUM, MALCOLM, Jacobite, tr. 28 July 1716, fr. Liverpool to Va, on *Godspeed,* arr. Md Oct. 1716.   (SPC.1716.310)(CTB.31.209)(HM388)

McCALLUM, NEIL, clergyman, sh. 1736 to Va.   (WMQ.2.20.126)

McCALMAN, JOHN, sh. 2 Nov. 1674, to St Mary's Co, Md, on the *Bachelor of Bristol.* (MSA.ESB.152)

McCANDLISH, ROBERT, tutor, res. Wigtownshire, sett. Essex Co, Va 1760. (SG.32.2.111)

McCANNON, JANE, b. 1808, sh. pre 1829 to Pa, mo. of John, Margaret, Thomas, Jane and Nathaniel, sett. Baltimore.   (N.A.-M432/277-99)

McCAUL, ALEXANDER, merchant, res. Glasgow, sett. Va pre 1776, Loyalist. (PRO.AO13.32.116)

McCAULL, JAMES, merchant, res. Glasgow, sett. Va pre 1746.   (SRO.CS16.1.78)

McCAW, JAMES, s. of William McCaw and Elizabeth Drew, surgeon and apothecary, res. Newton-Stewart, Wigtownshire, sh. 1769, sett. Norfolk, Va, m. Elizabeth Brough, fa. of James, Loyalist, d. Oct. 1779 N.Y.   (PRO.AO13.31.220)(SRO.CC8.8.220) (BLG2803)(DAB.11.575)

MACHEYNE, JAMES, res. Petic (?), sh. 1720, fr. Glasgow to Md, sett. Potomac River 1727.   (MdHistMag.1.347)

McCLEAN, JOHN, merchant, sett. Norfolk, Va, pre 1776, Loyalist.   (PRO.AO13.31.331)

McCLEAN, Miss J., b. 1798, arr. Norfolk, Va, 1823. (PA300)

McCLEMENT, JOHN, clergyman, edu. Edinburgh Uni., sh. 1718, fr. London to Philadelphia, sett. Rehobeth, Va. (AP192)

McCLOUD, - , d. June 1787, Richmond, Va. (VaGaz14.6.1787)

McCLOUD, WILLIAM, b. 1730, militiaman in Va Regt 1756. (VMHB.1/2)(L)

McCLOUGHTON, PETER, Jacobite, tr. 22 Apr. 1747, fr. Liverpool to Va, on *Johnson*, arr. Port Oxford, Md, 5 Aug. 1747. (PRO.T1.328)

McCLURE, DAVID, nat. 26 Dec. 1803 Norfolk City, Va, nat. 7 Apr. 1794 Princess Anne Co, Va.

McCONOCHIE, JAMES, b. 1785, clergyman and physician, sett. Culpepper Co, Va, 1796, m. Susan Slaughter, sett. Kentucky 1838. (VMHB.67.174)

McCONOCHIE, WILLIAM, clergyman, sh. 1710, sett. Portobacco, Potomac River, Md, d. 1742, pro. 21 Jan. 1743 Edinburgh. (SRO.CC8.8.107)(EMA43)

McCOULL, NEIL, b. 1740, merchant, sett. Fredericksburg, Va, d. 27 Apr. 1792. (VaHerald5.5.1792)

McCOULL, ROBERT, b. 1773, merchant, sh. pre 1809, m. Margaret -, fa. of Jane and Robert, sett. Baltimore. (N.A.-M432/277-99)

MacCOURTUIE, JAMES, b. 1757, servant, res. Kirkcudbright, thief, tr. 1771, fr. Port Glasgow to Md on *Crawford*, arr. Port Oxford, Md, 23 July 1771. (SRO.JC27.10.3)(AJ1167)

McCOY, H. B., b. 1795, plasterer, m. Ellen -, fa. of Agnes, Margaret, Sally, Susan, Rachel, Mary and Marcella, sett. Rockbridge Co, Va. (N.A.-M932/982)

McCOY, PATRICK, Jacobite, tr. 28 July 1716, fr. Liverpool to Va, on *Godspeed*, arr. Md, Oct. 1716. (SPC.1716.310)(CTB.31.209)(HM389)

McCOY, PETER, res. Bellie, Banffshire, Jacobite, tr. 22 Apr. 1747, fr. Liverpool to Va, on *Johnson*, arr. Port Oxford, Md, 5 Aug. 1747. (PRO.T1.328)(JAB.2.434)

McCRACKEN, ROBERT, b. 1777, merchant, res. Newton-Douglas, Galloway, sett. Richmond City, Va, nat. 19 Sep. 1799 Eastern District, Va. (US.D/C.1799.15)

McCRADIE, ROBERT, nat. 24 July 1786 Norfolk City, Va.

McCRAW, DANIEL, runaway, Fredericksburg, Va, 1746. (VaGaz14.8.1746)

McCRAY, JOHN, b. 1749, planter, sett. Louisa Co, Va. (VSA24296)

McCRONE, JOHN, b. 1795, iron manufacturer, sh. pre 1828, m. Sarah -, fa. of John, Alexander, Mary, Sarah, Andrew, Emily and Richard, sett. Baltimore. (N.A.-M432/982)

McCROSKREY, DAVID, s. of John McCroskrey, sett. Augusta Co, Va, m. Grizel Poage, d. 1788 Rockbridge, Va. (SG

McCUBBIN, HUGH, b. 1812, ropemaker, m. Ann -, fa. of Jane, sett. Petersburg, Dinwiddie Co, Va. (N.A.-M932/982)

MacCUBBIN, JOHN, b. 1630, s. of Sir John MacCubbin of Knockdolian, Ayrshire, planter, sett. Tinker Neck, Anne Arundel Co, Md, 1659, m. (1) Susan Howard (2) Elinor Campbell, fa. of John, Samuel, William, Zachariah, Moses and Elizabeth, d. 21 Sep. 1685.   (BLG2805)(CF.4.350)

McCUILLAN, WILLIAM, servant, res. Borrowston, Caithness, thief and housebreaker, tr. 1773, fr. Glasgow to Va, on *Donald*, arr. Port James, Upper District, Va, 13 March 1773.   (SRO.JC27.10.3)

McCULLOCH, ANNE, merchant, sett. Va, d. 4 Nov. 1794, Westfield, Bothwell, Lanarkshire. (GM.64.1150)

McCULLOCH, ANTHONY, res. Glasgow, sett. Queen Anne Co, Md, d. 1770, pro. 30 Apr. 1773. (SRO.CC8.8.122)

McCULLOCH, DAVID, b. 1718, s. of John McCulloch of Torhousekey, Galloway, merchant, sett. Joppa, Baltimore Co, Md, pre 1756, m. Mary Dick 1759, fa. of James, Margaret and Elizabeth, d. 17 Sep. 1766, bd. St John's, pro. 6 Oct. 1766 Anne Arundel Co, Md. (NGSQ.65.262)(MHS:All Hallows OPR.145)

McCULLOCH, RODERICK, clergyman, res. Ardwell, Wigtownshire, sh. 1727, sett. Westmoreland Co, Va, m. Elizabeth -, fa. of Roderick, d. 1745. (CAG.1.185/983)

McCULLOCH, THOMAS, merchant, res. Glasgow, sett. Gosport and Norfolk, Va, Loyalist, d. 4 Nov. 1794 Westfield, Bothwell, Lanarkshire, pro. 6 Jan. 1795 Edinburgh. (SRO.CC8.8.175)(SRO.CS16.1.175)(PRO.AO13.31.244)(GM.64.1150)

McCULLON, JOHN, Jacobite, tr. 29 June 1716, fr. Liverpool to Jamaica or Va, on Elizabeth and Anne.   (SPC.1716.310)(CTB.31.208)

McDANIEL, Jacobite, tr. 22 Apr. 1747, fr. Liverpool to Va, on *Johnson,* arr. Port Oxford, Md, 5 Aug. 1747.   (PRO.T1.328)

McDANIEL, JOHN, Jacobite, tr. 22 Apr. 1747, fr. Liverpool to Va, on *Johnson,* arr. Port Oxford, Md, 5 Aug. 1747.   (PRO.T1.328)

McDARRAN, ARCHIBALD, Jacobite, tr. 24 May 1716, fr. Liverpool to Md, on *Friendship*, arr. Md Aug. 1716.   (SPC.1716.311)(HM387)

McDERMOTT, ANGUS, Jacobite, tr. 28 July 1716, fr. Liverpool to Va, on *Godspeed,* arr. Md Oct. 1716.   (SPC.1716.310)(CTB.31.209)(HM389)

McDERMOTT, MARY, b. 1794, arr. Baltimore 1825.   (N.A.-M596)

MacDONALD, ALASTAIR, b. 1745, res. Lochaber, Invernessshire, m. Sarah - 1776, sh. 1803, fa. of John, sett. Baltimore.   (AA.7.233)

McDONALD, ALEXANDER, Jacobite, tr. 24 Feb. 1747, fr. Liverpool to Va, on *Gildart,* arr. Port North Potomac, Md, 5 Aug. 1747.   (PRO.T1.328)

McDONALD, ALEXANDER, res. Tarbert, Argyllshire, sett. Va 1770.   (SRO.CS16.1.141)

McDONALD, ALEXANDER, res. Reay, Caithness, shipwreck looter, tr. 1773, fr. Glasgow to Va, on *Donald*, arr. Port James, Upper District, Va, 13 Mar. 1773, runaway, Apr. 1773. (SRO.JC27.10.3)(AJ1091/8)(VaGaz15.4.1773)

McDONALD, ALEXANDER, b. 1742, schoolmaster, res. Edinburgh, m. - Hoff, sett. Frederickstown, Md, 1764, d. 1795. (Fred. Evang.Lutheran OPR)

McDONALD, ALEXANDER, b. 1800, wagonmaker, m. Ann -, fa. of Alexander, Elizabeth and Mary, sett. Alleghany Co, Md. (N.A.-M432-277/99)

McDONALD, ANGUS, b. 1727, m. Anna Thompson, sett. Frederick Co, Va, 1770, d.1778. (RAV64)

McDONALD, ANGUS, b. 1735, seaman, sett. King George Co, Va, militiaman in Va Regt 1757. (VMHB.1/2)(L)

McDONALD, ANGUS, tr. 1771, fr. Port Glasgow to Md, on *Matty,* arr. Port Oxford, Md, 17 Dec. 1771. (SRO.JC27.10.3)

MacDONALD, ANGUS, Jacobite, tr. 24 Feb. 1747, fr. Liverpool to Va, on *Gildart,* arr. Port North Potomac, Md, 5 Aug. 1747. (PRO.T1.328)

McDONALD, ANGUS, res. Glengarry, Invernessshire, sh. 1750, sett. Winchester Co, Va, d. 1779. (VaMag.20.83)(D.U.-McDonald PP)

McDONALD, ANN, res. Inverness, thief, tr. 1772, fr. Glasgow to Va, on *Brilliant,* arr. Port Hampton, Va, 7 Oct. 1772. (SRO.JC27.10.3)(AJ1274)

McDONALD, ARCHIBALD, b. 1705, farmer, Glenmoriston, Invernessshire, Jacobite, tr. 22 Apr. 1747, fr. Liverpool to Va, on *Johnson,* d. 4 June 1747 at sea. (P.3.48)(MR155)(PRO.T1.328)

McDONALD, COLIN, s. of Donald McDonald, assistant storekeeper, res. Glasgow, sett. Culpepper Co, Va, pre 1776. (SFV229)

McDONALD, DONALD, b. 1733, planter, sett. Dinwiddie Co, Va, pre 1776. (VSA24296)

McDONALD, DONALD, b. 1692, laborer, Camghouran, Rannoch, Perthshire, Jacobite, tr. 24 Feb. 1747, fr. Liverpool to Va, on Gildart, arr. Port North Potomac, Md, 5 Aug. 1747. (P.3.56)(MR156)(PRO.T11.328)

McDONALD, JEAN, tr. 1772, fr. Glasgow to Va, on *Brilliant,* arr. Port Hampton, Va, 7 Oct. 1772. (SRO.JC27.10.3)

McDONALD, JOHN, Jacobite, tr. 24 Feb. 1747, fr. Liverpool to Va, on *Gildart,* arr. Port North Potomac, Md, 5 Aug. 1747. (PRO.T1.328)

McDONALD, JOHN, b. 1734, planter, sett. Caroline Co, Va, militiaman in Va Regt 1756. (VMHB.1/2)(L)

McDONALD, JOHN. Jacobite, tr. 24 Feb. 1747, fr. Liverpool to Va, on *Gildart,* arr. Port North Potomac, Md, 5 Aug. 1747. (PRO.T1.328)

McDONALD, JOHN, Jacobite, tr. 22 Apr. 1747, fr. Liverpool to Va, on *Johnson,* arr. Port Oxford, Md, 5 Aug. 1747. (PRO.T1.328)

McDONALD, JOHN, b. 1752, husbandman, sh. July 1774, fr. London to Md, on *Peggy Stewart.* (PRO.T47.9/11)

McDONALD, M., b. 1799, arr. Baltimore 1820 on *Oryza.* (N.A.-M596)

McDONALD, RONALD, city guardsman, res. Edinburgh, Jacobite, tr. 24 Feb. 1747, fr. Liverpool to Va, on *Gildart,* arr. Port North Potomac, Md, 5 Aug. 1747. (P.3.76)(PRO.T1.328)

McDONALD, WILLIAM, cooper, sh. 1766, runaway, Suffolk Co, Va, 1767. (VaGaz1.10.1767)

McDOUGALL, ALEXANDER, Jacobite, tr. 24 May 1716, fr. Liverpool to Md, on *Friendship,* arr. Md Aug. 1716. (SPC.1716.311)(HM387)

McDOUGALL, JOHN, d. 1803, Va, pro. 15 Jan. 1805, Monroe Co, Va.

McDOUGAL, MARY, res. Greenock, Renfrewshire, m. - Donahue, pro. 13 Apr. 1760 Norfolk, Va.

McDOUGALL, ROBERT, b. 1720, sett. Hanover Co, Va, and Chillecottie, Ohio, fa. of John, d. 1816. (CAG.1.185)

McDOWALL, ANDREW, pro. 18 Apr.1796 Amherst, Va.

McDOWELL, JOHN, merchant, res. Glasgow, sett. Hanover Co, Va, 1750, Loyalist, sett. Glasgow. (PRO.AO13.31.275)

McDOWALL, PATRICK, blockmaker, Leith, Midlothian, m. Catherine Hardie, Va, 13 Jan. 1794. (Edinburgh OPR)

McDOWELL, SAMUEL, b. 1720, res. Newport, Glasgow, runaway fr. *The Berry,* 1752. (VaGaz27.3.1752)

McDOWELL, THOMAS, b. 1792, res. Wigtownshire, d. 9 July 1825 Sulphur Springs, Va. (SRO.AC27.7.1825)

McDUFF, JAMES, laborer, Ballicreughan, Perthshire, Jacobite, tr. 22 Apr. 1747, fr. Liverpool to Va, on *Johnson,* arr. Port Oxford, Md, 5 Aug. 1747. (P.3.84)(PRO.T1.328)(MR207)

McDUGALD, HUGH, Jacobite, tr. 28 July 1716, fr. Liverpool to Va, on *Godspeed,* arr. Md Oct. 1716. (SPC.1716.310)(CTB.31.209)(HM389)

McEWAN, ANDREW, thief, tr. 1775, on *Aeolis,* arr. Port North Potomac, Md, 17 Oct. 1775. (SRO.JC27.10.3)

McEWAN, JOHN, Jacobite, tr. 28 July 1716, fr. Liverpool to Va, on *Godspeed,* arr. Md Oct. 1716. (SPC.1716.310)(CTB.31.209)(HM388)

McEWAN, KATHERINE, b. 1707, res. Fort William, Invernessshire, Jacobite, tr. 22 Apr. 1747, fr. Liverpool to Va, on *Johnson*, arr. Port Oxford, Md, 5 Aug. 1747. (P.3.174)(PRO.T1.328)

McFAIN, DANIEL, b. 1730, planter, sett. Winchester, Va, militiaman in Va Regt 1756. (VMHB.1/2)(L)

McFARLAND, A. B., b. 1797, stonemason, m. Josephine -, fa. of Daniel and Walter, sett. Washington, D.C. (N.A.-M432/56-57)

McFARLAND, SARAH, b. 1790, mo. of John, sett. Washington, D.C. pre 1829. (N.A.-M432.277-99)

McFARLAND, JOHN, b. 1794, printer, m. Eliza -, sett. Richmond, Henrico Co, Va. (N.A.-M432/56-57)

McFARLAND, MARGARET, b. 1798, sh. pre 1826 to Va, mo. of Robert, John and Elizabeth, sett. Baltimore. (N.A.-M432/277-99)

McFARLANE, ALEXANDER, factor, res. Glasgow, sh. pre 1761, sett. Chaptico, Md. (SRA.CFI)

MacFARLANE, GEORGE, sh. Apr. 1756, fr. London to Md. (CLRO/AIA)

MacFARLANE, JAMES, sett. Va, fa. of William. (CAG.1.561)

MacFARLANE, ROBERT, runaway, Albemarle Co, Va, 29 Feb. 1752. (VaGaz5.3.1752)

MacFEARGHUIS, RODERICK, Jacobite, tr. 22 Apr. 1747, fr. Liverpool to Md, on *Johnson,* arr. Port Oxford, Md, 5 Aug. 1747. (P.3.86)(PRO.T1.328)

McGEORGE, JOHN, storekeeper, Surrey Co and Southampton Co, Va, pre 1777, Loyalist. (PRO.AO13.33.297)

McGIBBON, PETER, res. Strathblane, Stirlingshire, sett. Norfolk, Va, d. July 1788, on *Farmer of Glasgow*, pro. 2 Feb. 1789 Glasgow. (SRO.CC9.7.73)(SRO.RD4.244.418)

McGILL, ANDREW, b. 1749, blacksmith, res. Edinburgh, sh. Aug. 1774, fr. London to Va, on *Beith,* runaway, Williamsburg, Va, July 1775. (PRO.T47.9/11)(VaGaz20.7.1775)

McGILL, DANIEL, clergyman, edu. Edinburgh Uni., sh. 1712, sett. Patuxent, Md, 1714, d. 10 Feb. 1724. (F.7.664)(AP170)

MacGILL, JAMES, b. 1701, clergyman, sh. 1727, sett. Queen Caroline ph., Md, 1730, m. Sarah Hillary, fa. of Margaret -, d. 26 Dec. 1779. (EMA42)(CAG.1.381)

McGILL, JANET, res. Rackhead, Kilmarnock, Ayrshire, thief, tr. 1772, fr. Glasgow to Va, on *Brilliant*, arr. Port Hampton, Va, 7 Oct. 1772. (PRO.JC27.10.3)(AJ1270)

McGILL, JOHN, b. Mar. 1752, res. Auckland, Dumfries, sh. 1773 to Va, Loyalist, sett. St John, New Brunswick, 1784, d. 31 Dec. 1834 Toronto. (DCB.6.451)

McGILL, NATHAN, nat. 27 May 1793 Norfolk City, Va.

McGILLIS, DANIEL, Jacobite, tr. 22 Apr. 1747, fr. Liverpool to Va, on *Johnson*, arr. Port Oxford, Md, 5 Aug. 1747. (PRO.T1.328)

McGILLIVRAY, DANIEL, Jacobite, tr. 29 June 1716, fr. Liverpool to Jamaica or Va, on *Elizabeth and Anne*, arr. Va 1716. (SPC.1716.310)(CTB.31.208)(VSP.1.186)

McGILLIVRAY, FARQUHAR, Jacobite, tr. 24 May 1716, fr. Liverpool to Md, on *Friendship*, arr. Md 20 Aug. 1716. (SPC.1716.311)(HM386)

McGILLIVRAY, WILLIAM, Jacobite, tr. 24 May 1716, fr. Liverpool to Md, on *Friendship*, arr. Md. Aug. 1716. (SPC.1716.311)(HM386)

McGILLIVRAY, WILLIAM, Jacobite, tr. 29 June 1716, fr. Liverpool to Jamaica or Va, on *Elizabeth and Anne*, arr. Va. 1716. (SPC.1716.310)(CTB.31.208)(VSP.1.185)

McGILLIWIE, JOHN, b. 1791, s. of Peter McGilliwie and Janet Robertson, res. Wester Logerait, Perthshire, sett. Richmond, Va, d. 1820. (Logerait g/s)

McGIVEN, ALEXANDER, Jacobite, tr. 28 July 1716, fr. Liverpool to Va, on *Godspeed*, arr. Md Oct. 1716. (SPC.1716.310)(CTB.31.209)(HM389)

McGLASHAN, JOHN, res. Edinburgh, tr. 1696, fr. Newhaven, Midlothian, to Va. (SRO.RH15.14.58)

McGLASHAN, MARGARET, res. Edinburgh, tr. 1696, fr. Newhaven, Midlothian, to Va. (SRO.RH15.14.58)

McGOWAN, JOHN, sh. 2 Nov. 1674, to St Mary's Co, Md, on *Bachelor of Bristol*. (MSA.ESB.152)

McGRATH, HENRY, b. 1712, husbandman, res. Edinburgh, sh. Oct. 1734, fr. London to Va. (CLRO/AIA)

McGRAW, DONALD, runaway, Va, 1 July 1746. (VaGaz7.1746)

McGREGOR, ALEXANDER, b. 1610, tr. 1651, sett. Calvert Co, Md, m. (1) Margaret Braithwaite (2) Elizabeth Hawlan, fa. of Samuel, d. 1667. (BLG2814)

McGREGOR, DUNCAN, Jacobite, tr. 22 Apr. 1747, fr. Liverpool to Va, on *Johnson*, arr. Port Oxford, Md, 5 Aug. 1747. (PRO.T1.328)

McGREGOR, DUNCAN, farmer, res. Tarland, Aberdeenshire, Jacobite, tr. 24 Feb. 1747, fr. Liverpool to Va, on *Gildart*, arr. Port North Potomac, Md, 5 Aug. 1747. (P.3.92)(JAB.2.434)(MR202)(PRO.T1.328)

McGREGOR, GREGOR, Jacobite, tr. 31 July 1716, fr. Liverpool to Va, on *Anne*. (SPC.1716.310)(CTB.31.209)

McGREGOR, JOHN, Jacobite, tr. 28 July 1716, fr. Liverpool to Va, on *Godspeed*, arr. Md Oct. 1716. (SPC.1716.310)(CTB.31.209)(HM388)

McGREGOR, JOHN, laborer, res. Perthshire, Jacobite, tr. 22 Apr. 1747, fr. Liverpool to Md, on Johnson, arr. Port Oxford, Md, 5 Aug. 1747. (P.3.94)(MR94)(PRO.T1.328)

McGREGOR, MARK, b.1723, cook, res. Balnagowan, Perthshire, Jacobite, tr. 24 Feb. 1747, fr. Liverpool to Va, on Gildart, arr. Port North Potomac, Md, 5 Aug. 1747. (P.3.96)(MR40)(PRO.T1.328)

McGREGOR, N. M., b. 1803, merchant, m. S. C. -, sh. pre 1830, fa. of H., M., S., E., A., Robert and John, sett. Washington, D.C.   (N.A.-M432/56-57)

McGREGOR, PATRICK, farmer, res. Perthshire, Jacobite, tr. 22 Apr. 1747, fr. Liverpool to Va, on Johnson, arr. Port Oxford, Md, 5 Aug. 1747.   (P.3.220)(PRO.T1.328)

McGREGOR, SUSANNA, b. 1785, sett. Ritchie Co, Va, pre 1825, mo. of Joseph, Susan, and James.   (N.A.-M932/982)

MacGRUDER, ALEXANDER, b. 1610, s. of Alexander MacGruder and Margaret Campbell, res, Madderty, Perthshire, tr. 1651, sett. Turkey Buzzard Island, Calvert Co, Md, m. (1) Margaret Braithwaite (2) Sarah - (3) Elizabeth Hawkins, fa. of James, Samuel, John, Alexander, Nathaniel and Elizabeth, d. 1677.   (CF.6)(DAB.11.205)

MacHARDY, JOHN, Jacobite, tr. 28 July 1716, fr. Liverpool to Va, on Godspeed. (SPC.1716.310)(CTB.31.209)

McHARG, ALEXANDER, res. Minnigaff, Galloway, m. Elizabeth Watts, fa. of Mary, sett. Mecklenburg Co, Va, pro. 10 Oct. 1774 Mecklenburg, Va. (Mecklenburg Wills.1.194)

McHARG, EBENEZER, merchant, res. Minnigaff, Galloway, sett. Mecklenburg Co, Va, pre 1763.   (SRO.CS16.1.115)

McINDOE, WALTER, s. of Robert McIndoe, merchant, res. Carbeth, Strathblane, Stirlingshire, sett. Petersburg, Va, pre 1822.   (SRO>SH13.12.1822)(Strathblane g/s)

McINNIS, ARCHIBALD, Jacobite, tr. 22 Apr. 1747, fr. Liverpool to Va, on Johnson, arr. Port Oxford, Md, 5 Aug. 1747.   (PRO.T1.328)

McINNY, ALEXANDER, Jacobite, tr. 24 Feb. 1747, fr. Liverpool to Va, on Gildart, arr. Port North Potomac, Md, 5 Aug. 1747.   (PRO.T1.328)

McINTAGGART, PATRICK, Jacobite, tr. 22 Apr. 1747, fr. Liverpool to Va, on Johnson, arr. Port Oxford, Md, 5 Aug. 1747.   (P.3.100)(PRO.T1.328)

McINTOSH, ALEXANDER, Jacobite, tr. 28 July 1716, fr. Liverpool to Va, on Godspeed, arr. Md Oct. 1716.   (SPC.1716.310)(CTB.31.209)(HM388)

McINTOSH, ALEXANDER, b. 1678, laborer, Balnabrough, Perthshire, Jacobite, tr, 24 Feb. 1747, fr. Liverpool to Va, on Gildart, arr. Port North Potomac, Md, 5 Aug. 1747. (P.3.100)(PRO.T1.328)(MR74)

McINTOSH, DUNCAN, b. 1687, carpenter, res. Inverness, Jacobite, tr. 22 Apr. 1747, fr. Liverpool to Va, on Johnson, arr. Port Oxford, Md, 5 Aug. 1747. (P.3.102)(PRO.T1.328)(MR74)

McINTOSH, GEORGE, b. 1769, m. Elizabeth -, sh. pre 1826 to Va, fa. of Anthony. (N.A.-M932/982)

McINTOSH, JAMES, Jacobite, tr. 28 July 1716, fr. Liverpool to Va, on *Godspeed*, arr. Md Oct. 1716.   (SPC.1716.310)(CTB.31.209)(HM389)

MacINTOSH, JAMES, b. 1768, d. July 1788 Baltimore, bd. Presb. Cem. (MdJournal29.7.1788)

McINTOSH, JAMES, Jacobite, tr. 29 June 1716, fr. Liverpool to Jamaica or Va, on *Elizabeth and Anne*, arr. Va 1716.   (SPC.1716.310)(CTB.31.208)(VSP.1.186)

McINTOSH, JOHN, Jacobite, tr. 22 Apr. 1747, fr. Liverpool to Va, on *Johnson*, arr. Port Oxford, Md, 5 Aug. 1747.   (PRO.T1.328)

McINTOSH, JOHN, Jacobite, tr. 29 June 1716, fr. Liverpool to Jamaica or Va, on *Elizabeth and Anne*, arr. York, Va, 1716.   (SPC.1716.310)(CTB.31.208) (VSP.1.185)

McINTOSH, LACHLAN, Jacobite, tr. 28 July 1716, fr. Liverpool to Va, on *Godspeed*, arr. Md Oct. 1716.   (SPC.1716.310)(CTB.31.209)(HM388)

MacINTOSH, PETER, b. 1726, runaway, Patapsco Forest, Baltimore Co, Md, 1754. (MdGaz1.8.1754)

McINTOSH, WILLIAM, Jacobite, tr. 31 July 1716, fr. Liverpool to Va, on *Anne*. (SPC.1716.310)(CTB.31.209)

McINTOSH, -, b. 1781, merchant, arr. Baltimore 1826.   (N.A.-M596)

McINTYRE, ARCHIBALD, b. 1697, leadminer, res. Argyllshire, Jacobite, tr. 22 Apr. 1747, fr. Liverpool to Va, on *Johnson*, arr. Port Oxford, Md, 5 Aug. 1747. (P.3.104)(PRO.T1.328)

McINTYRE, DONALD, b. 1691, "quackdoctor", res. Argyllshire, Jacobite, tr. 22 Apr. 1747, fr. Liverpool to Va, on *Johnson,* arr. Port Oxford, Md, 5 Aug. 1747. (P.3.104)(PRO.T1.328)

McINTYRE, DANIEL, b. 1734, planter, sett. Fredericksburg, Va, militiaman in Va Regt 1756.   (VMHB.1/2)(L)

McINTYRE, FINLAY, Jacobite, tr. 28 July 1716, fr. Liverpool to Va, on *Godspeed*, arr. Md Oct. 1716.   (SPC.1716.310)(CTB.31.209)(HM389)

McINTYRE, GILBERT, b. 1798, res. Argyllshire, sh. 1831, nat. 17 Dec. 1832 Norfolk, Va.

McINTYRE, HUGH, Jacobite, tr. 28 July 1716, fr. Liverpool to Va, on *Godspeed,* arr. Md Oct. 1716.   (SPC.1716.310)(CTB.31.209)(HM389)

McINTYRE, JOHN, Jacobite, tr. 24 May 1716, fr. Liverpool to Va, on *Friendship*, arr. Md Aug, 1716.   (HM387)

McINTYRE, WILLIAM, b. 1717, plasterer, sett. Augusta Co, Va, militiaman in Va Regt 1757.   (VMHB.1/2)(L)

McIVER, CHARLES, bank clerk, res. Edinburgh, sett. Stafford Co, Va, pre 1767.
(SRO.CS16.1.130)

McIVER, COLIN, s. of William McIver of Tournaig, res. Isle of Lewis, Outer Hebrides, merchant, sett. Alexandria, Va, pro. 21 Jan. 1788 Fairfax, Va.
(SRO.SH26.6.1789)(SRO.RD2.254.922)

McIVER, JOHN, s. of William McIver of Tournaig, res. Isle of Lewis, Outer Hebrides, merchant, sett. Alexandria, Va, pre 1788.   (SRO.SH26.6.1789)(SRO.RD2.254.922)

MacKALL, James, b. 1630, sett. The Clifts, Calvert Co, Md, pre 1666, m. Mary Graham, fa. of James, John, Benjamin, Ann and Elizabeth, pro. 11 Dec. 1693 Md.
(CF.6.329)

MACKAY, ANDREW, Jacobite, tr. 22 Apr. 1747, fr. Liverpool to Va, on *Johnson*, d. 15 June 1747 at sea.   (PRO.T1.328)

McKAY, JOHN CHARLES, s. of William McKay, res. Glasgow, sh. 1711, fr. Glasgow to Va, sett. Essex Co, Va, 1712.   (Essex Deeds10.4.1712)

MACKAY, EBENEZER, merchant, res. Glasgow, sett. Va pre 1763, sett. Talbot Co, Md.
(MdMag.2.375(SRO.CS16.1.115)

McKAY, FINLAY, b. 1728, laborer, sett. Fort Cumberland, Md, militiaman in Va Regt 1756.   (VMHB.1/2)(L)

MACKAY, GEORGE, s. of John Mackay, sh. 1772 to Va.   (BM260)

McKAY, JAMES, b. 1751, runaway, Johnson's Ferry, Cecil Co, Md, 1776.
(PaGaz11.9.1776)

McKAY, MELASHUS, b. 1613, sh. 28 May 1635, fr. London to Va, on *Speedwell*.
(PRO.E157/20)

McKAY, ROBERT, merchant, res. Glasgow, sh. pre 1761, sett. Va.   (SRA.B1015.6729)

MACKAY, ROBERT, s. of _ and Jean Mackay, soldier, res. Rothesay, Isle of Bute, d. pre 1772 Va, pro. Sep. 1772 PCC.

MACKAY, WILLIAM, clergyman, sh. 1736 to Va.   (WMQ.2.20.126)

McKAY, WILLIAM, planter, res. Coxtoun, Golspie, Sutherland, sh. 1742 to Md, sett. Sugar Loaf Mountain, Montgomery Co, Md, pre 1790.   (SRO.RD3.276.974)(MdGaz27.2.1755)

McKAY, WILLIAM, b. 1781, teacher, m. Margaret -, sett. Ohio Co, Va.   (N.A.-M932/982)

MACKEALLY, THOMAS, mariner, res. Turnberry, Ayrshire, sh. 1695 to Va, on *Nicholas*, pro 12 Dec. 1695 Barbados.

McKECHNIE, GEORGE, upholsterer, sett. Richmond, Va, 1796.
(Richmond and Manchester Advertiser13.1.1796)

McKEDDIE, DANIEL, b. 1778, runaway, Caroline Co, Va, 1796.
(Richmond and Manchester Advertiser13.1 .1796)

MacKENNY, - , b. 1704, res. Argyllshire, sh. Feb. 1724, fr. London to Md. (CLRO/AIA)

McKENNY, ALEXANDER, Jacobite, tr. 29 June 1716, fr. Liverpool to Jamaica or Va, on
Elizabeth and Anne, arr. Va 1716.   (SPC.1716.310)(CTB.31.208)(VSP.1.185)

McKENNY, JOHN, Jacobite, tr. 28 July 1716, fr. Liverpool to Va, on Godspeed, arr.
Md Oct. 1716.   (SPC.1716.310)(HM388)(CTB.31.209)

McKENNY, JOHN, b. 1727, weaver, sett. Augusta Co, Va, pre 1776.   (VSA24296)

MacKENZIE, - ,res. Argyllshire, sh. 4 Feb. 1724, fr. London to Md.   (CLRO/AIA)

McKENZIE, ALEXANDER, merchant, sett. Hampton, Va, pre 1748. (SRO.CS16.1.80)

MACKENZIE, ALEXANDER, physician, sett. Va pre 1740.   (SA187)

McKENZIE, ALEXANDER, res. Va, burgess of Edinburgh 1729.   (BGBE130)

McKENZIE, ANN, b. 1687, knitter, Glen Garry, Invernessshire, Jacobite, tr. 22 Apr.
1747, fr. Liverpool to Va, on Johnson, arr. Port Oxford, Md, 5 Aug. 1747.
(P.3.114)(PRO.T1.328)

McKENZIE, DONALD, d. Rockbridge Co, Va, 1824. (Family Visitor14.2.1824)

MacKENZIE, ENEAS, b. 1675, clergyman, edu. Edinburgh Uni. and Aberdeen Uni.,
sh. 1705 to Staten Island, sett. Va.   (SCHR.14.149)(SPG.11.105)

McKENZIE, JAMES, merchant, res. Glasgow, d. Sep. 1748 Md.   (MdGaz21.9.1748)

McKENZIE, JAMES, mariner, nat. 1792 Fairfax Co, Va. (VSP.6.570)

McKENZIE, JOHN, b. 1725, weaver, sett. Westmoreland Co, Va, militiaman in
Va Regt 1756.   (VMHB.1/2)(L)

MacKENZIE, KENNETH, clergyman, sh. 1712, on Severn, sett. St James ph, Lawn Creek,
Va.   (SRO.NRAS0040)(EMA43)

MACKENZIE, KENNETH, m. Joanna Tyler, sett. Williamsburg, Va, d. 1755. (ANY.1.60)

McKENZIE, M., b. 1792, arr.Baltimore 1826.   (N.A.-M596)

McKENZIE, THOMAS, b. 1755, periwigmaker, res. Edinburgh, sh. Jan. 1774, fr.
London to Md, on Chance. (PRO.T47.9/11)

MACKENZIE, THOMAS, b. 1720, res. Inverness, sh. 1746, planter, sett. The Clifts,
Calvert Co, Md, m. (1) Rebecca Johnson (2) Ann Johns 1768, fa. of Cosmo, Elizabeth,
George and Colin. (CF.6.336)

McKETHRICK, JOHN, s. of William McKethrick, res. Bridgend, Dumfriesshire, rioter, tr. 1771, fr. Port Glasgow to Md, on *Matty,* arr. Port Oxford, Md, 17 Dec. 1771. (SRO.JC27.10.3)(SM.33.497)

MACKEWE, ROBERT, b. 1626, sh. 14 Aug. 1657, fr. London to Va, on *Conquer.* (PRO.CO1.13.29)

MACKIE, ALEXANDER, merchant, res. Glasgow, sett. Md pre 1748, pro.28 July 1766 Md (SRA.B10.5959/6653)(SRA.B10.15.7019)

MACKIE, JOHN, b. 1731, s,. of Patrick Mackie, res. Wigtown, d. Petersburg, Va, 11 Oct. 1750, bd. Old Blandford, Va. (Old Blandford g/s)(WMQ.5.237)

MACKIE, MARY, b. 1794, res. Thurso, Caithness, m. James Kinnaird, sh. 1816, fr. Leith, Midlothian, to Va, sett. Richmond City, Va, nat. 12 Oct. 1826 Eastern District, Va. (US.D/C.RB5/520)

MACKIE, RICHARD, merchant skipper, sett. Nansemond Co, Va, pre 1776, Loyalist, sett. N.S. (PRO.AO13.31.306)

MACKIE, THOMAS, b. 9 Jan. 1704, s. of John Mackie and Jean Scott, res. Forres, Morayshire, sett. Tanquier Co, Va, pre 1764. (SRO.CS16.1.117)(SRO.SH31.1.1767)

McKINLAY, WILLIAM, sh. 1767, sett. Md and Tennessee, fa. of William. (AA.9.145)

McKINNELL, JAMES, b. 1762, s. of John McKinnell, res. Wigtown, shipmaster, sett. Baltimore, m. Mary Dwyer 1801, fa. of Henry, William, Charles, Elizabeth, Maria and Anna, d. 28 Jan. 1843. (BLG2811)

McKINNY, ALEXANDER, b. 1790, sett. Baltimore. (N.A.-M432/277-299)

McKINNY, DONALD, Jacobite, tr. 24 Feb. 1747, fr. Liverpool to Va, on *Gildart,* arr. Port North Potomac, Md,5 Aug. 1747. (PRO.T1.328)

McKINNON, DONALD, b. 9 Sep. 1743, res. Sleat, Invernessshire, clergyman, edu. King's College, Aberdeen, 1764, sh. 1767, sett. Westwood, Prince William Co, Va. (FPA.25.105/18)

McKINNEY, MARGARET, b. 1800, sh. 1827 to Ohio, mo. of Elizabeth and Sophia, sett. Wood Co, Va. (N.A.-M932/982)

McKINNEY, WILLIAM, b. 1776, farmer, m. Martha -, fa. of John, Anna, Mary, Robert and Sarah, arr. Baltimore 1823. (N.A.-M596)

McKINVINE, DUNCAN, servant, res. Beach, Ross, Argyllshire, adulterer, tr. 2 Aug. 1733 to Va. (SRO.JC27.10.3)

McKITTERICK, JOHN, s. of William McKitterick, res. Bridgend, Dumfries, Dumfriesshire, rioter, tr. 1771, fr. Port Glasgow to Md, on *Matty,* arr. Port Oxford, Md, 17 Dec. 1771. (SRO.JC27.10.3)(SM.33.497)

McKITTRICK, ANTHONY, merchant, sett. va pre 1763. (SRO.CS16.1.115)

MACKWAY, WILLIAM, b. 1701, schoolmaster, res. Galloway, sh. Apr. 1721, fr. London to Md. (CLRO/AIA)

McLACHLAN, HENRY, sett. Georgetown, Md, pre 1776, Loyalist. (PRO.AO13.31.304)

McLACHLAN, JAMES, res. Dunbartonshire, sett. Kent, Co, Md, pro. 29 June 1768 Md.

McLACHLAN,JOHN, res. Greenock, Renfrewshire, sett. Portsmouth, Va, fa. of William, pro. 5 Feb. 1774 Norfolk, Va.

McLACHLAN, PETER, b. 1707, weaver, res. Fochabers, Morayshire, Jacobite, tr. 22 Apr 1747, fr. Liverpool to Va, on *Johnson,* arr. Port Oxford, Md, 5 Aug. 1747. (P.3.142)(MR122)

McLAIN, DANIEL, b. 1792, huckster, m. Margaret -, fa. of Mary, sh. pre 1830, sett. Baltimore. (N.A.-M432/277-299)

MacLAREN, ALEXANDER, res. Edinburgh, tr. 1696, fr. Newhaven, Midlothian, to Va. (SRO.RH15.14.58)

McLAREN, JAMES, Jacobite, tr. 28 July 1716, fr. Liverpool to Va, on *Godspeed*, arr. Md Oct. 1716. (SPC.1716.310)(CTB.31.209)(HM389)

MacLAREN, JOHN, b. 1706, barber, res. Edinburgh, sh. 20 Dec. 1737, fr. London to Md. (CLRO/AIA)

McLAREN, ROBERT, b. 1790, sh. pre 1822 to Pa, m. Margaret, fa. of Eliza and Isabella, sett. Brooke Co, Va. (N.A.-M932/982)

McLAUGHLAN, JAMES, merchant, sett. Va 1753, and Cecil Co, Md, 1763. (SRO.CS16.1.89/115)

McLAURINE, ROBERT, b. 1717, clergyman, sh. 1750, m. Elizabeth Blakely, sett. St James, Southam ph, Va, d. 5 July 1773. (EMA43)(OD17)(CCVC54)

McLEAN, ALLAN, Jacobite, tr. 24 May 1716, fr. Liverpool to Md, on *Friendship*, arr. Md Aug. 1716. (SPC.1716.311)(HM386)

McLEAN, ARCHIBALD, nat. 8 Dec. 1777 Norfolk City, Va.

McLEAN, DANIEL, b. 1730, sett. Winchester Co, Va, militiaman in Va Regt 1757. (VMHB.1/2)(L)

MacLEAN, DUNCAN, b. 1749, merchant, m. Janet Miln, sett. Petersburg, Va, d. 10 Apr. 1814 Va. (Dundee g/s)

McLEAN, DUNCAN, b. 1754, periwigmaker, res. Edinburgh, sh. Mar. 1775, fr. London to Md, on *Nelly Frigate.* (PRO.T47.9/11)

McLEAN, HUGH, Jacobite, tr. 22 Apr. 1716, fr. Liverpool to Va, on *Johnson*, arr. Port Oxford, Md, 5 Aug. 1747. (PRO.T1.328)

McLEAN, JAMES, b. 1746, runaway, Richmond, Va, 1774. (VaGaz27.10.1774)

MacLEAN, JOHN, Jacobite, tr. 24 May 1716, fr. Liverpool to Md, on *Friendship*, arr. Md Aug. 1716. (HM387)

McLEAN, JOHN, Jacobite, tr. 24 Feb. 1747, fr. Liverpool to Va, on *Gildart*, arr. Port North Potomac, Md, 5 Aug. 1747. (PRO.T1.328)

McLEAN, JOHN, b. 9 July 1757, s. of Malcolm McLean and Margaret McDowall, res. Glasgow, publisher in N.Y., 1783, and in Norfolk, Va, d. 18 May 1789. (ANY.1.212)(VaIndependentChronicle27.5.1789)

McLEAN, JOHN, b. 1771, physician and surgeon, res. Glasgow, sh. 1795 to N.J., Professor at the College of William and Mary, Va, 1812, d. 17 Feb 1814 N.J. (SA165)

McLEAN, LAUCHLAN, s. of Angus McLean, res. Isle of Mull, Argyllshire, thief, tr. Nov. 1704, fr. Leith, Midlothian, to Md. (SRO.PC2.28.307)

McLEAN, LAUCHLIN, b. 1733, planter, sett. Prince William Co, Va, militiaman in Va Regt 1757. (VMHB.1/2)(L)

McLEAN, LAUCHLAN, res. Aberdeenshire, thief, tr. 1773, on *Donald*, arr. Port James, Upper District, Va, 13 Mar. 1773. (AJ1292)(SRO.JC27.10.3)

McLEAN, MALCOLM,b. 1730, bricklayer, Jacobite, tr. 24 Feb. 1747, fr. Liverpool to Md, on *Gildart*, arr. Port North Potomac, Md, 5 Aug. 1747. (P.3.150)(PRO.T1.328)

McLEAN, MARY, res. Argyllshire, infanticide, tr. Aug. 1733. (JRA.2.464)

MacLEAN, NEIL, s. of - MacLean and Gillian Campbell, res. Kilmichael, Argyllshire(?), horsethief, tr. 1775, fr. Greenock, Renfrewshire, to Va, on *Rainbow,* arr. Port Hampton, Va, 3 May 1775. (SRO.JC27.10.3)

MacLEAN, WILLIAM, b. 1712, cooper,res. Portsoy, Banffshire, sh. Aug. 1734, fr. London to Md or Va. (CLRO/AIA)

McLEISH, ELIZA, b. 1777, sett. Alexandria, Va. (N.A.-M932/982)

McLELLAN, WILLIAM, merchant, sett. Va 1759, sett. N.C. 1766, Loyalist, d. 1779 Charlestown, S.C. (PRO.AO12.35)(PRO.AO13.121)

McLEOD, ALEXANDER, Jacobite, tr. 22 Apr. 1747, fr. Liverpool to Va, on the *Johnson* arr. Port Oxford, Md, 5 Aug. 1747. (PRO.T1.328)

McLEOD, ANGUS, tr. 1775, fr. Greenock, Renfrewshire, to Va, on *Rainbow*, arr. Port Hampton, Va, 3 May 1775. (SRO.JC27.10.3)

McLEOD, ANGUS, b. 1712, laborer, res. Invernessshire, Jacobite, tr. 22 Apr. 1747, fr. Liverpool to Va, on Johnson, arr. Port Oxford, Md, 5 Aug. 1747. (P.3.156)(MR159)(PRO.T1.328)

McLEOD, DONALD, b. 1801, cotton spinner, arr. Baltimore 1826. (N.A.-M596)

McLEOD, HENRIETTA, tr. 1775, fr. Greenock, Renfrewshire, to Va, on *Rainbow*, arr. Port Hampton, Va, 3 May 1775. (SRO.JC27.10.3)

McLEOD, JOHN, b. 1759, runaway, Portsmouth, Va, 1774. (VaGaz13.10.1774)

McLEOD, KENNETH, Jacobite, tr. 24 Feb. 1747, fr. Liverpool to Va, on *Gildart*, arr. Port North Potomac, Md, 5 Aug. 1747. (P.3.164)(PRO.T1.328)

McLEOD, MURDOCH, b. 1723, planter, sett. Westmoreland Co, Va, militiaman in Va Regt 1757. (VMHB.1/2)(L)

McLEOD, ROBERT, housepainter, sett. Annapolis, Md, pre 1750, fa. of Hugh. (SRO.CS16.1.84)

McLEOD, TORQUIL, m. Ann Clark, d. Essex Co, Va, 1752. (GKF315)

McLEOD, WILLIAM, b. 1747, s. of Hugh McLeod and Isabella Fraser, res. Geanes, Ross and Cromarty, factor and storekeeper, sett. Queen Anne Co, Md, 1774. (NLS.Acc5340/61)(MdHistSocMag76.45/61)

MacLIN, JOHN, res. Paisley, Renfrewshire, sett. James City Co, Va, pre 1704. (SG.30.108)

MacLIN, WILLIAM, res. Paisley, Renfrewshire, sett. James City Co, Va, pre 1704, d. 1757. (SG.30.108)(RAV59)

McLOCHLAN, DANIEL, nat. 16 Oct. 1809 Norfolk, Va.

McLOUGHLIN, ARCHIBALD, Jacobite, tr. 29 June 1716, fr. Liverpool to Jamaica or Va, on *Elizabeth and Ann*. (SPC.1716.310)(CTB.31.208)

MacMAIKEN, CORNELIUS, s. 2 Nov. 1674, to St Mary's Co, Md, on *Bachelor of Bristol*. (MSA.ESB.152)

MacMAN, JAMES, runaway, Snowden's Ironworks, Md, 1755. (MdGaz24.7.1755)

McMICKEN, HUGH, s. of Gilbert McMicken of Killantringan, merchant, sett. Portsmouth, Va, pro. July 1774 Norfolk, Va. (OD132)(SRO.CS16.1.143)(SRO.CC8.8.123)

McMILLAN, HENRY, butcher, sh. 1714, fr. Glasgow to the Potomac River, on the *American Merchant*. (TM202)

MacMILLAN, JAMES, sett. Va pre 1766. (SRO.CS16.1.125)

McNAB, JOHN, b. 1680, laborer, Jacobite, tr. 22 Apr. 1747, fr. Liverpool to Va, on *Johnson*, arr. Port North Potomac, Md, 5 Aug. 1747. (P.3.170)(MR25) (PRO.T1.328)

McNABB, THOMAS, Jacobite, tr. 24 May 1716, fr. Liverpool to Md, on *Friendship*, arr. Md Aug. 1716. (SPC.1716.311)(HM387)

McNAUGHTON, DUNCAN, clergyman, res. Perthshire, sett. Wicomico ph, Northumberland Co, Va, 1799-1805, St Stehen's ph, Northumberland Co, Va, 1805-1809, d. 16 May 1809.   (Northumberland g/s)(WMQ.2.19.41)

McNAUGHTON, MALCOLM, Jacobite, tr. 29 June 1716, fr. Liverpool to Jamaica or Va, on *Elizabeth and Anne*, arr. Va 1716.   (SPC.1716.310)(CTB.31.208)(VSP.1.185)

McNEILL, ARCHIBALD, tacksman, res. Garvart, Isle of Colonsay, Argyllshire, sh. 1739, sett. Princess Anne Co, Va, m. Elizabeth -, fa. of Malcolm and Alexander, d. 1741, pro. 17 July 1741 Norfolk, Va.   (SRO.SC54..2.53.3)

MacNEIL, DANIEL, sh. 2 Nov. 1674, to St Mary's Co, Md, on *Bachelor of Bristol.* (MSA.ESB.152)

McNEIL, GEORGE, ship's carpenter, pro. 1796 Baltimore.

McNEIL, JAMES, sett. Southampton Co, Va, d. Apr. 1795.   (PRO.T79.73)

McNICOLL, DONALD, merchant and factor, res. Glasgow, sh. pre 1760, sett. Pittsylvania Co, Va. (SRA.CFI)

McNICOLL, JOHN, b. 1717, res. Isle of Mull, Argyllshire, d. 14 Apr. 1792 Euston, Md. (Baltimore DailyRepository24.4.1792)

MacNISH, GEORGE, clergyman, sh. 1705, sett. Md, N.Y. and Va, d. 10 Mar. 1723 N.Y. (CCMC54)

McPHAILL, DONALD DOW, res. Argyllshire, tr. 1772, fr. Port Glasgow to Md, on *Dolphin,* arr. Port Oxford, Md, 1 Feb. 1773.   (SRO.JC27.10.3)

McPHAIL, DUNCAN, Jacobite, tr. 29 June 1716, fr. Liverpool to Jamaica or Va, on *Elizabeth and Anne,* d. at sea 1716.   (SPC.1716.310)(CTB.31.208)

McPHAIL, JOHN, b. 1773, m. Mary -, fa. of Lillias, sh. pre 1830, sett. Norfolk, Va. (N.A.-M932/982)

McPHEE, DANIEL, b. 1754, joiner, res. Glasgow, sh. Apr. 1775, fr. London to Md, on *Adventure.*   (PRO.T47.9/11)

McPHERSON, ARCHIBALD, b. 1705, res. Morayshire, m. Elizabeth -, d. 17 Aug. 1754, St George's, Fredericksburg, Va.   (Fredericksburg g/s)(WMQ.10.108)

McPHERSON, DAVID, b. 1800, constable, m. Ellen -, sh. pre 1830, fa. of Jonathan, sett. Washington, D.C.   (N.A.-M432/277-299)

MacPHERSON, DONALD, s. of James MacPherson, res. Culloden, Invernessshire, sett. Portobacco, Md, pre 1727.   (MdHistMag.1.347)

McPHERSON, DUNCAN, b. 1785, machinist,m. Gracey -, sett. Chesterfield Co, Va. (N.A.-M932/982)

McPHERSON, DUNCAN, b. 1790, laborer, m. Ann -, fa. of Ann, Mary and Angus, sett. Baltimore.   (N.A.-M432/277-299)

McPHERSON, JOHN, b. 1732, res. Glen Garry, Invernessshire, Jacobite, tr. 24 Feb. 1747, fr. Liverpool to Va, on *Gildart*, arr. Port North Potomac, Md, 5 Aug. 1747. (P.3.178)(MR159)(PRO.T1.328)

McPHERSON, JOHN, b. 1725, clergyman, sh. 1751, sett. St Anne's ph, Annapolis, and William and Mary ph, Charles Co, Md, d. 1785. (CCMC54)

McPHERSON, OWEN, Jacobite, tr. 29 June 1716, fr. Liverpool to Jamaica or Va, on *Elizabeth and Anne,* arr. York, Va, 1716. (SPC.1716.310)(CTB.31.208)(VSP.1.185)

McPHERSON, WILLIAM, Jacobite, tr. 28 July 1716, fr. Liverpool to Va, on *Godspeed,* arr. Md Oct. 1716. (SPC.1716.310)(CTB.31.209)(HM388)

McPHERSON, WILLIAM, b. 1737, planter, sett. Goochland Co, Va, militiaman in Va Regt 1757. (VMHB.1/2)(L)

McPHERSON, WILLIAM, b. 1783, farmer, m. Jane -, sett. Jackson Co, Va. (N.A.-M932/982)

McPHERSON, WILLIAM, b. 1790, sett. Alleghany Co, Md. (N.A.-M432/277-299)

McQUEEN, ALEXANDER, Jacobite, tr. 24 May 1716, fr. Liverpool to Md, on *Friendship,* arr. Md Aug. 1716. (SPC.1716.311)(HM387)

McQUEEN, DAVID, Jacobite, tr. 24 May 1716, fr. Liverpool to Md, on *Friendship,* arr. Md Aug. 1716. (SPC.1716.311)(HM387)

McQUEEN, DUGALL, Jacobite, tr. 24 May 1716, fr. Liverpool to Md, on *Friendship,* arr. Md Aug. 1716, m. Grace -, fa. of William, Francis and Thomas, d. 1746 Baltimore, pro. 1746 Baltimore. (SPC.1716.311)(HM386)

McQUEEN, GEORGE, clergyman, sh. pre 1703, sett. Va. (SCHR.14.149)

McQUEEN, HECTOR, Jacobite, tr. 24 May 1716, fr. Liverpool to Md, on *Friendship,* arr. Md Aug. 1716. (SPC.1716.311)(HM387)

McQUERRIST, JOHN, Jacobite, tr. 22 Apr. 1747, fr. Liverpool to Va, on *Johnson,* arr. Port Oxford, Md, 5 Aug. 1747. (P.3.180)(PRO.T1.328)

McQUERRIST, RODERICK, Jacobite, tr. 24 Apr. 1747, fr. Liverpool to Va, on *Johnson,* arr. Port Oxford, Md, 5 Aug. 1747. (P.3.180)(PRO.T1.328)

McQUHAY, ANTHONY, merchant, sett. Va pre 1778. (SRO.CS16.1.173)

McQUIN, DANIEL, Jacobite, tr. 29 June 1716, fr. Liverpool to Jamaica or Va, on *Elizabeth and Anne,* arr. Va 1716. (SPC.1716.310)(CTB.31.208)(VSP.1.185)

McQUIN, FLORA, b. 1737, Jacobite, tr. 22 Apr. 1747, fr. Liverpool to Va, on Johnson, arr. Port Oxford, Md, 5 Aug. 1747. (P.3.180)(PRO.T1.328)

McQUIRE, PATRICK, b. 1729, smith and farrier, runaway, Richmond, Va, 1774. (VaGaz27.10.1774)

MacRAE, ALLAN, merchant, sett. Dumfries, Prince William Co, Va, 1653, m. Amelia Pearson, fa. of John, Amelia and Mary.   (FKC134)

McRAE, ANDREW, merchant, sett. Va pre 1778.   (SRO.CS16.1.173)

McRAE, CHRISTOPHER, b. 1733, s. of Christopher McRae, Urquhart, Invernessshire, clergyman, edu. Marischal College, Aberdeen, 1753, sh. 1766, sett. Surrey Co, Va, Littleton ph, Cumberland Co, Va, and Powhatan Co, Va, d. 22 Dec. 1808.   (EMA43)(OD18)

MacRAE, PHILIP, sett. Richmond, Va, pro. 13 Oct. 1794 Richmond, Va.

McRAE, WILLIAM, merchant, sett. Va pre 1778.   (SRO.CS16.1.173)

McROBERTS, ARCHIBALD, clergyman, sh. 1761, sett. Dale ph and St Patrick's ph, Va.   (EMA43)(OD19)

McROBIE, A., b. 1804, merchant, arr. Baltimore 1821 on *Thomas Gibbons*.   (N.A.-M596)

McROUL, JOHN, sett. Va pre 1811.   (SRO.SH2.8.1811)

McTAGGART, HUGH, b. 1822, farmer, m. Decivinda -, fa. of Jean, sett. Wood Co, Va.   (N.A.-M932/982)

McTAGGART, WILLIAM, b. 1790, farmer, m. Jane -, sh. pre 1830, fa. of Hugh, Edward, William and Margaret, sett. Wood Co, Va.   (N.A.-M932/982)

MacVEY, JEFFERY, sh. 2 Nov. 1674, to St Mary's Co, Md, on *Bachelor of Bristol*.   (MSA.ESB.152)

McVICAR, ROBERT, res. Argyllshire, drowned Norfolk, Va, pre 1806.   (SRA.AGN321)

McWHANN, WILLIAM, merchant, sett. Blandford, Va, 1763, Loyalist.   (PRO.AO13.31.303)

McWILLIAM, WILLIAM, surgeon apothecary, sett. Md, fa. of Janet, d. pre 1764.   (SRO.RH9.7.173)

McWILLIAM, WILLIAM, runaway, *Donald,* Richmond, Va, Apr. 1773.   (VaGaz15.4.1773)

MABEN, DAVID, b. 1789, farmer, sett. Amelia Co, Va.   (N.A.-M932/982)

MABEN, MATTHEW, b. 1777, merchant, res. Dumfries, Dumfriesshire, d. 8 Jan. 1822, Petersburg, Va.   (Blandford g/s)

MABEN, MICHAEL, res. Dumfriesshire, d. Petersburg, Va, 1818.   (SRA.NRAS.0118)

MAIN, JOHN, b. 1725, fisherman, res. Footdee, Aberdeen, Jacobite, tr. 22 Apr. 1747, fr. Liverpool to Va, on *Johnson,* arr. Port Oxford, Md, 5 Aug. 1747.   (P.3.4)(MR129)(PRO.T1.328)

MAITLAND, DAVID, b. 1796, res. Kirkcudbright, nat. 28 Oct. 1822 Norfolk City, Va.

MAITLAND, JOSEPH, b. 1801, merchant, res. Kirkcudbrightshire, sh. Liverpool to USA, sett. Norfolk, Va, nat. 15 Dec. 1823 N.Y.

MAITLAND, WILLIAM, merchant, sett. Williamsburg, Va, 1771, Loyalist. (PRO.AO13.31.344)

MAITLAND of VALLEYFIELD, WILLIAM jr, b. 1756, merchant, sett. Petersburg, Va, d. 1812 Valleyfield. (SM.74.646)

MALCOLM, ALEXANDER, clergyman, sh. 1739, sett. Annapolis, Md. (EMA43)(SPG.3.20)

MALCOLM, JAMES, Jacobite, tr. 29 June 1716, fr. Liverpool to Jamaica or Va, on *Elizabeth and Anne*, arr. York, Va, 1716. (SPC.1716.310)(CTB.31.208)(VSP.1.186)

MALCOLM, JOHN, s. of - and Jean Malcolm, res. Madderty, Perthshire, d. pre 1793 Norfolk, Va, pro. Dec. 1799 PCC.

MALLONE, JAMES, Jacobite, tr. 28 July 1716, fr. Liverpool to Va, on *Godspeed,* arr. Md Oct. 1716. (SPC.1716.310)(CTB.31.209)(HM388)

MANN, WILLIAM, Jacobite, tr. 24 May 1716, fr. Liverpool to Md, on *Friendship,* arr. Md Aug. 1716. (SPC.1716.311)(HM387)

MANN, WILLIAM, woolcomber, res. Aberdeen, conspirator, tr. Aug. 1772, fr. Glasgow to Va, on *Brilliant,* arr. Port Hampton, Va, 7 Oct. 1772. (SRO.JC27.10.3)(AJ1272)

MARJORYBANKS, GEORGE, Jacobite, tr. 29 June 1716, fr. Liverpool to Jamaica or Va, on *Elizabeth and Anne,* arr. York, Va, 1716. (SPC.1716.310)(CTB.31.208)(VSP.1.185)

MARKLEY, JOANNAH, b. 1786, sett. Alexandria, Va. (N.A.-M932/982)

MARNO, JAMES, b. 1786, nat. 23 Mar. 1814 Norfolk City, Va.

MARR, ALEXANDER, sh. 1740, sett. Caroline Co, Va. (WMQ.2.22.345)

MARR, ALEXANDER, Jacobite, tr. 22 Apr. 1747, fr. Liverpool to Va, on *Johnson,* arr. Port Oxford, Md, 5 Aug. 1747. (P.3.8)(MR123)(PRO.T1.328)

MARR, ANN, tr. 1764, on *Boyd,* arr. Norfolk, Va, 24 Aug. 1764. (SRO.JC27.10.3)

MARSHALL, JAMES, factor, res. Glasgow, sh. 1747, fa. of Chloe, William, Mary, Eleanor and Mary-Anne, d. Apr. 1803 Frederick Co, Md. (DPCA71)(UNC/Williams pp)

MARSHALL, JOHN, merchant, sett. Louisa Co, Va, pre 1779. (SRO.CS16.1.175) (VSP.3.251)

MARSHALL, MUNGO, clergyman, sh. 1744, sett. St Thomas ph, Orange Co, Va, m. Susanna Morye, d. 1758. (WMQ.2.1.154)(EMA44)

MARTIN, ALEXANDER, res Aberdeenshire, thief, tr. Aug. 1753, fr. Aberdeen to Va, on *St Andrew.* (SM.15.260)(AJ294)

.MARTIN, JAMES, res. Glasgow, storekeeper in Va pre 1776, Loyalist. (PRO.AO13.30.473)

MARTIN, JAMES, b. 1800, machinist, m. Jane -, sh. pre 1827 to Va, fa. of James, Elizabeth and William, sett. Petersburg, Dinwiddie Co, Va.   (N.A.-M932/982)

MARTIN, PETER, b. 1739, linen weaver, sh. Dec. 1774, fr. London to Va, on *William.*   (PRO.T47.9/11)

MARTIN, ROBERT, m. Mary - , fa. of John and Mary, sett. Snowhill, Somerset Co, Md. d. 1725, pro. 16 June 1725 Md.

MARTIN, WILLIAM, tr. Nov. 1750, fr. Aberdeen to Va or the West Indies, on *Adventure.* (AJ152/70)

MARTIN, WILLIAM, Jacobite, tr. 29 June 1716, fr. Liverpool to Jamaica or Va, on *Elizabeth and Anne*, arr. York, Va, 1716.   (SPC.1716.310)(CTB.31.208) (VSP.1.185)

MARTIN, WILLIAM, tr. 1764 to Va, on *Boyd,* arr. Norfolk, Va, 24 Aug. 1764. (SRO.JC27.10.3)

MARTISON, JOHN, Jacobite, tr. 24 May 1716, fr. Liverpool to Md, on *Friendship*, arr. Md Aug. 1716.   (SPC.1716.311)(HM387)

MASON, JANET, tr. 1696, fr. Newhaven, Midlothian, to Va.   (SRO.RH15.14.58)

MASSIE, LAWRENCE, tr. 1696, fr. Newhaven, Midlothian, to Va.   (SRO.RH15.14.58)

MATHIE, ALEXANDER, b. 1732, s. of Gabriel Mathie, merchant, res. Greenock, Renfrewshire, sett. Appomattox Co, Va, d. 30 July 1752, pro 5 Mar. 1753 Henrico Co. (Hanover g/s)

MATHIESON, WALTER, servant, housebreaker, tr. 1772, fr. Port Glasgow to Md, on *Matty,* arr. Port Oxford, Md, 16 May 1772.   (SRO.JC27.10.3)

MAXWELL, ANDREW, b. 1793, res. Renfrewshire, nat. 26 Aug. 1833 Norfolk City, Va.

MAXWELL, GEORGE, b. 1759, distiller, res. Paisley, Renfrewshire, sh. 1790, sett. N.Y., d. 13 Dec. 1837 Baltimore.   (ANY.1.314)

MAXWELL, MATTHEW, s. of James Maxwell, merchant, res. Pollockshields, Glasgow, sett. Md and Va pre 1759.   (SRO.CS16.1.103)

MAXWELL, WILLIAM, Jacobite, tr. 29 June 1716, fr. Liverpool to Jamaica or Va, on *Elizabeth and Anne*, arr. York, Va, 1716.   (SPC.1716.310)(CTB.31.208) (VSP.1.186)

MAYO, ELIZABETH, b. 1800, mo. of Isabella, sett. Richmond, Henrico Co, Va. (N.A.-M932/982)

MEIKLE, RICHARD, nat. 27 May 1806 Norfolk City, Va.

MEIKLE, ROBERT, res. Paisley, Renfrewshire, thief, tr. 1771, fr. Port Glasgow to Md, on *Polly*, arr. Port Oxford, Md, 16 Sep. 1771.   (SRO.JC27.10.3)(AJ1175)

MEIN, ANDREW, res. Edinburgh, sett. Talbot Co, Md, m. Ann -, pro. 2 Aug. 1770 Md. (MSA.MdWill.39.388)

MELDRUM, WILLIAM, clergyman, sh. 1756 to Va.   (EMA45)

MELVILLE, WILLIAM, miner, Aberdeen, Jacobite, tr. 22 Apr. 1747, fr. Liverpool to Md, on *Johnson*, arr. Port Oxford, Md, 5 Aug. 1747.   (P.3.188)(JAB.2.436)(MR211) (PRO.T1.328)

MENZIES, ADAM, clergyman, sh. 1750 to Va.   (EMA45)

MENZIES, ALEXANDER, b. 1764, carpenter, m. Mary -, arr. Baltimore 1826. (N.A.-M596)

MENZIES, ARCHIBALD, Jacobite, tr. 29 June 1716, fr. Liverpool to Jamaica or Va, on *Elizabeth and Anne*, arr. York, Va, 1716.   (SPC.1716.310)(CTB.31.208) (VSP.1.185)

MENZIES, DONALD, thief, tr. Apr. 1754, fr. Leith, Midlothian, to Va.   (AJ324/6)

MENZIES, JAMES, colonial administrator, sh. 1753 to Va, Loyalist. (PRO.AO13.31.622)

MENZIES, JAMES, clerk, sett. Va 1763, Loyalist.   (PRO.AO12.54.136) (PRO.AO12.109.208)

MENZIES, NINIAN, merchant, res. Glasgow, sett. Richmond, Va pre 1775, Loyalist, d. 18 Feb. 1781, pro.14 Feb. 1799 Edinburgh.   (SRO.CC8.8.131)(PRO.AO13.33.297)

MENZIES, PETER, b. 1736, tailor, sett. Fredericksburg, Va, militiaman in Va Regt 1757.   (VMHB.1/2)(L)

MENZIES, ROBERT, Jacobite, tr. 29 June 1716, fr. Liverpool to Jamaica or Va, on *Elizabeth and Anne*, arr. York, Va, 1716.   (SPC.1716.310)(CTB.31.208) (VSP.1.186)

MERCER, HUGH, b. 16 Jan. 1726, s. of Rev. William Mercer and Ann Munro, res. Pitsligo, Aberdeenshire, physician and soldier, edu. King's College, Aberdeen, 1744, sh. 1746 fr. Leith to Philadelphia, sett. Green Castle, King George Co, Va, m. Isabella Gordon, f, of Anne, John, William, George and Hugh, d. 12 Jan.1777 Princeton, N.J., pro. 20 Mar. 1777 Spotsylvania Co, Va.   (KCA.2.315)(OD43)(SA188) (Spotsylvania Deeds E169)(WMQ.2.22.97)

MERCER, JOHN, lawyer, sh. 1720 to Va, fa. of James.   (WMQ.2.22.47)

MERCER, THOMAS, sh. 2 Nov. 1674, to St Mary's Co, Md, on *Bachelor of Bristol*. (MSA.ESB.152)

MESSENGER, JOSEPH, clergyman, res. Dumfriesshire, m. Mary -, sett. St John's, Pitscataway, Md, pre 1776, fa. of Mary.   (St John's OPR.415)

MESTON, Colonel, res. Va, burgess of Glasgow, Mar. 1720. (BGBG347)

MICHIE, JOHN, Jacobite, tr. 29 June 1716, fr. Liverpool to Jamaica or Va, on Elizabeth and Anne, arr. York, Va, 1716, fa. of Robert, d. 1776. (SPC.1716.310)(VSP.1.186)(CAG..1.726)

MIDDLETON, ALEXANDER, physician, sett. Va pre 1776, Loyalist, sett. Jamaica. (PRO.AO13.31.530)

MIDDLETON, JAMES, res. Aberdeenshire, thief, tr. Aug. 1753, fr. Aberdeen to Va, on St Andrew. (AJ281/294)

MILL, DAVID, Jacobite, tr. 24 May 1716, fr. Liverpool to Md, on Friendship, arr. Md Aug. 1716. (SPC.1716.311)(HM386)

MILL, JAMES, Jacobite, tr. 22 Apr. 1747, fr. Liverpool to Va, on Johnson, arr. Port Oxford, Md, 5 Aug. 1747. (PRO.T1.328)

MILL, JAMES, s. of James Mill of Penlocthan(?), Angus, m. Anne Brett 1752, sett. King William Co, Va, fa. of Elizabeth, Ann, Barbara, James, Mary, Jane and John, d. 4 Mar. 1767. (WMQ.20.208)

MILLAN, HUGH, merchant, sett. Blandford, Prince George Co, Va, 1757, d. London, pro. 1 Dec. 1761 PCC. (VMHB.10.323)

MILLEN, ROBERT, runaway, Va, 1752. (VaGaz10.4.1752)

MILLER, ANDREW, b. 1775, farmer, m. Isobel -, sh. pre 1820 to Va, fa. of James, Eleanor and Christiana, sett. Monroe Co, Va. (N.A.-M932/982)

MILLAR, DANIEL, shoemaker, sh. 1714, fr. Glasgow to the Potomac River, on the American Merchant. (TM202)

MILLER, DAVID, s. of John Miller of Wellhouse, d. 14 Oct. 1798 Norfolk, Va. (GC1145)(NorfolkHerald16.10.1798)

MILLER, FARQUHAR, b. 1697, gardener, res. Edinburgh, Jacobite, tr. 24 Feb. 1747, fr. Liverpool to Va, on Gildart, arr. Port North Potomac, Md, 5 Aug. 1747. (P.3.194)(MR194)(PRO.T1.328)

MILLER, GEORGE, b. 1 Sep. 1743, s. of Rev. John Miller, res. Penninghame, planter in Va, US Consul in London. (F.2.374)

MILLER, HUGH, s. of Hugh Miller, res. Galloway, sett. Mecklenburg Co, Va, pre 1777. (SRO.RD2.224.234)(SRO.CS16.1.175)

MILLER, JAMES, b. 1734, sett. Port Royal, Caroline Co, Va, m. Elizabeth Roy pre 1760, fa. of Thomas, d. 1808 Port Royal, Va. (CAG.1.111)(WMQ.2.113.61)

MILLER, JAMES, merchant, sett. Portsmouth, Va, 1764, Loyalist, sett. Shelburne, N.S., 1783. (PRO.AO12.109.24)(PRO.AO12.55.5)(PRO.AO13.31.592)(LNS152)

MILLER, JAMES, b. 1787, farmer, m. Ann -, sh. pre 1822, sett. Monroe Co, Va, fa. of Alice, Andrew, Isabel, Ruth and Mary. (N.A.-M932/982)

MILLER, ROBERT, sh. 1749 , sett. Va, merchant and customs controller, Loyalist, sett. England. (PRO.AO12.56.58)(PRO.AO12.109.212)

MILLER, THOMAS, b. 1800, farmer, m. Margaret -, fa. of William, Margaret, James, Salina and Margaret, sett. Monroe Co, Va. (N.A.-M932/982)

MILLER, WILLIAM, merchant, res. Glasgow, sett. Va pre 1749. (SRO.CS16.1.81)

MILLER, WILLIAM, army deserter, Va, 1777. (VaGaz19.9.1777)

MILLIGAN, LILIAN, servant, Dumfries, Dumfriesshire, infanticide, tr. 1775, fr. Greenock, Renfrewshire, to Va, on *Rainbow*, arr. Port Hampton, Va, 3 May 1775. (SRO.JC27.10.3)

MILLIGAN, WILLIAM, weaver, Dumfries, Dumfriesshire, rioter, tr. 1771, fr. Port Glasgow to Md, on *Matty*, ar. Port Oxford, Md, 17 Dec. 1771. (SRO.JC27.10.3)(AJ1232)

MILLIKEN, M., b. 1790, arr. Baltimore 1820 on *Oryza*. (N.A.-M596)

MILLS, JAMES, b. 1732, hatter, sett. Leedstown, Va, militiaman in Va Regt 1757. (VMHB.1/2)(L)

MILLS, WILLIAM, res. Aberdeen, sett. Goochland Co, Va, pre 1743, m. Elizabeth -.

MILNE, ANDREW, tr. 5 Feb. 1753, fr. Aberdeen to Va, on *Planter*. (AJ265)

MILNE, CARD JAMES, res. Strathbogie, Aberdeenshire, adulterer, tr. 1669 to Va. (RSM139)

MILN, JANET, res. Dundee, Angus, m. Duncan McLean, sett. va pre 1814. (Dundee g/s)

MILTOUN, MARY, tr. 1696, fr. Newhaven, Midlothian, to Va. (SRO.RH15.14.58)

MITCHELL, ALEXANDER, b. 1766, s. of John Mitchell and Janet Tait, res. Ayr, physician, edu. Edinburgh Uni. 1788, sett. Shepherdstown, Jefferson Co, Va, 1790, m. (1) Elizabeth Kearsley (2) Ann -, fa. of John and Alexander, d. 29 Sep. 1804 Bladensburg, Va. (DAB.13.54)(GM.75.183)(SG7/2.12)

MITCHELL, ALEXANDER WILLIAM, physician, sett. Va, m. Elizabeth Fowler, 1808. (SM.70.555)

MITCHELL, COLIN, innkeeper, sett. Portobacco, Md, pre 1747. (LIM.2.243)

MITCHELL, DAVID, Jacobite, tr. 29 June 1716, fr. Liverpool to Jamaica or Va, on *Elizabeth and Anne*, arr. York, Va, 1716. (SPC.1716.310)(CTB.31.208) (VSP.1.185)

MITCHELL, GEORGE, res. Old Machar, Aberdeenshire, Jacobite, tr. 24 Feb. 1747, fr. Liverpool to Va, on *Gildart*, arr. Port North Potomac, Md, 5 Aug. 1747. (P.3.198)(JAB.2.437)(PRO.T1.328)(MR106)

MITCHELL, GEORGE, assistant factor, res. Kilmarnock, Ayrshire, sett. Winchester, Va, pre 1765.   (SRO.CS16.1.133)(SRO.CS16.1.122)

MITCHELL, GEORGE, clergyman, sett. Frederickstown, Md, 1769, Loyalist. (PRO.AO12.102.173)(PRO.AO13.62.21)

MITCHELL, HENRY, merchant, res. Glasgow, sh. 1757, sett. Fredericksburg, Va, Loyalist, sett. Glasgow.   (PRO.AO13.31.635)(SRA.CFI)

MITCHELL, HENRY, b. 1804, blacksmith, sh. pre 1828, fa. of William, Jane, Martina, Mary, Susan and Henry, sett. Alleghany Co, Md.   (N.A.-M432-277/99)

MITCHELL, HUGH, res. Glasgow, sett. Charlestown, Charles Co, Md, 1760. (MSA.Charles Deeds G3.435/L.536)

MITCHELL, JAMES, Jacobite, tr. 24 May 1716, fr. Liverpool to Md, on *Friendship,* arr. Md Aug. 1716.   (SPC.1716.311)(HM387)

MITCHELL, JAMES, merchant, res. Glasgow, d. 9 June 1787 Alexandria, Va. (SM.59.413)(SRA.B10.15.7118)

MITCHELL, JAMES, nat. 22 Apr. 1805 Norfolk City, Va.

MITCHELL, JOHN, s. of John Mitchell and Janet Warden, merchant, res. Glasgow, sh. pre 1776, sett. Fredericksburg and Culpepper Co, Va.   (SRO.CS17.1.1)(SRA.T79.32) (SRO.RD2.241.382)

MITCHELL, JOHN, merchant, res. Glasgow, sett. Charles Co, Md, 1761. (MSA.Charles Co Deeds G3.435/L536)

MITCHELL, JOHN, nat. 27 Aug. 1794 Norfolk City, Va.

MITCHELL, JOHN, b. 1803, merchant, arr. Balt. 1824.   (N.A.-M596)

MITCHELL, MARGARET, da. of John Mitchell, res. Spotsylvania Co, Va, m. 25 June 1792 Walter Logan jr, merchant, Glasgow.   (EEC11563)

MITCHELL, MARK, b. 1755. perukemaker, res. Glasgow, sh. 26 Jan. 1774, fr. London to Va, on *Planter,* arr. Hampton, Va, 28 Apr. 1774.   (PRO.T47.9/11)

MITCHELL, ROBERT, b. 1704, schoolmaster, res. Edinburgh, sh. Nov. 1723, fr. London to Md.   (CLRO/AIA)

MITCHELL, SPENCER COCHRANE, s. of John Mitchell and Agnes Tait, physician and surgeon, res. Ayr, Ayrshire, sh. 1800 to Md, sett. Washington, D.C., fa. of John, Mary, Spencer, A. and F.   (SG.7.12)(N.A.-M432/56-57)

MITCHELL, SUSAN, b. 1810, arr. Baltimore 1825.   (N.A.-M596)

MITCHELL, THOMAS, merchant, sett. Fredericksburg, Va, pre 1776. (VaGaz29.6.1776)

MITCHELL, WILLIAM, supercargo of *Katherine of London*, d. 1685, pro.1 Sep. 1685, Accomack Co, Va.

MITCHELL, WILLIAM, b. 1745, husbandman, sh. Dec. 1773, fr. London to Md, on *Etty*. (PRO.T47.9/11)

MITCHELL, WILLIAM, res. Glasgow, sett. Richmond City, Va, pro. 12 Feb. 1805 Richmond.

MITCHELL, W., b. 1805, arr. Baltimore 1825.   (N.A.-M596)

MICHELSON, JOHN, s. of James Michelson, res. Edinburgh, d. Yorktown, Va. (PCC.Glazier.227)

MOCHLINE, JOHN, res. Rutherglen, Lanarkshire, sett. Va, pre 1749.   (SRO.RD2.168.10)

MOCHLINE, WILLIAM, res. Rutherglen, Lanarkshire, sett. St Andrews ph, Brunswick Co, Va, pre 1749.   (SRO.RD2.168.10)

MOFFAT, JOHN, b. 1796, m. Janet, sh. to Pa, fa. of Thomas, William, Elizabeth, Hugh and Robert, sett. Baltimore.   (N.A.-M432/277-299)

MOIR, A. A., b. 1792, merchant, m. Mary -, fa. of Alexander, John, William, Margaret and Cycella, sett. Patrick Co, Va.   (N.A.-M932/982)

MOLISON, THOMAS, b. 1709, clerk or writer, res. Brechin, Angus, sh.Mar. 1730, fr. London to Md.   (CLRO/AIA)

MONCRIEFF, ARCHIBALD, merchant, sett. Md, d. 6 Jan. 1803, pro. 30 Nov. 1818 Edinburgh.   (SRO.CC8.8.144)

MONCRIEFF, HENRY, b. 1747, runaway, Frederick Co, Va, 1777.   (VaGaz12.9.1777)

MONCRIEFF, PHILIP, s. of Colonel Moncrieff, merchant, sett. Warwick Co, Va, 1771, Loyalist, sett. India.   (PRO.AO13.31.640)

MONCURE, JOHN, b. 24 Apr. 1710, s. of Robert Moncure and Jean Grant, res. Kinneff, Kincardineshire, clergyman and teacher, sh. 1733, sett. Overwharton ph, Stafford Co, Va, m. Frances Brown, fa. of John, Frances, Anne and Jean, d.10 Mar. 1764, bd. Aquia, Stafford Co, Va.   (VG424)(AA.9.22)(CCVC37)(Aquia g/s)

MONDELL, JOHN, Jacobite, tr. 29 June 1716, fr. Liverpool to Jamaica or Va, on *Elizabeth and Anne*, arr. York, Va, 1716.   (SPC.1716.310)(CTB.31.208) (VSP.1.185)

MONROE, ANDREW, s. of David Monroe, sett. St Mary's Co, Md, 1641, and Northumberland Co, Va, 1650, m. Elizabeth Alexander, fa. of William and Andrew, d. 1668.   (WMQ.2.13.231)(WMQ.2.4.45)(BLG2829)

MONROE, HUGH, nat. 24 Jan. 1791 Norfolk City, Va.

MONROE, WILLIAM, b. 1781, farmer, fa. of Mary, arr. Baltimore 1823.   (N.A.-M596)

MONTGOMERY, HEW, merchant, sh. Oct. 1685, fr. Port Glasgow to Va, on *Boston.* (SRO.E72.19.8)

MONTGOMERIE, HUGH, b. 1800, contractor, m. Jane, fa. of Robert, Jean, Frederick and Ann, sh. pre 1828, sett. Campbell Co, Va. (N.A.-M932/982)

MONTGOMERIE, HUGH. s. of Robert and Jean Montgomerie, res. Craighouse, Beith, Ayrshire, sh. pre 1820 to Va. (HAF.2.290)

MONTGOMERY, JOHN, sh. 2 Nov. 1674, to St Mary's Co, Md, on *Bachelor of Bristol.* (MSA.ESB.152)

MONTGOMERY, JOHN, merchant, sett. James River, Va, pre 1776 (SRO.CS16.1.170)

MONTGOMERY, NICHOLAS, Jacobite, tr. 29 June 1716, fr. Liverpool to Jamaica or Va, on *Elizabeth and Anne.* (SPC.1716.310)(CTB.31.208)

MONTGOMERIE, ROBERT WILSON, s. of John and Margaret Montgomerie, merchant, res. Giffen, Beith, Ayrshire, sh. pre 1775 to Va, Loyalist, sett. Scotland. (HAF.1.290)

MONTGOMERY, THOMAS, merchant, sett. Norfolk, Va, pre 1776, Loyalist, sett. Ayr. (PRO.AO13.31.643)

MONTGOMERIE, THOMAS, b. 1746, s. of Alexander Montgomerie of Coilsfield, Ayrshire, sett. Dumfries, Va, pre 1786, d. 13 Aug. 1792, pro.3 Sep. 1792 Prince William Co, Va. (HAF.2.241)(MOM.1.146)(SM.54.518)

MOODY, JOHN, b. 1787, res. Glasgow, sh. 1818, nat. 21 May 1833 Norfolk, Va.

MOORE, JAMES, sh. 1786, sett. Georgetown, D.C., nat. 1814 D.C.

MOOR, JOSIAS, res. Rothesay, Isle of Bute, sett. Dorchester, Md, pro. 18 Dec. 1766 Md. (MSA.Wills.36.596)

MORGAN, JAMES, b. 1785, fa. of Isla, sett. Petersburg, Dinwiddie Co, Va. (N.A.-M932/982)

MORGAN, PATRICK, res. Foginell, Aberdeenshire, Jacobite, tr. 22 Apr. 1747, fr. Liverpool to Va, on *Johnson,* arr. Port Oxford, Md, 5 Aug. 1747. (MR207) (JAB.2.438)(PRO.T1.328)(P.3.210)

MORRIS, GEORGE, b. 1810, s. of Alexander Morris, res. Paisley, Renfrewshire, clergyman, edu. Glasgow Uni. 1822, sett. Silverspring, Pa, d. 16 Dec 1883, Baltimore. (MAGU334)

MORRIS, WILLIAM, b.1770, merchant, res. Glasgow, set. Baltimore Md, (MSA.Baltimore Wills.24.217)(N.A.-M432/277-299)

MORRISON, ALEXANDER, res. Aberdeen, sett. King George Co, Va, pre 1750. (K.G.Courtbook2.472)

MORRISON, ALEXANDER, robber, tr. 1773, fr. Port Glasgow to Va, on *Thomas of Glasgow,* arr. James River, Va, 3 July 1773. (SRO.JC27.10.3)

MORRISON, ANDREW, robber, tr. 1773, fr. Port Glasgow to Va, on *Thomas of Glasgow*, arr. Upper District, James River, Va, 5 June 1773. (SRO.JC27.10.3)

MORRISON, ANN, b. 1753, sett. Frederick Co, Md. (N.A.-M432/277-299)

MORRISON, CHARLES, surgeon, res. Greenock, Renfrewshire, sh. 1753, tobacco merchant in Va, d. Va. (VMHB.22.201)

MORRISON, HARRIET, b. 1802, sh. pre 1828, sett. Frederick Co, Md, mo. of Harriet, Phoebe and Virginia. (N.A.-M932/982)

MORRISON, JAMES, tr. 1696, fr. Newhaven, Midlothian, to Va. (SRO.RH15.14.58)

MORRISON, JOHN, clergyman, sh. 1699 to Va, sett. Nevis. (EMA46)(DP335)

MORRISON, JOHN, res. Aberdeen, sett. King George Co, Va, fa. of John, d. 1750. (King George Co Court Bk.2.472)

MORRISON, MARY, res. Va, d. 11 June 1829 Edinburgh. (SRO.C237)

MORRISON, ROBERT, s. 2 Nov. 1674, to St Mary's Co, Md, on *Bachelor of Bristol*. (MSA.ESB.152)

MORRISON, THOMAS, sett. Norfolk, Va, pre 1776, Loyalist. (PRO.AO13.31.647)

MORSON, ARTHUR, b. 3 Nov. 1734, factor, res. Greenock, Renfrewshire, sh. 14 Feb. 1751, on Greenock Snow, arr Rappahannock, Va, 29 June 1751, sett. Falmouth, Va, m. Marion Andrew 1758, fa. of Alexander, Margaret and Marion, d. 23 May 1798 Hartwood, Stafford Co, Va. (SRA.B10.15.7174)(VG654)

MORTIMER, ALEXANDER, Jacobite, tr. 24 May 1716, fr. Liverpool to Md, on *Friendship*, arr. Md Aug. 1716. (SPC.1716.311)(HM387)

MORTON, ALEXANDER, sh. 1768 to Md. (MdGaz27.9.1770)

MORTON, ROBERT, b. 1798, merchant, m. Margaret -, sett. Baltimore. (N.A.-M432/277-299)

MOUBRAY, WILLIAM, Jacobite, tr. 24 May 1716, fr. Liverpool to Md, on *Friendship*, arr. Md Aug. 1716. (SPC.1716.311)(HM387)

MOWAT, HENRY, b. 1734, s. of Captain Patrick Mowat, sett. N.H. 1773, Loyalist, d. Cape Henry, Va, 14 Apr. 1798, bd. Hampton, Va. (LOM215)

MUIR, ADAM, merchant, res. Edinburgh (?), sett. Va pre 1756. (SRO.CS16.1.99)

MUIR, ALEXANDER, b. 1752, weaver, sh. Dec. 1773, fr. London to Va, on *Virginia*. (PRO.T47.9/11)

MUIR, GEORGE, merchant, sett. Fredericksburg, Va, Loyalist, sett. London 1781. (PRO.AO13.31.653)

MUIRE, JAMES, sett. Va, pro. 1689 PCC.

MUIR, JAMES, tr. 1775, fr. Greenock, Renfrewshire, to Va, on *Rainbow,* arr. Port Hampton, Va, 3 May 1775. (SRO.JC27.10.3)

MUIR, JAMES, b. 12 Apr. 1756, s. of Rev. George Muir and Isabella Wardlaw, res. Catrine, Ayrshire, clergyman and teacher, edu. Glasgow Uni. and Edinburgh Uni., sh. 1781 to Bermuda, m. Elizabeth Wellman 1783, sh. 1787 to USA, sett. Alexandria, Va, 1789, d. 8 Aug. 1820. (F.3.172)(F.7.661)(WMQ.2.20.256)(MAGU97)

MUIR, JOHN, tailor, res. Annapolis, Md, to Scotland 1748. (MdGaz16.3.1748)

MUIR, JOHN, b. 1731, s. of Hugh Muir, merchant, res. Dumfries, Dumfriesshire, sett. Alexandria, Va, d. 20 Mar. 1791. (Christchurch g/s)

MUIR, JOHN, b. 1750, banker and politician, d. 30 Aug. 1810, Annapolis, Md. (MdGaz5.9.1810)

MUIR, ROBERT, b. 1748, s. of Hugh Muir, merchant, res. Dumfries, Dumfriesshire, sett. Alexandria, Va, d. 21 Dec. 1786. (Christchurch g/s)

MUIR, THOMAS, s. of John Muir, res. Newstead, Roxburghshire, sett. Alexandria, Va, pre 1802. (SRO.SH29.9.1802)

MUIR, WILLIAM, res. Kirkcudbright, sh. pre 1796 to Va, sett. Lynchburg and Richmond, Va. (SRO.NRAS.0118)

MUIR, WILLIAM, b. 1785, banker, sett. Fredericksburg, Spotsylvania Co, Va. (N.A.-M932/982)

MUIRHEAD, JOHN, shoemaker, sh. 1763, sett. Norfolk, Va, Loyalist. (PRO.AO13.31.659)

MULLIKEN, JAMES, sett. 'The Level', Prince George Co, Md, fa. of Mary, d. 1715. (CF.7.91)

MUNRO, JAMES, b. 1747, res. Orbiston, Morayshire, clergyman, edu. King's College, Aberdeen, 1772, sh. 1785, sett. West Nottingham, Md, 1785-1792, sett. N.S., d. 17 May 1819. (F.6.397)

MUNRO, JOHN, res. Catewell, Ross and Cromarty, clergyman, sh. 1650, sett. St John's, Pamunkey River, King and Queen Co, Va, m. Christian Blair, fa. of John and Andrew, d. 1724. (WMQ.2.13.231)(Munro Tree 1734)

MUNROE, WILLIAM, sett. Dinwiddie Co, Va, 1830, fa. of Benjamin. (CAG.1.739)

MURDOCH, ALEXANDER, b. 1802, merchant, m. Susan -, fa. of William. Thomas, Charles, Alexander, John, Mary and Caroline, sh. pre 1828, sett. Baltimore. (N.A.-M432/277-299)

MURDOCH, GEORGE, clergyman, sh. 1720, sett. Prince George Co, Md, fa. of William, d. 1775. (TSA

MURDOCH, GILBERT, b. 1753, d. 9 Sep. 1822 Md. (MdGaz12.9.1822)

MURDOCH, JOHN, b. 1753, merchant, sh. June 1774, fr. Whitehaven, Cumberland, to Va, on *Lonsdale.* (PRO.T47.9/11)

MURDOCH, SAMUEL, b. 1755, merchant, sh. June1774, fr. Whitehaven, Cumberland, to Va, on *Lonsdale.* (PRO.T47.9/11)

MURDOCH, THOMAS, b. 1757, merchant, sh. June 1774, fr. Whitehaven, Cumberland, to Va, on *Lonsdale.* (PRO.T47.9/11)

MURDOCH, WILLIAM, b. 1707, wool merchant, res. Callendar, Perthshire, Jacobite, tr. 22 Apr. 1747, fr. Liverpool to Va, on *Johnson,* arr. Port Oxford, Md, 5 Aug. 1747. (P.3.216)(PRO.T1.328)

MURDOCH, WILLIAM T., b. 1799, merchant, sh. pre 1826, m. Mary -, fa. of Alexander, Mary, Alice, Marion, Helen, Susan, Annie, Margaret, Russell, Louisa and Elizabeth, sett. Baltimore.   (N.A.-M432/277-299)

MURRAY, ADAM, merchant, d. 20 Feb. 1823, Richmond, Va.   (S.335.199)

MURRAY, ALEXANDER, tr. 1651, clergyman, sett. Ware ph, Mockjack Bay, Va, 1653-1672, d. pre 1703.   (SPG.11.152)(CCVC38)(WMQ.2.2.157)(RoyalSoc.MSS.I.369)

MURRAY, ALEXANDER, Jacobite, tr. 31 July 1716, fr. Liverpool to Va, on *Anne.* (SPC.1716.310)(CTB.31.209)

MURRAY, ALEXANDER, b. 29 Jan. 1734, merchant-skipper, res. Glasgow, sett. Osburne, Va, 1762, m. Betty Clay, Loyalist, sett. Shelburne, N.S. 1783. (PRO.AO12.55.61)(PRO.AO12.109.218)(LNS152)

MURRAY, DAVID, Jacobite, tr. 31 July 1716, fr.Liverpool to Va, on *Anne.* (SPC.1716.310)(CTB.31.209)

MURRAY, DUNCAN, b. 1728, seaman, sett. Fairfax Co, Va, militiaman in Va Regt 1757. (VMHB.1/2)(L)

MURRAY, HENRY, Jacobite, tr. 24 May 1716, fr. Liverpool to Md, on *Friendship,* arr. Md Aug. 1716.   (SPC.1716.311)(HM387)

MURRAY, JAMES, merchant, res. Leith, Midlothian, sett. Va pre 1744. (SRO.CS16.1.173)

MURRAY, JAMES, Jacobite, tr. 29 June 1716, fr. Liverpool to Jamaica or Va, on *Elizabeth and Anne,* arr. York, Va, 1716. (SPC.1716.310)(CTB.31.208)(VSP.1.186)

MURRAY, JAMES, former Captain of Queen's American Rangers, d. Norfolk, Va, 29 Mar. 1789.   (SM.51.361)

MURRAY, JAMES, res. Glasgow, sett. Joppa, Md, d. 13 Aug. 1762. (SRO.SH16.12.1775)

MURRAY, JANE, res. Edinburgh, m. Alexander Schawfield, sett. Va, pre 1799. (SRO.SH10.4.1799)

MURRAY, JOHN, b. 1732, 4th Earl of Dunmore, Governor of Va 1771-1776, d. 25 Feb. 1809. (SP.3.388)

MURRAY, JOHN B., b. 1755, merchant, sh. pre 1780, m. Martha McClenachan, sett. Alexandria, Va, and N.Y. (ANY.2.9)

MURRAY, JOHN, tobacco factor, res. Glasgow, sh. pre 1770, sett. Aquia, Va. (SRA.T79.21)

MURRAY, PATRICK, farmer, res. Perthshire, Jacobite, tr. 22 Apr. 1747, fr. Liverpool to Va, on Johnson, arr. Port Oxford, Md, 5 Aug. 1747. (P.3.220)(PRO.T1.328)

MURRAY, WILLIAM, merchant, res. Va, m. Margaret Robertson, 1662, Edinburgh. (SRO.RD3/5)(Edinburgh OPR)

MURRAY, WILLIAM, b. 1708, physician, sett. Md, 1735, d. 1769. (SA178)

MURRAY, WILLIAM, merchant, res. Edinburgh, sett. Va, d. 2 Jan. 1791 London. (GM.61.91)

MURRAY, WILLIAM, b. 1800, machinist, sh. pre 1824, m. Elizabeth -, fa. of Mary, Agnes, Francis, William, Edward, Margaret, David and Alonzo, sett. Baltimore. (N.A.-M432/277-299)

MUSHET, JOHN, s. of ... Mushet of Lendricks, Stirlingshire, sett. Portobacco, Md, pre 1747. (LIM.2.243)

MUSCHET, Dr, s. of ...Mushet of Lendricks, Stirlingshire, physician, sett. Portobacco, Md, pre 1747. (LIM.2.243)

MUTTER, JOHN, sett. Richmond, Va, d. 20 Jan. 1819 Naples, Italy. (S.111.19)

NAPIER, PATRICK, b. 1610, s. of Robert Napier, physician, res. Edinburgh, sh. 1655, sett. Va, m. Elizabeth Booth, fa. of Robert, d. 1669. (BLG2839)

NAPIER, WILLIAM, b. 1811, patternmaker, sh. pre 1830, m. Mary -, fa. of Thomas, sett. Baltimore. (N.A.-M432/277-299)

NASMITH. JOHN, s. of James Nasmith of Earlshaugh, merchant, res. Edinburgh, sett. Va, d. 1747, pro. 9 July 1752 Edinburgh. (SRO.CC8.8.114)

NAISMITH, JOHN, b. 22 Mar. 1726, s. of Robert Naismith and Jean Young, res. Dundee, Angus, Jacobite, tr. 22 Apr. 1747, fr. Liverpool to Va, on Johnson, arr. Port Oxford, Md, 5 Aug. 1747, mail-carrier, Euston, Md, d. 20 Aug. 1793. (P.3.224)(MR107) (PRO.T1.328)(MdHerald27.8.1793)

NAUGHTY, JOHN, b. 1732, planter, sett. Stafford Co, Va, militiaman in Va Regt 1757. (VMHB.1/2)(L)

NEAVE, ALEXANDER, Jacobite, tr. 24 May 1716, fr. Liverpool to Md, on Friendship, arr. Md Aug. 1716. (SPC.1716.311)(HM386)

NEILSON, GEORGE, Jacobite, tr. 28 July 1716, fr. Liverpool to Va, on *Godspeed,* arr. Md Oct. 1716, founder Tuesday Club, Annapolis, Md, 1745. (SPC.1716.310) (CTB.31.209)(HM388)

NEILSON, HUGH, merchant, sett. Lewisburg, Loudoun Co, Va, 1770, m. Sarah Heale, fa. of Joseph, d. 1813. (CAG.1.741)(SRO.CS16.1.1165)

NEILSON, JAMES, tr. 1696, fr. Newhaven, Midlothian, to Va. (SRO.RH15.14.58)

NEILSON, JAMES, s. of Gilbert Neilson, merchant, res. Edinburgh, d. 4 July 1821, Baltimore, Md. (SRO.RD5.84.625)(BM.10.239)

NEILSON, JOHN, sh. pre 1768, storekeeper, sett. Dumfries, Va, d. 1772. (SFV60)

NELSON, THOMAS, b. 1677, merchant, sh. 1690, sett. York, Va, m. (1)Margaret Reid (2)Mrs Tracker, burgess of Glasgow 1716, fa. of William, d. 1745. (CAG.1.986/725)(BGBG1716)

NEILSON, WILLIAM, merchant, sett. Lewisburg, Va, pre 1775. (SRO.CS16.1.165)

NEVERY, JAMES, Jacobite, tr. 24 May 1716, fr. Liverpool to Md, on *Friendship,* arr. Md Aug. 1716. (SPC.1716.311)(HM386)

NEWLANDS, JAMES, b. 1700, sh. 1732 fr. Glasgow, sett. Va. (VaGaz14.4.1738)

NEWTON, ANDREW, customs collector, Accomack Co, Va, m. Katherine Goldie, fa. of Christina, d. pre 1784. (SRO.RD2.246.29)

NEWTON, CATHERINE, sett. Accomack, Va, pro. 17 Oct. 1788 Edinburgh. (SRO.CC8.8.127)

NICHOLSON, JAMES, b. 1711, res. Inverness, Steward of William and Mary College, Va, d. 22 Jan. 1773 Williamsburg. (Bruton g/s)(WMQ.4.45)(VaGaz28.1.1773)

NICHOLSON, ROBERT, s. of Thomas Nicholson, sett. Williamsburg, Va, pre 1775, m. Elizabeth Digges, fa. of George. (CAG.1.299)

NICHOLSON, WILLIAM, merchant, res. Berwickshire, sett. Anne Arundel Co, Md, pro. 28 Dec. 1731. (MSA.Wills.20.306)

NICOLL, JAMES, nat. 24 Dec. 1804 Norfolk City, Va

NICOLL, JOHN, s. of John Nicoll, res. Bo'ness, West Lothian, thief, sh. 28 Nov. 1704, fr. Leith to Md. (SRO.PC2.28.307)

NIMMO, JAMES, merchant, res. Linlithgow, West Lothian, sett. Princess Anne Co, Va, pre 1748. (WMQ.5.134)
...
NIMMO, WILLIAM, attorney, res. Blackridge, Linlithgow, West Lothian, sett. Va, pro. 10 Aug. 1748. (WMQ.5.134)

NIMMO, WILLIAM, merchant, sett. Va, fa. of Robert, d. pre 1817. (SRO.SH26.9.1817)

NINIAN, GRIZEL, res. Largs, Ayrshire, infanticide, tr. 1772, fr. Glasgow to Va, on *Brilliant*, arr. Port Hampton, Va, 7 Oct. 1772. (SRO.JC27.10.3)(AJ1270)

NISBET, ALEXANDER, b. 26 June 1777, s. of Charles Nisbet and Anne Tweedie, res. Montrose, Angus, sh. 1784, judge, sett. Baltimore, Md, m. Mary Owings, fa. of Ann, d. 22 Nov. 1857. (N.A.-M432/277-299)(Montrose, Md, G/s)

NISBET, JAMES, Jacobite, tr. 29 Sep. 1716, fr. Liverpool to Jamaica or Va, on *Elizabeth and Anne*, arr. Va 1716. (SPC.1716.310)(CTB.31.208)(VSP.1.185)

NISBET, ROBERT, b. 1746, weaver, res. Ayrshire (?), sett. Richmond City, Va, nat. 4 Nov. 1800. (US.D/C.1800.38)

NIVISON, JOHN, clergyman, edu. Glasgow Uni., sett. St Anne's ph, Albemarle Co, Va, 24 Apr. 1751. (FPA307)

NIXON, WILLIAM, b. 1786, merchant, res. Edinburgh, sett. Richmond, Va, nat. 27 Oct. 1800. (US.D/C.1800.37)

NOBLE, JAMES, merchant, res. Mauchline, Ayrshire, sett. Norfolk, Va, d. 30 May 1810. (EA.4869.183)

NOBLE, THOMAS, b. 1704, merchant, res. Newmill, Banffshire, edu. Aberdeen Uni., sett. Md and Va, m. Molly Gilbert. (GKF677)

NOBLE, WILLIAM, Jacobite, tr. 29 Sep. 1716, fr. Liverpool to Jamaica or Va, on *Elizabeth and Anne*, arr. York, Va, 1716. (SPC.1716.310)(CTB.31.208) (VSP.1.186)

NORRIS, ALEXANDER, house carpenter, runaway, Dumfries, Va, 1775. (VaGaz31.3.1775)

NORVIL, ADAM, Jacobite, tr. 22 Apr. 1747, fr. Liverpool to Va, on *Johnson*, arr. Port Oxford, Md, 5 Aug. 1747. (P.3.230)(PRO.T1.328)

NOUGHTIE, JAMES, b. 1747, tailor, runaway, Petersburg, Va, 1769. (VaGaz20.4.1769)

OCHILTREE, DANIEL, s. of ... Ochiltree and Margaret McGlashan, tr. 1696, fr. Newhaven, Midlothian, to Va. (SRO.RH15.14.58)

OCHILTREE, HUGH, s. of ... Ochiltree and Margaret McGlashan, tr. 1696, fr.Newhaven, Midlothian, to Va. (SRO.RH15.14.58)

OUCHTERLONY, PATRICK, mariner, res. Arbroath, Angus, sett. Calvert Co, Md, m. Elizabeth -, d. 18 May 1753, pro 1758 Edinburgh. (SRO.CC8.8.117) (SRO.CS16.1.100)

OGILVIE, ALEXANDER, b. 1802, nat. 29 Nov. 1821 Norfolk City, Va.

OGILVIE, DAVID, b. 1663, s of Alexander Ogilvie, res. Banff, Banffshire, sh. July 1684, fr. London to Md, on *Benedict Leonard*. (CLRO/AIA)
OGILVIE, ISOBEL, Banff, infanticide, tr. 25 May 1749, fr. Aberdeen to Va, on *Dispatch of Newcastle*. (AJ68)

OGILVIE, JAMES, res. Banff, clergyman, sh. 1771, sett. Charles City, Va, 1772, Loyalist.   (PRO.AO13.32.166)(AOB.2.427)(EMA48)

OGILVY, JAMES, thief, tr. 4 May 1666, fr. Leith to Va, on *Phoenix of Leith.* (ETR107)

OGILVIE, JANET, res. Aberfoyle, Stirlingshire, tr. May 1770, fr. Port Glasgow to Md, on *Crawford,* arr. Port Oxford, Md, 23 July 1771.   (SRO.JC27.10.3)(AJ1170)

OGILVY, JOHN, Jacobite, tr. 29 June 1716, fr. Liverpool to Jamaica or Va, on *Elizabeth and Anne,* arr. York, Va, 1716.   (SPC.1716.310)(CTB.31.208) (VSP.1.186)

OGILVIE, JOHN, b. 1722, servant, Jacobite, tr. 24 Feb. 1747, fr. Liverpool to Va, on *Gildart,* arr. Port North Potomac, Md, 5 Aug. 1747.   (P.3.238)(PRO.T1.328) (MR107)

OGILVIE, WILLIAM, s. of William Ogilvie and Janet Webster, res. Shielhill, physician, sett. Va 1713.   (SRO.SH27.4.1713)

OGILVIE, WILLIAM, b. 1728, s. of James Ogilvie of Auchiries, Aberdeenshire, Jacobite, d. 1750 Va.   (JAB.2.369)

OGLEBY, DAVID, b. 1772, sett. Washington, D.C., 1793, nat. 1802 D.C.

OGSTON, JAMES, Jacobite, tr. 15 July 1716, fr. Liverpool to Va, on *Elizabeth and Anne* (CTB.311.209)

OLD, JOHN, merchant, res. Glasgow, sett. Va, pro. 28 Oct. 1803 Edinburgh. (SRO.CC8.8.134)

OLIPHANT, JOHN, res. Glasgow, sh. 1775 to Va.   (SRO.GD136)

OMAND, MARGARET, m. Captain Charles Gregory, sett. Va, sett. Stromness, Orkney Islands, 1790.   (SRO.SH5.11.1790)

ORR, JOHN, b. 25 July 1726, s. of Rev. Alexander Orr and Agnes Dalrymple, merchant, res. Hoddam ph, Berwickshire, sett. Leestown, Loudon Co, Va, m. Susannah Grayson, fa. of Alexander, Benjamin, John, William, Ann, Eleanor, Elizabeth and Susanna, d. after 1788. (SOF151)(VG105)(Tylers Qrtly4.49)

ORR, JOHN, s. of Rev. David Orr, res. Shotts, Lanarkshire, storekeeper, Alexandria, Fairfax Co, Va, pre 1770.   (SRO.CS16.1.141)

ORR, ROBERT, sh. 2 Nov. 1674, to St Mary's Co, Md, on *Bachelor of Bristol.* (MSA.ESB.152)

ORROCK, ALEXANDER, Jacobite, tr. 28 July 1716, fr. Liverpool to Va, on *Godspeed,* arr. Md Oct. 1716.   (SPC.1716.310)(CTB.31.209)(HM388)

OSWALD, ANDREW, b. 1662, s. of James Oswald, clerk, res. Edinburgh, sh. July 1684, fr. London to Va.   (CLRO/AIA)

OSWALD, HENRY, b. 1694, s. of Thomas Oswald, surgeon, res. Kirkcaldy, Fife, sh. pre 1725, sett. essex Co, Va, m. Mary -, fa. of Ludovic, John, Mary and Elizabeth, d. 1726, pro. 1726 Essex Co. (BGBG376)

PALMER, PHILIP, b. 1788, rigger, m. Mary -, sett. Norfolk, Va. (N.A.-M432/277-299)

PALMER, WILLIAM, b. 1799, farmer, arr. Baltimore 1822. (N.A.-M596)

PARK, JOHN, merchant, res. Greenock, Renfrewshire, sett. Va pre 1752. (SRO.CS16.1.88)

PARK, JOHN, b. 1805, boatbuilder, m. Jane -, fa. of Samuel and Mary, sh. pre 1825, sett. Washington Co, Md.   (N.A.-M432/277-299)

PARK, THOMAS, Jacobite, tr. 24 May 1716, fr. Liverpool to Md, on *Friendship*, arr. Md Aug. 1716.   (SPC.1716.311)(HM388)

PARKER, JAMES, b. 1729, s. of Patrick Parker, merchant, res. Port Glasgow, sh. 1754, sett. Norfolk, Va, m. Margaret Elligood, Loyalist.   (PRO.AO13.32.229) (PRO.AO13.134)(SRO.SH24.8.1754)(Col.Williamsburg.M.77.1/3)

PARKER, JOHN, s. of Patrick Parker, merchant, res. Port Glasgow, sett. Va pre 1760. (SRO.CS16.1.107)

PATERSON, DAVID, nat. 24 Mar. 1789 Norfolk City, Va.

PATTERSON, ELIZABETH, tr. 1696, fr. Newhaven, Midlothian, to Va. (SRO.RH15.14.58)

PATTERSON, GEORGE, nat. 21 Aug. 1806 Norfolk Co, Va.

PATTERSON, JAMES, Jacobite, tr. 29 June 1716, fr. Liverpool to Jamaica or Va, on *Elizabeth and Anne*, arr. York, Va, 1716. (SPC.1716.310)(CTB.31.208)(VSP.1.186)

PATTERSON, JEAN, stabler's servant, res. Aberdeen, assailant, tr. July 1772, fr. Glasgow to Va, on *Brilliant*, arr. Port Hampton, Va, 7 Oct. 1772. (SRO.JC27.10.3)(AJ1272)

PATTERSON, JOHN, b. 1751, gardener, res. Aberdeen, sh. Dec. 1773, fr. London to Va, on *Elizabeth*.   (PRO.T47.9/11)

PATTERSON, JOHN, b. 1780, sett. Petersburg, Dinwiddie Co, Va. (N.A.-M932/982)

PATTERSON, ROBERT, b. 1732, res. Renfrew, Renfrewshire, sh. 1763, sett. Cross Roads, Churchville, Md, sh. May 1767, sett. Pictou, N.S., d. 30 Sep. 1808, N.S. (DCB. 3 .659)

PATERSON, SIMON, clerk, sett. Va pre 1774, Loyalist.   (PRO.AO12.101.190) (PRO.AO12.101.305)(PRO.AO12.109.242)
PATERSON, THOMAS, ropemaker, res. Leith, Midlothian, sett. Baltimore. Md, fa. of William, d. pre 1780.   (SRO.SH.24.2.1780)(SRO.CS16.1.175/9)

PATON, JOHN, Jacobite, tr. 24 Feb. 1747, fr. Liverpool to Va, on *Gildart,* arr. Port North Potomac, Md, 5 Aug. 1747. (PRO.T1.328)

PATON, JOHN, nat. 2 Apr. 1812 Norfolk City, Va.

PATON, ROBERT, Covenanter, tr. 1669 to Va. (PC.3.22)

PATTISON, GRANVILLE SHARP, b. 1791, s. of Thomas Pattison, res. Glasgow, physician, edu. Glasgow Uni., sh. 1819 to Philadelphia, Professor of Anatomy at Uni. of Md, d. 12 Nov. 1851 N.Y. (ANY198)

PATRICK, MARGARET EASSON, da. of William Patrick, res. Beith, Ayrshire, m. Dandridge Henley, Va, 1821. (SRO.SH14.7.1823)

PATRICK, WILLIAM, s. of James Patrick and Anne Sheddan, res. Beith, Ayrshire, sh. pre 1790, sett. Va, fa. of Margaret, d. 1807. (HA.1.296)(SRO.SH28.5.1821)

PATTON, ROBERT, merchant factor, res. Glasgow, sh. pre 1776, sett. Culpepper Co, Va, m. Ann Mercer 1793, d. 1827. (AA.10.41)(SFV230)(SRA.CFI)

PATTULLO, GEORGE ALEXANDER, b. 1720, sh. 1740, sett. Va, m. Martha Varner 1757, fa. of James, William, David, John, Samuel, Sarah, Mary and Jane, d. 9 June 1798 Charlotte Co, Va. (PF145)

PATTULLO, HENRY, b. 1726, merchant and clergyman, sh. 1735 to Va, sett. N.C., d. 1801. (DAB.14.295)

PATTULLO, JAMES, Jacobite, tr. 29 June 1716, fr. Liverpool to Jamaica or Va, on *Elizabeth and Anne,* arr. York, Va, 1716. (SPC.1716.310)(CTB.31.208)(VSP.1.185)

PAUL, ALEXANDER, b. 1804, engineer, m. Agnes -, sh. pre 1820, fa. of Thomas, R., Agnes and Alexander, sett. Baltimore. (N.A.-M432?277-299)

PAUL, HUGH, b. 1731, planter, militiaman in Va Regt 1757. (VMHB.1/2)(L)

PAUL, WILLIAM, b. 1738, s. of John Paul and Jean McDuff, res. Arbigland, Kirkbean, Stewartry of Galloway, sett. Fredericksburg, Spotsylvania Co, Va, bd. St George's, Fredericksburg, pro. 16 Dec. 1774 Spotsylvania Co.

PEARSON, JOHN, sh. 2 Nov. 1674, to St Mary's Co, Md, on *Bachelor of Bristol.* (MSA.ESB.152)

PEARSON, MARGARET, b. 1760, sett. Mecklenburg Co, Va. (N.A.-M932/982)

PEDDIE, JOHN, b. 6 july 1703, s. of John Peddie and Jean Smith, merchant, res. Arbroath, Angus, Jacobite, tr. 24 Feb. 1747, fr. Liverpool to Va, on Gildart, arr. Port North Potomac, Md, 5 Aug. 1747. (P.2.250)(PRO.T1.328)

PEDENE, JAMES, s. of James Pedene of Midauchenlungford, sett. Va pre 1780. (SRO.CS16.1.179)

PEEBLES, DAVID, merchant, res. Edinburgh, sett. Powell's Creek, Va, 1650. (EBR.129)(WMQ.2.13.132)

PENDIN, JAMES, clergyman, edu. Glasgow Uni., sh. pre 1732, sett. Va. (SCHR.14.148)

PERCY, JAMES, b. 1800, innkeeper, m. Ellen -, sett. Alleghany Co, Md. (N.A.-M432.277-299)

PERKLE, JAMES, b. 1752, printer, res. Edinburgh, sh. Sep. 1774, fr. London to Md, on *Neptune.*   (PRO.T47.9/11)

PETER, JAMES, Jacobite, tr. 29 June 1716, fr. Liverpool to Jamaica or Va, on *Elizabeth and Anne,* arr. York, Va, 1716. (SPC.1716.310)(CTB.31.208)(VSP.1.186)

PETER, JOHN, Jacobite, tr. 29 June 1716, fr. Liverpool to Jamaica or Va, on Elizabeth and Anne, arr. York, Va, 1716. (SPC.1716.310)(CTB.31.208)(VSP.1.185)

PETER, JOHN, Jacobite, tr. 24 May 1716, fr. Liverpool to Md, on *Friendship,* arr. Md Aug. 1716.   (SPC.1716.311)(HM386)

PETER, JOHN, b. 31 May 1722, s. of Thomas Peter and Janet Frew, merchant, res. Glasgow, sett. Surrey Co, Va pre 1760, d. 1763.   (CD43)

PETER, ROBERT, b. 1726, s. of Thomas Peter and Jane Dunlop, merchant, res. Crossbasket, Lanarkshire, sett. Georgetown, Frederick Co, Md pre 1775, m. Elizabeth Scott 1767.   (SRO.CS16.1.165)(HM.1.732)

PETER, WALTER, s. of Thomas Peter, merchant, res. Glasgow, sett. Surrey Co, Va, pre 1763, d. pre 1787.   (SRO.SH30.11.1787)(SRO.CS16.1.174)

PETRIE, ALEXANDER, b. 1745, res. Elgin, Morayshire, sett. King William Co, Va, pre 1776.   (VSL.23816)

PETTIGREW, JAMES, b. 20 Feb. 1715, s. of John Pettigrew and Jean Cleland, merchant, res. Glasgow, sett. Va pre 1780, fa. of John and Gavin. (SRO.CS16.1.181)

PHILIPS, GEORGE, b. 1787, res. Edinburgh, sh. July 1817, fr. Kirkcaldy, Fife, to Norfolk, Va, nat. Washington, D.C. 1824.

PHILIPS, Mrs, b. 1781, sett. Wshington, D.C.   (N.A.-M432/56-57)

PHILP, GEORGE, physician, res. Huntly, Aberdeenshire, abortionist, tr. 1772,   arr. Port of James River, Upper District, Va, 29 Apr. 1772.   (SRO.JC27.10.3)(AJ1238)

PHINN, JOHN, res. Edinburgh, sett.Jamaica, pro. 15 June 1761 Norfolk, Va.

PIKE, RICHARD, b. 1718, baker, sett. King William Co, Va, militiaman in Va Regt 1757.   (VMHB.1/2)(L)

PINMURRAY, JANET, Jacobite, tr. 22 Apr. 1747, fr. Liverpool to Va, on *Johnson,* arr. Port Oxford, Md, 5 Aug. 1747.   (P.3.254)(PRO.T1.328)

PIRIE, ERIC, physician, res. Aberdeen, sett. Va pre 1774.   (NLS.Acc5340/61)

PIRIE, MARGARET, res. Banff, Banffshire, infanticide, tr. 25 May 1749, fr. Aberdeen to Va, on *Dispatch of Newcastle*. (AJ68)

POLLOCK, ALLAN, s. of Allan Pollock, merchant, res. Glasgow, sett. Richmond, Va, d. Jan. 1816 Chelsea, Va, pro. 26 Jan. 1819 Edinburgh. (SRO.CC8.8.145) (SRO.SC70.1.18)

POLLOCK, Mrs Anne, b. 1791, mo. of David, Andrew, James, William, Colin and Robert, arr. Baltimore 1829. (N.A.-M529)

POLLOCK, GEORGE, b. 10 Apr. 1646, s. of George Pollock and Helen Orr, res. Glasgow, edu. Glasgow Uni. 1664, m. Elizabeth Douglas, sett. Va. (HHG11)

POLLOCK, JOHN, b. 17 Jan. 1783, s. of Allan Pollock and Janet Morris, res. Glasgow, lawyer, edu. Glasgow Uni. 1795, d. 28 Apr. 1817 Yancieville, Va. (MAGU179)

POLLOCK, MORRIS, b. 22 Mar. 1787, s. of Allan Pollock and Janet Morris, res. Glasgow, manufacturer, sett. Va pre 1819. (SRO.CC8.8.145)

POLLOCK, ROBERT, b. 12 Mar. 1775, s. of Allan Pollock and Janet Morris, merchant, res. Glasgow, d. 19 May 1811 Petersburg, Va. (SM.73.558)(SRO.CC8.8.139) (SRO.SC70.1.8)(Blandford g/s)

POLLOCK, WILLIAM, b. 1800, farmer, m. Janet, sett. Stafford Co, Va, fa. of John, Aitchison and Matthew. (N.A.-M932/982)

POLSON, WILLIAM, s. of John Polson and Janet Mackay, res. Navidale, Sutherland, Captain of Va Rangers, d. 1755 Monogahela River. (BOM295)

PORTEOUS, EDWARD, s. of Robert Porteous and Elizabeth Keith, merchant, res. Dalkeith, Midlothian, sh. July 1675, fr. London to Va, on *Barnaby,* sett. Petsworth ph, Gloucester Co, Va, fa. of Robert, d. 23 Feb. 1694, pro. 24 Oct. 1700 Gloucester Co, pro. 1700 PCC. (PRO.E190.62.5)(SRO.GD297.114)(VMHB.13.311) (Gloucester g/s)

PORTEOUS, JAMES, baker, sh. 1714, fr. Glasgow to the Potomac River, on the *American Merchant.* (TM202)

PORTEOUS, JOHN, Jacobite, tr. 29 June 1716, fr. Liverpool to Jamaica or Va, on *Elizabeth and Anne.* (SPC.1716.310)(CTB.31.208)

PORTER, WILLIAM, sett. Va pre 1811. (SRO.SH18.12.1811)

POTTS, TIM, b. 1790, hatter, m. Rebecca -, sett. Louis Co, Va. (N.A.-M932/982)

POTTS, THOMAS, Jacobite, tr. 24 May 1716, fr. Liverpool to Md, on *Friendship,* arr. Md Aug. 1716. (SPC.1716.311)(HM387)

POUSTOUN, JOHN, patent of denization, 4 Mar. 1634 Md. (MSA.3.490)

PRATT, WILLIAM, b. 29 Aug. 1703, merchant, res. Peterhead, Aberdeenshire, sett. Gloucester Co, Va. (GGE936)

PRICE, RALPH, b. 1713, miller, Jacobite, tr. 24 Feb. 1747, fr. Liverpool to Va, on *Gildart*, arr. Port North Potomac, Md, 5 Aug. 1747. (P.2.258)(PRO.T1.328)

PRIMROSE, JOHN, blacksmith, sett. Queen Anne Co, Md, m. Elizabeth -, fa. of John, William, George, Archibald, Tulip, Violet, Lilly and Elizabeth, pro. 27 Mar. 1723 Md.

PRIMROSE, WILLIAM, b. 1792, patternmaker, sh. pre 1825, fa. of Janet, William, John, Margaret and Samuel, sett. Baltimore. (N.A.-M932/982)

PROCTOR, WILLIAM, res. Banff or Elgin, Morayshire, clergyman and schoolmaster, edu. Aberdeen Uni. 1733, sh. 1740, sett. Nottway ph, Amelia Co, Va, d. Dec. 1761. (VMHB.10.298)(SM.24.167)(AJ741)(GM.32.145)

PROPHET, SYLVESTER, Jacobite, tr. 29 June 1716, fr. Liverpool to Jamaica or Va, on *Elizabeth and Anne*, arr. York, Va, 1716. (SPC.1716.310)(CTB.31.208)(VSP.1.185)

PROUDFOOT, JOHN, b. 1732, hairdresser, res. Edinburgh, sh. Nov. 1774, fr. London to Va, on Elizabeth, m. Eleanor Hitt, d. 1823, bd. Barbour Co, WVa. (PRO.T47.9/11)

PROVAN, HUGH jr, s. of Hugh Provan of Auchinloch, sett. Isle of Wight Co,Va, d. Govan, Glasgow, pro. 9 Jan. 1790 Glasgow. (SRO.CC10.5.12)

PROVAN, MATTHEW, res. Dunbartonshire, sh. pre 1726, sett. Md, fa. of William. (SRO.RS10..5.384/405)

PROVAN, ROBERT, shopbreaker, tr. 1773, fr. Port Glasgow to Va, on *Thomas of Glasgow*, arr. James River, Upper District, Va, 5 June 1723. (SRO.JC27.10.3)

PUGH, THEOPHILIUS, res. Va, pro. 15 Nov. 1748 Glasgow. (SRO.CC9.-)

PULLER, CHARLES, b. 1750, barber or hairdresser, sh. 1775, fr. London to Baltimore, on Nancy, runaway, Md, 1776. (PRO.T47.9/11)(MdGaz12.3.1776)

RADDOCK, SAMUEL, apothecary, d. Annapolis Royal, Md, Apr. 1769. (SM.31.334)

RAE, GEORGE, merchant, sett. Va pre 1776, Loyalist. (PRO.AO13.32.315)

RAE, JAMES, farmer, Cushnie, Aberdeenshire, Jacobite, tr. 29 June 1716, fr. Liverpool to Jamaica or Va, on *Elizabeth and Anne*, ar. York, Va, 1716. (SPC.1716.310)(CTB.31.208)(JAB.1.151)(VSP.1.186)

RAE, JAMES, b. 19 Nov. 1723, s. of Robert Rae and Elizabeth Dunlop, merchant, edu. Glasgow Uni. 1736, res. Govan, Glasgow, d. 1763 Va. (SM.26.290)(MAGU17)

RAE, JAMES, b. 1794, manufacturer, m. Catherine -, fa. of Isabel, sett. Richmond, Va. (N.A.-M932/982)

RAE, MARGARET, res. Echt, Aberdeenshire, cattlethief, sh. June 1755, fr. Aberdeen to Va, on *Hope*. (AJ350/388)

RAE, ROBERT, b. 1723, s. of Robert Rae and Elizabeth Dunlop, merchant, res. Little Govan, Glasgow, sett. Falmouth, Va, d. 30 May 1753. (Bruton g/s)

RAITT, MARGARET, b. 4 Sep. 1677, da. of Robert Raitt, res. Montrose, Angus, sett. Va, d. 1714. (SRO.GD45.17.916)

RALSTON, DAVID, merchant, res. Glasgow, sh. pre 1762, sett. Cabin Point, James River, Va. (SRA.CFI)

RALSTON, GAVIN, b. 1735, s. of William Ralston and Marion Ewing, res. Beith, Ayrshire, sh. pre 1744, sett. Va, m. Annabella Pollock 1758, d. 1819 Scotland. (HAF.1.269)

RAMAGE, ROBERT, m. Janet Liston, sett. Md pre 1820. (SRO.RD5.282.356)

RAMSAY, ANDREW, merchant, m. Catherine Graham, sett. Alexandria, D.C., and Washington, D.C., fa. of George (b.1802) (DAB.15.340)

RAMSAY, GEORGE, physician, m. Sarah -, fa. of John and James, sett. Norfolk, Va, pro. 22 June 1756 Norfolk, Va.

RAMSAY, JOHN, Jacobite, tr. 24 May 1716, fr. Liverpool to Md, on *Friendship,* arr. Md Aug. 1716. (SPC.1716.311)(HM387)(MdArch.34.164)

RAMSAY, JOHN, clergyman, sh. 1751 to Va. (EMA51)

RAMSAY, JOHN, b. 1701, res. Dalry, Galloway, sh. Sep. 1721, fr. London to Md. (CLRO/AIA)

RAMSAY, JOHN, b. 1800, farmer, arr. Norfolk, Va, Sep. 1820. (PA111)

RAMSAY, PATRICK, b. 20 June 1736, s. of Andrew Ramsay and Janet Houstoun, res. Glasgow, sett. Bristol ph, Va, pre 1760. (SRA.CFI)

RAMSAY, SAMUEL, d. 3 Mar. 1798 Va. (VaGaz11.9.1798)

RAMSAY, WILLIAM, b. 1716, merchant, res. Galloway, sett. Alexandria, Va, m. Ann McCarty, fa. of Dennis and William, d. 1785. (SRO.SC15.55.2)(SRO.RS19.376) (VG88)

RAY, ADAM, b. 1800, ploughmaker, m. Elizabeth -, sh. pre 1825, fa. of Francis, William, Margaret, Sarah, Mary, Robert, Ann, Janet and Eliza, sett. Baltimore. (N.A.-M432/277-299)

RANDAL, ROBERT, b. 1753, printer and bookbinder, res. Edinburgh, sh. July 1774, fr. London to Md, on *Russia Merchant.* (PRO.T47.9/11)

RANKIN, WILLIAM, sett. Portsmouth, Va, pre 1776, Loyalist, sett. Shelborne, N.S. (PRO.AO13.26.387)

RATTRAY, ANN, res. Aberdeen,murderer, tr. 1728, fr. Glasgow to Md, on *Concord of Glasgow*, arr. Charles Co, Md, 24 May 1728. (SRO.JC.11.6)(SRO.JC27.10.3)

RAY, ADAM, b. 1800, ploughmaker, m. Elizabeth -, sh. pre 1825, fa. of Francis, William, Margaret, Sarah, Mary, Robert, Ann, Janet and Eliza, sett. Baltimore, Md. (N.A.-M432/277-299)

REID, ADAM, res. Ayrshire, sett. Urbanna, Middlesex Co, Va, d. pre Sep. 1763. (ref. JasReid pro.3.1.1764 Williamsburg,Va)

REID, ALEXANDER, res. Alford, Aberdeenshire, Jacobite, tr. 24 May 1716, fr. Liverpool to Md, on *Friendship*, sett. Reidbourne, Chester River, Calvert Co, Md, d. 14 Oct. 1718 inestate. (MSA.MdProvCourt.DeedsE18/6)

REID, CHARLES, b. 4 Apr. 1800, s. of George Reid and Elizabeth Taylor, grocer, res. Forfar, Angus, sh. 1801, sett. Portsmouth and Norfolk, Va, m. Lucretia Nash 1825, fa. of Charles, George, Robert, James, Lucretia, Harriet and Rebecca, d. 17 Jan. 1899, Norfolk, Va. (ANY.2.261)(N.A.-M932/982)(LNA.149)

REID, DAVID, b. 1754, weaver, sh. Dec. 1773, fr. London to Md, on *Etty*. (PRO.T47.9/11)

REID, GEORGE, gentleman, res. Aberdeenshire (?), sett. Calvert Co, Md, d. 1718. (MSA.MdProvCourt. DeedsE18/6)

REID, GEORGE, s. of William Reid, res. Forfar, Angus, m. Elizabeth Taylor 1799, sh. 1801, sett. Norfolk, Va, fa. of Andrew and Charles, nat. 28 Sep. 1808 Norfolk City, Va, d. 1849. (CF.7.392)

REID, HUGH, b. 1751, woolcomber, sh. Nov. 1774, fr. London to Va, on *Elizabeth*. (PRO.T47.9/11)

REID, JAMES, res. Ayrshire (?), sett. Urbanna, Middlesex Co, Va, pro. 3 Jan. 1764 Williamsburg, Va.

REID, JAMES, nat. 26 Mar. 1792 Norfolk Co, Va.

REID, JAMES, tutor and poet, res. Edinburgh, sett. Sweet Hall, King William Co, Va, pre 1768. (VMHB.79.3)

REID, JOHN, s. of George Reid, res. Dalgairn, Sorn, Ayrshire, pro. 25 Feb. 1747 Westmoreland Co, Va.

REID, JOHN, merchant, res. Dumfries, Dumfriesshire, sett. Va 1740, d. 29 Oct. 1791 Norfolk, Va. (SM.53.568)

REID, KATHERINE, b. 1755, da. of Rev. Alexander Reid, res. Kemnay, Aberdeenshire, m. Andrew Harper, d. Oct. 1788 Portsmouth, Va. (Norfolk, Portsmouth Journal22.10.1788)

REID, ROBERT, farmer, res. Mid Clova, Aberdeenshire, Jacobite, tr. 29 June 1716, fr. Liverpool to Jamaica or Va, on *Elizabeth and Anne*. (SPC.1716.310)(CTB.31.208)(JAB.1.151)

REID, THOMAS, merchant, sett. Richmond, Va, pre 1776, Loyalist. (PRO.AO12.54.161)

REID, THOMAS, merchant, sett. Amherst Co, Va, 1762, Loyalist. (PRO.AO13.32.367) (Cunningham District Arch.A34.40)

REID, THOMAS, nat. 28 June 1791 Norfolk City, Va.

REID, WILLIAM, merchant, res. Aberdeen, sett. Reidburn, Chester River, St Mary's Co, Md, 1722.　(MSA.MdProvCt.L5/39;LEi/6)

REID, WILLIAM, merchant and tobacco factor, res. Glasgow, sh. pre 1769, sett. Fredericksburg, Va, Loyalist.　(PRO.AO12.56.292)(SRA.T79.1)

RENNEY, ROBERT, clergyman, edu. Glasgow and Aberdeen Unis. 1755, sh. 1764, sett. Overwharton, Va.　(EMA52)(FPA308)

RENTON, JAMES, Jacobite, tr. 28 July 1716, fr. Liverpool to Va, on Godspeed, arr. Md Oct. 1716.　(SPC.1716.310)(CTB.31.209)(HM389)(MdArch.25.347)

RHEA, G., b. 1805, m. Elizabeth -, fa. of Elizabeth and Allan, arr. Baltimore 1823. (N.A.-M596)

RHEA, J., b. 1805, farmer, m. Elizabeth -, fa. of John, arr. Baltimore 1823. (N.A.-M596)

RHEA, JOSHUA, b. 1805, farmer, fa. of Margaret and William, arr. Baltimore 1823. (N.A.-M596)

RHIND, ALEXANDER, Jacobite, tr. 24 May 1716, fr. Liverpool to Md, on *Friendship,* arr. Md Aug. 1716.　(SPC.1716.310)(HM387)(MdArch.34.164)

RICHARDSON, JOHN, b. 1795, m. Jane -, fa. of Joseph, Samuel and Elizabeth, arr. Baltimore 1824.　(N.A.-M596)

RICHARDSON, THOMAS, sett. Baltimore Co, Md, d. Kingston, Jamaica, pro. 12 Mar. 1768 Md.　(MSA.Wills.35.478)

RICHARDSON, WILLIAM, b. 1752, printer, res. Edinburgh, sh. July 1774, fr. London to Md, on *Elizabeth.*　(PRO.T47.9/11)

RICHMOND, HELEN, res. Edinburgh, tr. 1696, fr. Newhaven, Midlothian, to Va. (SRO.RH15.14.58)

RIDDELL, ALEXANDER, b. 23 Sep. 1752, s. of Alexander Riddell and Agnes Fergus, merchant, res. Glasgow, sett. Baltimore, Md, d. 1825 Glasgow, pro. Baltimore. (MSA.Baltimore Wills.8.406)

RIDDELL, GEORGE, s. of George Riddell and Christian Paterson, merchant and physician, res. Kinglass, West Lothian, sett. Yorktown, Va, 1751, m. Susannah -, sett. Williams-burg, Va, Loyalist, d. 20 Jan. 1779 Va.　(PRO.AO13.8.161)(SRO.CS16.1.117)(OD40) (SN.3.342)(SM.41.79/167)(PRO.AO13.32.396)

RIDDELL, HENRY, merchant, res. Glasgow, sett. Pitscataway, Md, pre 1776, sett. Colchester, Fairfax Co, Va, 1779, Loyalist.　(SRO.CS16.1.179)(SRA.AO12.9) (PRO.AO12.80.17)

RIDDELL, JOHN, merchant, res. Glasgow, sh. pre 1769, sett.Dumfries, Prince William Co, Va.　(SRA.CFI)

RIDDELL, ROBERT, b. 1760, merchant, res. Glasgow, sett. Baltimore, d. 5 May 1809, pro. Baltimore. (MSA.Baltimore Wills.8.406)

RIDDELL, WILLIAM, b. 1619, sh. 6 July 1635, fr. London to Va, on *Paull*. (PRO.E157.20)

RIDDLE, D., b. 1799, plasterer, arr. Baltimore 1820 On *Oryza*. (N.A.-M596)

RIDDLE, WILLIAM, b. 1751, res. Aberdeen, runaway, Bedford Co, Va, 1769. (VaGaz14.9.1769)

RIDDOCH, COLIN, surgeon, res. Perthshire, m. Jean -, sett. Port Royal, Va, 1756, and Newcastle, Hanover Co, Va, 1774. (SRO.CS16.1.98)(SRO.RD4.216.288)

RIDDOCH, PETER, b. 1721, slater, res. Doune, Stirlingshire, Jacobite, tr. 22 Apr. 1747, fr. Liverpool to Va, on *Johnson,* arr. Port Oxford, Md, 5 Aug. 1747. (P.3.272)(MR45)(PRO.T1.328)

RIGHTREE, JAMES, d. 20 Dec. 1751 Charles ph, York Co, Va. (Charles OPR)

RITCHIE, ARCHIBALD, merchant and factor, sett. Caroline Co, Va, 1740, and Tappahannock, Essex Co, Va, 1749, m. (1) Sarah Roane 1753 (2) Isabella Toushee, fa. of Thomas, John, Archibald and William, Loyalist, d. 1784, pro. 20 Apr. 1784 Essex Co, Va. (DAB.15.628)(VMHB..7.2.40)(WMQ.2.18.90)(WMQ.2.22.345)

RITCHIE, HENRY, merchant, sett. Hobshole, Va, pre 1775. (SA59)

RITCHIE, JAMES, merchant, sett. Hobshole, Va, pre 1775. (SA59)

RITCHIE, JOHN, b. 1755, s. of Alexander Ritchie, res. Kirkcudbright, thief, tr. 1771, fr. Port Glasgow to Md, on *Crawford,* arr. Port Oxford, Md, 23 July 1771. (SRO.JC27.10.3)(AJ1167)

RITCHIE, NATHANIEL, nat. 27 May 1817 Norfolk City, Va.

RITCHIE, WILLIAM, b. 1814, carpenter, sett. Alleghany Co, Va. (N.A.-M932/982)

RITCHIE, WILLIAM, res. Perth, sett. Baltimore, Md, pre 1799. (SRO.SH14.8.1799)

RITCHLEY, KATHERINE, res. Ayr, sh. 5 Sep. 1698, fr. Liverpool to Va, on *Eleanor of Liverpool.* (LRO.Town Book)

ROBB, JAMES, s. of William Robb, res. Glasgow, sh. pre 1753, sett. Port Royal, Va. (SRA.T-MJ)

ROBB, PETER, b. pre 1743, baker, runaway, Hobshole, Va, 1773. (VaGaz26.8.1773)

ROBERTS, E., b. 1803, arr. Baltimore 1822 on *Arethusa.* (N.A.-M596)

ROBERTS, J., b. 1805, tailor, arr. Baltimore 1822 on *Arethusa.* (N.A.-M596)

ROBERTS, WILLIAM, b. 1794, farmer, m. Nancy -, sett. Ritchie Co, Va. (N.A.-M932/982)

ROBERTSON, AGNES, res. Edinburgh, thief and whore, tr. 28 Nov. 1704, fr. Leith, Midlothian, to Md. (SRO.PC2.28.307)

ROBERTSON, ALEXANDER, sh. pre 1769, sett. Wicomico River, Somerset Co, Md. (SRO.NRAS.0247)

ROBERTSON, ANDREW, b. 1716, physician, sett. Va, d. 1795. (SA188)

ROBERTSON, ANDREW, assistant storekeeper, sett. James River, Va, pre 1776. (SFV231)

ROBERTSON, ARCHIBALD, s. of William Robertson, merchant, res. Edinburgh, sh. pre 1743, sett. Petersburg, Va, m. Elizabeth Fitzgerald 1748, fa. of George, William, etc. (VMHB.34.77)(WMQ.5.237)(WMQ.5.185)(SRO.SC36.63.2)

ROBERTSON, CHARLES, sett. Va pre 1776, Loyalist. (PRO.AO13.32.421)

ROBERTSON, DAVID, b. 1797, merchant, arr. Baltimore 1820, on *Andromache* (PA58)

ROBERTSON, DONALD, Jacobite, tr. 24 May 1716, fr. Liverpool to Md, on *Friendship,* arr. Md Aug. 1716. (SPC.1716.311)(HM387)

ROBERTSON, DONALD, b. 27 Sep. 1717, s. of Charles Robertson and Isabella McDonald, res. Aberdeenshire(?), schoolmaster, edu. Aberdeen and Edinburgh Unis., sh. 29 Mar. 1753, m. (1) Henrietta Maxwell (2) Rachel Rogers, sett. Drysdale ph, King and Queen Co, Va, 1758-1769, d. 7 Nov. 1792. (VMHB.10.224)(VMHB.30.194)

ROBERTSON, EDWARD, sh. pre 1785, sett. Va, m. Mary Thompson, fa. of Thompson. (CAG.1.119)

ROBERTSON, ELIZABETH, res. Edinburgh, m. M. Sully, sett. Richmond, Va, pre 1827. (SRO.SH10.9.1827)

ROBERTSON, GEORGE, b. 1668, res. Struan, Perthshire, clergyman and schoolmaster, edu. St Andrews Uni. 1683, sh. 1693, sett. Bristol ph, Va, 1693-1739, m. Mary -, fa. of George, John, James and Elizabeth, d. 1739. (SCHR.14.142)(OD12)

ROBERTSON, HUGH, b. 6 Dec. 1717, s. of Thomas Robertson and Margaret Coul, laborer, res. Inverness, sh. Jan. 1736, fr. London to Md. (CLRO/AIA)

ROBERTSON, JAMES, clergyman, sh. 1717, sett. Va. (EMA52)

ROBERTSON, JAMES, Jacobite, tr. 24 May 1716, fr. Liverpool to Md, on *Friendship,* arr. Md Aug. 1716. (SPC.1716.311)(HM387)

ROBERTSON, JAMES, s. of James Robertson, waggon-maker, res. Currie, Midlothian, sett. Fells Point, Md, fa. of James, Ann and Elizabeth. (MdJournal18.8.1786)

ROBERTSON, JANET, res. Edinburgh, thief and whore, tr. 28 Nov. 1704, fr. Leith to Md. (SRO.PC2.28.307)

ROBERTSON, JEFFREY, b. 1654, sh. pre 1709, on *Blessing,* m. Elizabeth Bowman, fa. of George, Jeffrey, Richard, William and Martha, d. 1734 Henrico Co, Va. (SG25.3.87)

ROBERTSON, JOHN, Jacobite, tr. 24 May 1716, fr. Liverpool to Md, on *Friendship,* arr. Md Aug. 1716. (SPC.1716.311)(HM386)

ROBERTSON, JOHN, b. 1754, schoolmaster, sh. Apr. 1775, fr. London to Md, on *Nancy.* (PRO.T47.9/11)

ROBERTSON, JOHN, b. 1750, gardener, sh. Feb. 1774, fr. London to Md, on *Jenny.* (PRO.T47.9/11)

ROBERTSON, JOHN, merchant, res. Glasgow, sett. Va pre 1754. (SRO.CS16.1.95)

ROBERTSON, JOHN, s. of John Robertson and Agnes Gillies, merchant, res. Saltcoats, Ayrshire, sett. Portsmouth, Va, pre 1791. (SRO.RD4.258.895)

ROBERTSON, JOHN, schoolmaster, sh. fr. Glasgow to Va, m. Sarah Brand, sett. Albemarle Co, 1791, and Culpepper Co, Va, fa. of William, d. 1810. (DAB.16.29)

ROBERTSON, LEONARD, Jacobite, tr. 24 May 1716, fr. Liverpool to Md, on *Friendship,* arr. Md Aug. 1716. (SPC.1716.311)(HM386)(MdArch.34.164)

ROBERTSON, MALCOLM, Jacobite, tr. 22 Apr. 1747, fr. Liverpool to Va, on *Johnson,* arr. Port Oxford, Md, 5 Aug. 1747. (PRO.T1.328)

ROBERTSON, MARGARET, res. Jedburgh, Roxburghshire, gypsy, tr. 1 Jan. 1715, fr. Glasgow to Va. (GR530)

ROBERTSON, MARY, b. 1684, res. Kindeace, Ross and Cromarty, sh. 1705 to Va, m. John Drummond 1706, d. 1739 Prince William Co, Va. (OWC7/6)

ROBERTSON, NATHANIEL, b. 1680, res. Kindeace, Ross and Cromarty, sh. 1705 to Va, m. Mary Drewry 1705, fa. of Nathaniel, John and Christopher, d. 1711 Surrey Co, Va. (OWC6)

ROBERTSON, NEIL, cordiner, res. Logerait, Perthshire, Jacobite, tr. 22 Apr. 1747, fr. Liverpool to Va, on *Johnson,* arr. Port Oxford, Md, 5 Aug. 1747. (P.3.278)(MR27)(PRO.T1.328)

ROBERTSON, PATRICK, Jacobite, tr. 24 May 1716, fr. Liverpool to Md, on *Friendship.* (SPC.1716.311)

ROBERTSON, RICHARD, tr. 1773, fr. Port Glasgow to Va, on *Thomas of Glasgow,* arr. Upper District, James River, Va, 5 June 1773. (SRO.JC27.10.3)

ROBERTSON, ROBERT, sh. 1727, sett. Caroline Co, Va. (WMQ.2.22.345)

ROBERTSON, ROWLAND, Jacobite, tr. 28 July 1716, fr. Liverpool to Va, on *Godspeed,* arr. Md Oct. 1716. (SPC.1716.310)(CTB.31.209)(HM389)

ROBERTSON, WALTER, merchant, res. Glasgow, sh. pre 1765, sett. Petersburg, Va. (SRO.CS16.1.173)(SRA.T.MJ)

ROBERTSON, WILLIAM, b. 1650, res. Kindeace, Ross and Cromarty, m. Mary McKenzie 1671, sh. 1705 to Va, fa. of John, George, Thomas, Nathaniel, William, Mary, Catherine, Elspeth, Isabella and Anne, d. 1709 James City, Va. (OWC.7.6)

ROBERTSON, WILLIAM, s. of Archibald Robertson, res. Edinburgh, colonial official, sh, 1745, m. Elizabeth Fitzgerald 1748, fa. of Archibald, William, John, Christian and Susan. (CF.6.443)

ROBERTSON, WILLIAM, s. of William Robertson, merchant, res. Forfar, Angus, sett. Petersburg, Va, pre 1816. (SRO.RD5.187.241)(SRO.SH28.1.1818)

ROBESON, JOHN, b. 1776, farmer, m. Christianna -, sett. Monroe Co, Va. (N.A.-M932/982)

ROBINSON, DANIEL, Jacobite, tr. 24 Feb. 1747, fr. Liverpool to Va, on *Gildart*, arr. Port North Potomac, Md, 5 Aug. 1747. (P.3.282)(PRO.T1.328)

ROBINSON, JAMES, Jacobite, tr. 29 June 1716, fr. Liverpool to Jamaica or Va, on *Elizabeth and Anne,* arr. York, Va, 1716. (SPC.1716.310)(CTB.31.208) (VSP.1.185)

ROBINSON, JAMES, b. 1735, shoemaker, sett. King George Co, Va, militiaman in Va Regt 1757. (VMHB.1/2)(L)

ROBINSON, JAMES, tobacco merchant, sh. 1767, sett. Falmouth, Rappahannock River, Va, pre 1776, Loyalist. (PRO.AO12.56)(SRA.CFI)

ROBINSON, JAMES, b. 1758, whitesmith, sh. Mar. 1775, fr. London to Va, on *Betsey.* (PRO.T47.9/11)

ROBINSON, JOHN, Jacobite, tr. 29 June 1716, fr. Liverpool to Jamaica or Va, on *Elizabeth and Anne,* arr. York, Va, 1716. (SPC.1716.310)(CTB.31.208)(VSP.1.186)

ROBINSON, JOHN, factor, sett. Falmouth, Va, 1767-1774. (SRO.John C Brodie pp)

ROBINSON, JOHN, b. 1696, runaway, Queen Anne Co, Va, 1720. (Amer.Wkly.Mercury4.8.1720)

ROBINSON, JOHN, b. 11 Nov.1708, s. of William Robertson, res. Fordyce, Banffshire, sh. Feb. 1724, fr. London to Md. (CLRO/AIA)

ROBINSON, JOHN, b. 1736, planter, sett. Fredericksburg, Va, militiaman in Va Regt 1757. (VMHB.1/2)(L)

ROBINSON, ROBERT, Jacobite, tr. 29 June 1716, fr. Liverpool to Jamaica or Va, on *Elizabeth and Anne,* arr. York, Va, 1716. (SPC.1716.310)(CTB.31.208)(VSP.1.186)

ROBINSON, ROBERT, b. 1747, joiner and carpenter, sh. 1775, fr. Glasgow to Va, on *Friendship*, runaway Va 1775. (VaGaz23.6.1775)

ROBISON, JAMES, s. of Andrew Robison, clerk and factor, res. Dalry, Ayrshire, sh. Apr. 1761, fr. Glasgow to Va. (SRO.NRAS.1892)

RODAN, HOMER, sh. Dec. 1698, fr. Liverpool to Va, on *Globe*. (LRO.HO325.2Fre)

ROGERS, JOHN, b. 1726, sett. Md 1750, m. Elizabeth Reynolds 1760, fa. of John, d. 1791. (BLG2893)

ROLL, JOHN, b. 1752, gardener, res. Aberdeen, sh. May 1774, fr. London to Md. on *Minerva*. (PRO.T47.9/11)

RONALD, ALEXANDER. clergyman, sh. 1760 to Va. (EMA52)

ROSE, ALEXANDER, s. of John Rose and Margaret Grant, sett. King George Co, Va, 1768, d. 2 June 1786 Grantwood, Va. (SM.48.622)(WMQ.33.82)

ROSE, ALEXANDER, b. 1738, merchant, sh. pre 1755, sett. Va and N.C., m. Eunice Lea 1774, d. 12 Apr. 1807 Person Co, N.C. (RSA78)

ROSE, ALEXANDER, merchant, sett. Jamaica, d. 28 Nov. 1800 Fredericksburg, Va, bd. St George's. (Fredericksburg g/s)

ROSE, CHARLES, merchant, res. Tain, Ross and Cromarty, sh. pre 1776, sett. Smithfield, Va. (SRO.CS.GMB55)(SRO.AC.7.50)

ROSE, CHARLES, clergyman, res. Alves, Morayshire, sh. 1731, sett. Cople ph, Va, fa. of Robert, d. 1761. (OD16)(SA31)(EMA53)(WMQ.2.22.532)

ROSE, DUNCAN, merchant, res. Glasgow, sh. pre 1764, sett. Va. (SRA.B10.15.6969)

ROSE, JOHN, s. of John Rose and Margaret Grant, merchant, res. Forres, Morayshire, m. Anne Cumming 1735, fa. of Jean, Margaret, William, Patrick, Rachel and Alexander, d. 1762 Va. (DRF

ROSE, ROBERT, b. 12 Feb. 1704, s. of John Rose and Mary Grant, clergyman, res. Wester Alves, Morayshire, sh. 1725, sett. St Anne's ph, Essex Co, Va, 1725-1746, St Anne's ph, Albemarle Co, Va, 1747-1751, m. (1)Mary Tennant (2)Anne Fitzhugh, fa. of John and Hugh, d. 30 June 1751, bd. Richmond, Va. (VMHB.87.361)(BLG3017)(OD102)

ROSIER, EDWARD JAMES, b. 11 Aug. 1751, s. of James Rosier, res. South Ronaldsay, Orkney Islands, sailor in Va, gs. of Edward Rosier of Sucquoy, South Ronaldsay, Orkney Islands, (SRO.SH9.4.1801)

ROSS, ANDREW, s. of Professor Andrew Ross, merchant, edu. Glasgow Uni., d. 9 June 1752 Va. (SM.14.365)(MAGU3)

ROSS. ANDREW, b. 3 Feb. 1800, merchant, sett. Richmond, Va, pre 1830, m. Harriet Buckingham (2) Helen -, sett. N.Y. (ANY.2.270)

ROSS, DANIEL, b. 14 July 1760, res. Sutherland, sett. Baltimore, m. Mollie McDonald, Indian trader in Tennessee. (SG

ROSS, DAVID, b. 1664, carpenter, runaway, Bruton ph, York Co, Va, 18 Sep. 1699. (NCSA.CCR192)

ROSS, DAVID, s. of David Ross of Invercharron, sett. Baltimore, d. Sep. 1794, pro. 9 July 1804 Edinburgh. (SRO.CC8.8.135)

ROSS, DAVID, physician and merchant, sett. Bladenburg, Md, pro. 23 Feb. 1778. (MSA.Chancery48/390)(MSA.Prince George Co. Wills.T1.107)

ROSS, GEORGE, res. Ross and Cromarty, clergyman, edu. Edinburgh Uni., sett. Newcastle, Va, 1705. (SCHR.14.147)

ROSS, JAMES, b. 1765, sett. Fredericksburg, Spotsylvania Co, Va. (N.A.-M932/982)

ROSS, JANET, res. Edinburgh, thief and whore, tr. 28 Nov. 1704, fr. Leith, Midlothian, to Md. (SRO.PC2.28.307)

ROSS, JEAN, res. Jedburgh, Roxburghshire, gypsy, tr. 1 Jan. 1715, fr. Glasgow to Va. (GR530)

ROSS, JOHN, forger, tr. Feb. 1670, fr. Leith, Midlothian, to Va, on *Ewe and Lamb.* (PC.3.650)

ROSS, JOHN, Jacobite, tr. 24 May 1716, f. Liverpool to Md, on *Friendship,* arr. Md Aug. 1716. (SPC.1716.311)(HM387)

ROSS, JOHN, res. Island of Bute, sh. pre 1663, fr. Bristol to Va. (BRO.04220)

ROSS, JOHN, b. 1730, runaway, Fredericksburg, Va, 1746. (VaGaz7.8.1746)

ROSS, JOHN, merchant, res. Aberdeen, sett. Norfolk, Va, pre 1760. (MSA.Prince George Co Record Book 12.5.1760)

ROSS, JOHN, clergyman, edu. Aberdeen Uni., sh. 10 Oct. 1754, sett. All Hallows ph, Worcester Co, Md, d. 1780 Snowhill, Eastern Shore, Md. (SRO.CS16.1.179)(EMA53)

ROSS, JOHN, m. - Ritchie, sh. Glasgow to Md, sh. Philadelphia to Pictou, N.S., 1765 on *Hope.* (SC96)

ROSS, JOHN, , 1726, brewer, sett. Caroline Co, Va. (VSA.24296)

ROSS, JOHN, b. 1755, runaway, Va, 1773. (VaGaz30.9.1773)

ROSS, JOHN, merchant, res. Tain, Ross and Cromarty, sett. Philadelphia, m. Clementina Cruickshank, fa. of Charles, Clementina, Jean, Helen and Mary, pro. 19 Apr. 1809 Baltimore.

ROSS, RODERICK, sett. Grenada, d. 15 Oct. 1799 Norfolk, Va. (GC1301)

ROSS, THOMAS, b. 1683, laborer, res. Aberdeen, Jacobite, tr. 22 Apr. 1747, fr. Liverpool to Md, on Johnson, arr. Port Oxford, Md, 5 Aug. 1747. (P.3.290)(JAB.2.442)(PRO.T1.328)

ROSS, THOMAS, b. 1782, clerk, res. Tain, Ross and Cromarty, sett. City Point, Va, 1799, nat. Richmond, Va. (VSA,List of Aliens 1799)

ROSS, WILLIAM, b. 1731, planter, sett.Caroline Co, Va, militiaman in Va Regt 1757. (VMHB.1/2)(L)

ROWSAY, JOHN, res. Orkney Islands(?), goldsmith and jeweller, sett. Va pre 1773. (SRO.SH1.6.1773)

ROXBURGH, ANTHONY, sett. Nansemond, Va, 1767, Loyalist, sett. St Augustine, Florida, 1780. (PRO.AO13.32.455/462)

ROXBURGH, JAMES, b. 1758, husbandman, sh. Mar. 1774, fr. Whitehaven, Cumberland, to Va, on Ann. (PRO.T47.9/11)

RUSSELL, DAVID, b. 1727, glover, res. Aberdeen, Jacobite, tr. 22 Apr. 1747, fr. Liverpool to Md, on Johnson, arr. Port Oxford, Md, 5 Aug. 1747. (P.3.294)(PRO.T1.328)

RUSSELL, DAVID, merchant, sett. Blandford, Va, Loyalist, sett. Glasgow 1776. (PRO.AO12.109.260)(PRO.AO13.134.577)

RUSSELL, JAMES, b. 23 Apr. 1708, s. of James Russell and Anne Wightman, res. Kingseat, Slipperfield, Fife, sett. Nottingham Town, Prince George Co, Md, 1730, m. - Lee, burgess of Edinburgh 1753, (MdHistMag.72.165)

RUSSELL, JAMES, b. 1805, res. Lanarkshire, nat. 26 Aug. 1833 Norfolk City, Va.

RUSSELL, JOHN, b. 1723, sailmaker, res. Barry, Angus, Jacobite, tr. 24 Feb. 1747, fr. Liverpool to Va, on Gildart, arr. Port North Potomac, Md, 5 Aug. 1747. (P..3.294)(PRO.T1.328)

RUSSELL, WILLIAM, b. 1797, merchant, arr. Baltimore 1824. (N.A.-M596)

RUTHERFORD, GEORGE, Jacobite, tr. 29 June 1716, fr. Liverpool to Jamaica or Va, on Elizabeth and Anne. (SPC.1716.310)(CTB.31.208)

RUTHERFORD, JAMES, Jacobite, tr. 28 July 1716, fr. Liverpool to Va, on Godspeed, arr.Md Oct. 1716. (SPC.1716.310)(CTB.31.209)(HM389)

RUTHERFORD, JOHN, Jacobite, tr. 29 June 1716, fr. Liverpool to Jamaica or Va, on Elizabeth and Anne, arr. York, Va, 1716. (SPC.1716.310)(CTB.31.208)(VSP.1.186)

RUTHERFORD, JOHN, b. 1761, kidnapper, Frederick Co, Va, 1789. (VaGaz21.10.1789)

RUTHERFORD, RICHARD, b. 1791, farmer,sh. 1825, m. Ellen -, fa. of Ann, George, Susanna, Margaret, Isobel, Catherine and James, sett. Ritchie Co, Va. (N.A.-M932/982)

RUTHERFORD, ROBERT, merchant, set, Winchester, Va, pre 1765. (SRO.CS16.1.122)

RUTHERFORD, ROBERT, b. 20 Oct. 1728, edu. Edinburgh Uni., m. Mary D. Howe, sett. Fredericksburg, Va, d. Oct. 1803 Charlestown, Va. (WA530)

RUTHERFORD, THOMAS, b. 7 Jan. 1766, s. of Thomas Rutherford and Janet Meldrum, merchant, res. Kirkcaldy, Fife, edu. Glasgow Uni., sh. 1783, fr. Dublin to Va, sett. Richmond, Henrico Co, Va, m. Sallie Winston, fa. of John, d, 31 Jan. 1852 Richmond. (MAGU123)(BLG2897)(N.A.-M932/982)

SALKRIG, JAMES, b. 1709, tailor, runaway, Wonsbury, Va, 1739. (VaGaz23.3.1739)

SALMON, GEORGE, b. 1727, planter, sett. Stafford Co, Va, militiaman in Va Regt 1757. (VMHB.1/2)(L)

SAMPSON, GEORGE LESLIE, b. 2 Apr. 1798, merchant, res. Kirkcaldy, Fife, sett. Richmond, Va, d. Feb. 1866 N.Y. (ANY183)

SAMPSON, SAMUEL, currier, sett. Petesburg, Va, pre 1828. (SRO.SH1.12.1828)

SAMPSON, THOMAS, b. 1795, manufacturer, sett. Richmond, Va. (N.A.-M932/982)

SANDERS, JOHN, b. 1770, m. Helen -, sett. Frederick Co, Md. (N.A.-M432/277-299)

SANDERS, MARGARET, b. 1782, sett. Baltimore pre 1826, mo. of Matilda and James. (N.A.-M432/277-299)

SANDERS, ROBERT, b. 1796, farmer, sh. pre 1826, m. Susan -, fa. of William, Robert and Sarah, sett. Carroll Co, Md. (N.A.-M432/277-299)

SANDERSON, DANIEL, servant, res. Tyningham, East Lothian, vagabond, tr. Sep. 1668, fr. Leith, Midlothian, to Va, on *Convertin.* (PC.2.534)

SANGSTER, THOMAS, sett. N.S and Fairfax Co, Va, pre 1770, m. Mary Fuller, fa. of James. (CAG.1.457)

SAWERS, JOHN, res. Edinburgh, sett. Richmond, Va, d. 30 Sep. 1832. (SRO.D1299)

SAYERS, JOHN, merchant, sh. Aug. 1683, fr. Leith, Midlothian, to Va, on *Ewe and Lamb.* (SRO.E72.15.12)

SCHAW, JOHN, sett. Va pre 1776, Loyalist. (PRO.AO13.32.482)

SCHEVIZ, ALEXANDER, merchant, sett. Blandford, Prince George Co, Va, pre 1776, Loyalist, sett. Glasgow. (PRO.AO13.4.195)

SCHOLLER, BARBARA, b. 1659, da. of Edward Scholler, res. Stronsay, Orkney Islands, sh. Aug. 1685, fr. London to Va, m. - Whitefield. (CLRO/AIA)

SCOTT, ALEXANDER, b. 20 July 1686, s. of John Scott and Marjory Stuart, clergyman, sh. 1710, sett. Overwharton, Stafford Co, Va, m. Sarah Gibbs, d. 1 Apr. 1738, pro. 9 Jan. 1739. (SRO.CC8.8.101)(EMA53)(OD14)(SNQ.2.24)(F.6.402)(Aquia g/s)

SCOTT, ALEXANDER, merchant, res. Glasgow, sh. pre 1755, sett. Norfolk, Va. (SRA.CFI)

SCOTT, ANDREW, merchant and surgeon, res. Mallemy, Midlothian(?), sett. Md 1748. (SRO.CS16.1.80)

SCOTT, ARCHIBALD, b. 1745, clergyman, sh. to Pa, sett. Princed Edward Co, Va, 1777, d. 1799. (SA103)

SCOTT, CHARLES ROBERT, res. Edinburgh, planter, sett. Alexandria, pre 1797. (SRO.SH29.3.1797)

SCOTT, DAVID, tailor, res. Arbroath, Angus, Jacobite, tr. 24 Feb. 1747, fr. Liverpool to Va, on *Gildart,* arr. Port North Potomac, Md, 5 Aug. 1747. (P.3.300)(PRO.T1.328)(MR109)

SCOTT, EBENEZER, s. of Rev. Ebenezer Scott, res. Minnigaff, Galloway, sett. Va pre 1794. (SRO.RD3.267.50)

SCOTT, FRANCIS, merchant, res. Dumfries, Dumfriesshire, sett. Va pre 1748. (SRO.CS16.1.80)

SCOTT, GEORGE, res. Malenie, Midlothian, d. 1771 Prince George Co, Md. (HM.1.732)

SCOTT, HUGH, b. 27 May 1773, s. of William Scott and Elizabeth Ross, weaver, res. Glasgow, sh. 1801, sett. Norfolk, Va. (1812)

SCOTT, JAMES, b. 1699, s. of Rev. John Scott and Helen Grant, clergyman, res. Dipple, Elgin, Morayshire, sh. pre 1719, sett. Overwharton ph, Stafford Co, Va, and Dettingen ph, Prince William Co, Va, m. Sarah Brown 1738, fa. of Helen, Alexander, Catherine, James, Christian, John, Robert, William and Gustavus, d. 1782 Va. (VG593)(SA32) (SRO.RS29.5.228/7.216/8.172)(AA.9.163)

SCOTT, JAMES, b. 1704, smith, sett. Norfolk, Va, militiaman in Va Regt 1756. (VMHB.1/2)(L)

SCOTT, JAMES MUIR, physician, gs. of Rev. Scott, d. Waterford, Va, 20 Sep. 1821. (SM.89.559)

SCOTT, JAMES, b. 1778, tobacconist, sett. Va 1798, d. 1861 Richmond, Va. (VMHB.84.349)

SCOTT, JAMES, b. 1790, manufacturer, m. Ann -, fa. of John, Ellen, Anna and Mary, sett. Isle of Wight Co, Va. (N.A.-M932/982)

SCOTT, JOHN, Va, m. Betty Gordon, da. of Prof. Thomas Gordon, Aberdeen, 14 Nov. 1798. (AJ1768)

SCOTT, JOHN, clergyman, res. Dettingen ph, Prince William Co, Va, m. Elizabeth Innes, fa. of Robert and John, pro. 27 Apr. 1785 Fauquier Co, Va.

SCOTT, JOHN, b. 1718. planter, sett. Prince William Co, Va, militiaman in Va Regt. 1757. (VMHB.1/2)(L)

SCOTT, JOHN, b. 1728, sailor, sett. Prince William Co, Va, militiaman in Va Regt 1757. (VMHB.1/2)(L)

SCOTT, JOHN, merchant, m. Frances -, sett. Fredericksburg, Va, pre 1800. (WMQ.2.2.232)

SCOTT, ROBERT, b. 1708, husbandman, res. Berwickshire, sh. 1 Jan. 1736 to Md. (CLRO/AIA)

SCOTT, ROBERT, s,. of George Scott, watchmaker, res. Leith, Midlothian, sett. Fredericksburg, Va, pre 1781.   (SRO.CS16.1.183)(SRO.SH21.5.1779)

SCOTT, ROBERT, merchant, sett. Caroline Co, Va, pre 1764. (SRO.RD2.197.470)

SCOTT, ROBERT, clerk, res. Dundee, Angus, (?), sett. St Mary's Co, Md (MSA.Wills.20.836)

SCOTT, ROBERT, b. 2 Oct. 1745, mathematician and engraver, res. Edinburgh, sett. Va, m. Eunice Beall 1783, d. 3 Nov. 1823 Philadelphia.   (AP312)

SCOTT, THOMAS, merchant, res. Glasgow, sett. Blandford, Va, 1771, Loyalist. (PRO.AO13.4.195)(PRO.AO13.31.303)

SCOTT, THOMAS, tailor, runaway, Westmoreland Co, Va, 1774.   (VaGaz28.7.1774)

SCOTT, WALTER, merchant, res. Glasgow, sett. md pre 1752, pro. 14 Mar. 1752 Md.

SCOTT, WATSON, s. of Rev. Ebenezer Scott, res. Minnigaff, Galloway, sett. Va pre 1794. (SRO.RD3.267.50)

SCOTT, WILLIAM, sett. Va pre 1694.   (NEHGS:Scots Society MS)

SCOTT, WILLIAM, s. of Walter Scott, res. Kelso, Roxburghshire, sett. Prince William Co, Va, pre 1794.   (SRO.RD4.256.881)

SCOUGALL, JAMES, clergyman, res. Paisley, Renfrewshire, sh. pre 1743, sett. Ferry, Worcester Co, Md, 1746.   (F.7.665)

SCRAGGS, THOMAS, sh. to Md, on Mediterranean, pro. 31 May 1740.   (SRO/MEP)

SCRIMGEOUR, JOHN, clergyman, sett. Nomine, Westmoreland Co, Va, pro. 1693 PCC.

SEMPLE, JAMES, b. 18 May 1730, s. of Rev. James Semple and Margaret Glennie, clergyman, res. Dreghorn, Ayrshire, sh. 1755, sett. St Peter's, New Kent Co, Va, m. Rebecca Allen 1763, d. 1787. (WMQ.1.26.176)

SEMPLE, JOHN, b. 17 Oct. 1727, s. of Rev. James Semple and Margaret Glennie, res. Dreghorn, Ayrshire, sh. 1752, sett. Rosemount, King and Queen Co, Va, m. Elizabeth Walker 1761, fa. of John, Elizabeth, James and Robert, d. 1773, pro. 6 May 1783 Prince William Co, Va.   (WMQ.2.22.345)(CAG.1.900)(AGB.1.243)(WMQ.1.9.175) (VMHB.92.282)(SRA.B10.15.7082)(SRO.CS230.19.21)

SETON, JOHN, s. of Sir David Seton of Parbroath and Mary Gray, res. Fife, sh. 7 Aug. 1635, fr. London to Va. (PRO.E157/20)(AOF196)

SETON, WILLIAM, b. 24 Apr. 1746, s. of John Seton and Elizabeth Seton, sh. 1758, m. Rebecca Curzon, Baltimore 1767, fa. of William, James, John and Anna, merchant and banker, Loyalist, d. 9 June 1798. (FOS.1.303)

SHAFTOE, JOHN, Jacobite, tr. 28 July 1716, fr. Liverpool to Va, on *Godspeed*, arr. Md. (SPC.1716.310)(CTB.31.209)(MdArch.34.164)

SHANNINGTON, ELISABETH, b. 1788, sett. Baltimore. (N.A.-M432/277-299)

SHARP, JOHN, clergyman, edu. King's College, Aberdeen, sh. 1699 to Va, sett. Va and N.Y. (F.Ab.442)(EMA54)(KCA99)

SHARP, JOHN, b. 1792, merchant, arr. Baltimore 1824. (N.A.-M596)

SHAW, ALEXANDER, merchant, sett. Va pre 1778. (SRO.CS16.1.173)

SHAW, ANGUS, Jacobite, tr. 29 June 1716, fr.Liverpool to Jamaica or Va, on *Elizabeth and Anne*, arr. York, Va, 1716. (SPC.1716.310)(CTB.31.208)(VSP.1.185)

SHAW, DONALD, Jacobite, tr. 29 June 1716, fr. Liverpool to Jamaica or Va, on Elizabeth and Anne, arr. York, Va, 1716. (SPC.1716.310)(CTB.31.208) (VSP.1.185)

SHAW, JAMES, Jacobite, tr. 28 July 1716, fr. Liverpool to Va, on *Godspeed,* arr. Md Oct. 1716. (SPC.1716.310)(CTB.31.209)(HM389)

SHAW, JAMES, Jacobite, tr. 24 May 1716, fr. Liverpool to Va, on *Friendship,* arr. Md. (SPC.1716.311)(HM387)

SHAW, JOHN, cabinetmaker, sh. 1772, sett. Annapolis, Md. (SRA.CFI)

SHAW, JOHN, physician, m. Jane -, pro. 3 May 1809 Baltimore.

SHAW, JOHN, Jacobite, tr. 29 June 1716, fr. Liverpool to Jamaica or Va, on *Elizabeth and Anne,* arr. York, Va, 1716. (SPC.1716.310)(CTB.31.208)(VSP.1.186)

SHAW, MARGARET, b. 1732, spinner, res. Perthshire, Jacobite, tr. 22 Apr. 1747, fr. Liverpool to Va, on *Johnson,* arr. Port Oxford, Md, 5 Aug. 1747. (P.3.308)(PRO.T1.328)

SHAW, MARGARET, da. of John Shaw, res. Edinburgh, m. Dr John Feild, Prince George Co, Va, d. 1772. (SEV33)

SHAW, MARY, b. 1707, res. Inverness, Jacobite, tr. 22 Apr. 1747, fr. Liverpool to Va, on *Johnson,* arr. Port Oxford, Md, 5 Aug. 1747. (P.3.308)(PRO.T1.328)

SHAW, MATTHEW, sh. 2 Nov. 1674, to St Mary's Co, Md, on *Bachelor of Bristol.* (MSA.ESB.152)

SHAW, ROBERT, b. 1753, baker, sh. Apr. 1774, fr. London to Md, on *Diana,*
runaway, Alexandria, Va, 1775.   (PRO.T47.9/11)(VaGaz17.6.1775)

SHAW, THOMAS, Jacobite, tr. 28 July 1716, fr. Liverpool to Va, on *Godspeed,* arr. Md
Oct. 1716.   (SPC.1716.310)(CTB.31.209)(HM388)

SHAW, WILLIAM, Jacobite, tr. 28 July 1716, fr. Liverpool to Va, on *Godspeed,* arr, Md
Oct. 1716.   (SPC.1716.310)(CTB.31.209)(HM389)

SHEDDAN, JOHN, b. 1743, s. of Robert Sheddan of Roughwood and Jean Harvey, merchant,
res. Beith, Ayrshire, sett. Va pre 1770, d. Whitehaven, Cumberland.
(SRO.CS17.1.2)(HAF.1.274)

SHEDDAN, ROBERT, s. of Robert Sheddan and - Dobie, merchant, res. Beith, Ayrshire,
sh. 1759, sett. Portsmouth, James River, Va, Loyalist, d. Sep. 1826 London.
(SRO.CS16.1.161)(HAF.1.274)(PRO.AO13.33.78)(PRO.AO12.56.104)
(PRO.AO12.109.268)

SHEDDAN, ROBERT, s. of William Sheddan, merchant, res. Beith, Ayrshire, sett. Va
pre 1767.   (SRO.SH17.11.1767)

SHEDDAN, WILLIAM RALSTON, b. 23 Apr. 1747, s. of John Sheddan and Jean Ralston,
merchant, res. Roughwood, Beith, Ayrshire, sett. Hobshole, Rappahannock River, Va,
pre 1770, Loyalist, sett. Bermuda 1776-1783, sett. N.Y., d. 1798.
(HA.1.275)(SRO.CS16.1.161)(PRO.AO13.83.389)

SHEPHERD, ANDREW, b. 16 Aug. 1759, s. of George Shepherd and Isabel Smith,
merchant, res. Aberdeen, edu. King's College and Marischal College, Aberdeen,
sett. Va.   (SFV188)(KCA.2.342)(MCA.2.342)

SHEPHERD, JOHN, b. 1727, inn servant, res. Ferryden, Montrose, Angus, Jacobite,
tr. 24 Feb. 1747, fr. Liverpool to Va, on *Gildart,* arr. Port North Potomac, Md,
5 Aug. 1747.   (P.3.310)(PRO.T1.328)(MR109)

SHERIDAN, THOMAS, soldier, thief, tr. 1772, fr. Port Glasgow to Md, on Matty, arr.
Port Oxford, Md, 16 May 1772.   (SRO.JC27.10.3)

SHERIFF, JOHN, s. of Matthew Sheriff, sett. Md, Loyalist, sett. St Thomas, West Indies.
(SRO.CS16.1.179)(SRO.RD4.234.764)

SHERIFF, WILLIAM, Commisary at Annapolis, Md. 1717.   (NEHGS:Scots Society MS)

SHIELDS, JAMES, tr. 24 Apr. 1666, fr. Leith, Midlothian, to Va, on *Phoenix of Leith.*
(ETR107)

SHIELDS, JOHN, b. 1740, runaway, Anne Arundel Co, Md, 1770.   (Md Gaz13.9.1770)

SHIELDS, THOMAS, sh. 1725. m. Ann Bayard, sett. Bohemia Manor, Md.   (AABB207)

SHONGER, ALEXANDER, Jacobite, tr. 24 May 1716, fr. Liverpool to Va, on *Friendship,*
arr. Md Aug. 1716.   (SPC.1716.311)(HM311)

SHORT, JAMES jr, s. of John Short, sett. Va, pro. 26 Sep. 1787 Edinburgh. (SRO.CC8.8.127)

SHORT, JOHN, res. Edinburgh (?), sett. Va 1783, fa. of John. (SRO.CS17.1.2)(SRO.RD3.15.247)

SHORT, THOMAS, runaway, Va, 1752.   (VaGaz10.4.1752)

SHORT, THOMAS, optician (?). res. Edinburgh (?), sett. Va pre 1783. (SRO.CS17.1.2)(SRO.RD3.15.247)

SHORTREID, JOHN, sett. Va, d. 1792, pro. 29 Jan. 1801 Edinburgh. (SRO.CC8.8.132)

SIBBET, PETER, res, Haddington, East Lothian, d. pre 1678 Va, pro. July 1678 PCC.

SIM, ALEXANDER, sh. 2 Nov. 1674, to St Mary's Co, Md, on *Bachelor of Bristol.* (MSA.ESB.152)

SIMM, WILLIAM, Jacobite, tr. 24 May 1716, fr. Liverpool to Va, on *Friendship*, arr. Md Aug. 1716.   (SPC.1716.311)(HM386)

SIMMS, JAMES, tailor, res. Angus, sett. Annapolis, Md, pro. 4 Apr. 1735 Md. (MSA.Wills.21.457)

SIMPSON, ARCHIBALD, m. Eleanor -, fa. of John, sett. Dorchester Co, Md, d. 1738, pro. 14 Mar. 1739 Md.

SIMPSON, HOUSTON, shipmaster, d. 24 Sep. 1806 Baltimore. (GM.76.1168)

SIMPSON, JAMES, b. 1727, shoemaker, Arbroath, Angus, Jacobite, tr. 22 Apr. 1747, fr. Liverpool to Va, on *Johnson*, arr. Port Oxford, Md, 5 Aug. 1747. (P.3.314)(PRO.T1.328)(MR110)

SIMPSON, PATRICK, set. Md pre 1727. (NEHGS.Scots Char. Soc. MS)

SIMPSON, THOMAS, factor, sett. Hanover Town, Va, pre 1775. (SFV182)

SIMPSON, WILLIAM, Jacobite, tr. 28 July 1716, fr. Liverpool to Va, on *Godspeed*, arr. Md. Oct. 1716.   (SPC.1716.310)(CTB.31.209)(HM388)

SINCLAIR, AGNES, sh. 2 Nov. 1674, to St Mary's Co, Md, on *Bachelor of Bristol.* (MSA.ESB.152)

SINCLAIR, ALEXANDER, res. Glasgow, sh. 19 Oct. 1698, fr. Liverpool to Va, on *Loyalty.*   (LRO.HQ325.2.Fre)

SINCLAIR, ARTHUR, merchant skipper, res. Scalloway, Shetland Islands, sh. 1745, sett. Surrey Co, Va, d. 1791.   (VMHB.31.309)

SINCLAIR, JAMES, Jacobite, tr. 28 July 1716, fr. Liverpool to Va, on *Godspeed,* arr. Md Oct. 1716.
(SPC.1716.310)(CTB.31.209)(HM388)(MdArch.34.164)

SINCLAIR, JOHN, b. 1732, sett. Fredericksburg, Va,militiaman in Va Regt. 1757. (VMHB.1/2)(L)

SINCLAIR, JOHN, planter, sett. Leesburg, Va, d. 1800. (SCl406)

SINCLAIR, ROBERT, b. 1685, clergyman, sett. Va 1709-1711. (SCHR.14.147)

SINCLAIR, THOMAS, b. 1760, sh. 1783, fr. Nantz, France, to Baltimore. (MdGaz21.6.1785)

SINCLAIR, WILLIAM, Jacobite, tr. 31 July 1716, fr. Liverpool to Va, on *Anne*. (SPC.1716.310)(CTB.31.209)

SINCLAIR, WILLIAM, b. 1807, farmer, m. Mary -, arr. Baltimore 1829. (N.A.-M596)

SKENE, ROBERT, s. of Alexander Skene, res. Dyce, Aberdeenshire, sh. 1700, sett. Md, d. 1736, pro. 20 Oct. 1741 Edinburgh. (SRO.CC8.8.105)(APB.3.101)

SKINNER, CHARLES, b. 1746, husbandman, sh. June 1774, fr. London to Md, on *Industry*. (PRO.T47.9/11)

SKINNER, JAMES, b. 1800, farmer, m. Barbara -, arr. Baltimore 1834 , on *Herald*. (N.A.-M596)

SKINNER, JOHN, m. Eleanor, d. 1806 Baltimore Co, Md, pro. 16 Apr. 1806 Baltimore.

SKIRVIN, WILLIAM, sett. Somerset Co, Md, d. 1720, pro. 13 Jan. 1721 Md. (MSA.Wills.16.297)

SLOAN, ELIZABETH, b. 1790, sett. Baltimore. (N.A.-M432/277-299)

SLOAN, JAMES HALL, nat. 30 June 1821 Norfolk City, Va.

SLOANE, JOHN, sh. 2 Nov. 1674, to St Mary's Co, Md, on *Bachelor of Bristol*. (MSA.ESB.152)

SMALL, ANDREW, b. 28 Aug. 1794, s. of Andrew Small, teacher, res. Lochee, Dundee, Angus, sh. 1829, d. 6 Apr. 1847, Washington, D.C., bd. Darnestown, Montgomery Co. (Montgomery Co g/s)

SMALL, JAMES, Jacobite, tr. 24 May 1716, fr. Liverpool to Md, on *Friendship*, arr. Md Aug. 1716. (SPC.1716.311)(HM387)

SMALLWOOD, Mrs I. B., b. 1791, sh. pre 1830, sett. Washington, D.C., mo. of George, James, I., William and H. (N.A.-M432/277-99)

SMITH, ALEXANDER, Jacobite, tr. 24 May 1716, fr. Liverpool to Md, on *Friendship*, arr.Md Aug. 1716. (SPC.1716.311)(HM386)

SMITH, ALEXANDER, b. 1727, Jacobite, tr. 22 Apr. 1747, fr. Liverpool to Va, on *Johnson*, arr. Port Oxford, Md, 5 Aug. 1747. (P.3.318)(PRO.T1.328)

SMITH, ALEXANDER, b. 7 Dec. 1727, teacher, edu. Aberdeen Uni. 1743-1747, res. Slains, Aberdeenshire, sh. 1751 to N.Y., founder Washington College, Chestertown, Md, 1780, d. 14 May 1813. (SA132)

SMITH, ALEXANDER, b. 1791, m. Lydia -, fa. of Lydia, Elizabeth, Mary, Alexander and Jessie, sett. Baltimore. (N.A.M432.277/299)

SMITH, ANDREW, b. 1716, s. of Patrick Smith and Elizabeth Kerr, husbandman, res. Meldrum, Aberdeenshire, Jacobite, tr. 24 Feb. 1747, fr. Liverpool to Va, on *Gildart,* arr. Port North Potomac, Md, 5 Aug. 1747. (P.2.320)(JAB.2.443)(PRO.T1.328)

SMITH, ANDREW, b. 1729, weaver, res. Edinburgh, Jacobite, tr. 24 Feb. 1747, fr. Liverpool to Va, on *Gildart,* arr. Port North Potomac, Md, 5 Aug. 1747. (P.3.320)(MR207)(PRO.T1.328)

SMITH, B., hatter, arr. Baltimore 1821 on *Fairplay.* (N.A.-M596)

SMITH, CHARLES, Jacobite, tr. 29 June 1716, fr. Liverpool to Jamaica or Va, on *Elizabeth and Anne.* (SPC.1716.310)(CTB.31.208)

SMITH, CHARLES JEFFREY, clergyman, sett. Va and Md pre 1770, d. 1771. (VaGaz1.3.1770)

SMITH, ELIZABETH, tr. Aug. 1756, fr. Aberdeen to Va, on *St Andrew.* (AJ451)

SMITH, EUPHAME, tr. 1696, fr. Newhaven, Midlothian, to Va. (SRO.RH15.14.58)

SMITH, HENRY, b. 1789, farmer, m. Jeanetta -, sett. Alexandria Co, Va. (N.A.-M932/982)

SMITH, HUGH, b. 1796, sett. Alleghany Co, Md. (N.A.-M432.277/299)

SMITH, J., b. 1798, farmer, arr. Baltimore Sep. 1823. (PA300)

SMITH, JAMES, res. Strathspey, Morayshire, Jacobite, tr. 24 Feb. 1747, fr. Liverpool to Va, on *Gildart,* arr. Port North Potomac, Md, 5 Aug. 1747. (P.3.322)(MR193)(PRO.T1.328)

SMITH, JAMES, weaver, Kinninmonth, Aberdeenshire, tr. 1772, fr. Glasgow to Va, on *Brilliant,* arr. Port Hampton, Va, 7 Oct. 1772. (SRO.JC27.10.3)(AJ1272)

SMITH, JAMES, b. 1712, res. Ayr, sh. Jan. 1729, fr. London to Md. (CLRO/AIA)

SMITH, JAMES, b. 1798, farmer, arr. Baltimore 1823. (N.A.-M596)

SMITH, JOHN, runaway, Soldiers' Delight, Baltimore, 1758. (MdGaz17.8.1758)

SMITH, JOHN, b. 1738, physician, sh. to N.C. 1763, sett. Charles Co, Md, and Norfolk, Va, pre 1776, Loyalist. (PRO.AO12.6.72)(PRO.AO12.109.276)(SA178) (PRO.AO13.62.193)

SMITH, JOHN, gs. of John Smith in Drongan, sett. Va pre 1779. (SRO.SH16.1.1779)

SMITH, JOHN, nat. 23 June 1806 Norfolk City, Va.

SMITH, JOSEPH, res. Essex Co, Rappahannock River, Va, burgess of Glasgow 1716. (BGBG325)

SMITH, NICHOLAS, res. Richmond, Va, burgess of Glasgow 1716. (BGBG325)

SMITH, PATRICK, Jacobite, tr. 27 July 1716, fr. Liverpool to Va, on *Godspeed*, arr. Md Oct. 1716. (SPC.1716.310)(HM388)

SMITH, ROBERT, Jacobite, tr. 29 June 1716, fr. Liverpool to Jamaica or Va, on *Elizabeth and Anne*, arr. York, Va, 1716. (SPC.1716.310)(CTB.31.208)(VSP.1.185)

SMITH, ROBERT, b. 1756, husbandman, sh. Mar. 1774, fr. Whitehaven, Cumberland, to Va on *Anne*. (PRO.T47.9/11)

SMITH, THOMAS, Jacobite, tr. 24 May 1716, fr. Liverpool to Md, on *Friendship*, arr. Md Aug. 1716. (SPC.1716.311)(HM387)

SMITH, THOMAS, b. 1778, cabinet-maker, m. Cecilia -, fa. of Patrick, James, Mary, and Isabella, sh. pre 1829, sett. Baltimore. (N.A.-M432/277-299)

SMITH, WILLIAM, s. of William Smith, sh. July 1684, fr. London to Md. (CLRO/AIA)

SMITH, WILLIAM, res. Dunbar, East Lothian, m. Jane Bulcraig, sett. Va, pro. Jan. 1738 PCC.

SMITH, WILLIAM, Jacobite, tr. 24 Feb. 1747, fr. Liverpool to Va, on *Gildart*, arr Port North Potomac, Md, 5 Aug. 1747. (PRO.T1.328)

SMITH, WILLIAM, b. 1727, clergyman,res. Aberdeen, sett. Chester ph, Kent Co, Md, m. - Tilghman, Archbishop of Md, d. 1803. (DAB.17.353)

SMITH, WILLIAM, b. 1750, runaway, Newcastle, Va, 10 Dec. 1774. (VaGaz5.1.1775)

SMITH, WILLIAM, sh. 1806, sett. Newport, Dumfries, Va. (1812)

SNEDDON, JAMES, b. 1800, papermaker, sett. Baltimore. (N.A.-M432/56-57)

SNODGRASS, JOHN, factor, res. Glasgow, sh. pre 1776, sett. Goochland, Va. (SRA.B10.12.4)

SNODGRASS, NEIL, merchant, res. Paisley, Renfrewshire, sett. Norfolk, Va, d. 1782 N.Y., pro. 10 Apr. 1788 Edinburgh, pro. Apr. 1785 PCC. (SRO.CC8.8.127)(SRO.CS16.1.114)

SNODGRASS, WILLIAM, s. of John Snodgrass and Anne Nisbet,merchant, res. Dreghorn, Ayrshire, sett. Richmond, Va, Loyalist. (SRO.CS.GMB58)(HAF.1.452)

SOMERVILLE, ANDREW, b. 1758, physician, sett. Va, d. 1833. (SA188)

SOMERVILLE, JAMES, b. 1693, s. of James Somerville of Kennox, res. Ayrshire, physician, Jacobite , tr. 28 July 1716, fr. Liverpool to Va, on *Godspeed*, arr. Md Oct. 1716, m. Sarah Howe, fa. of Rebecca, John and James, d. 15 Feb. 1751 Calvert Co, Md. (SPC.1716.310)(CTB.31.209)(HM389)(SG.37.111)(CF.2.691) (MdArch25.347/9)(SRO.208.430)

SOMERVILLE, JAMES, b. 1731, planter, sett. Fredericksburg, Va, militiaman in Va Regt 1757.   (VMHB.1/2)(L)

SOMERVILLE, JAMES, b. 1744, s. of John Somerville and Margaret Cunningham. Midlothian, merchant, sett. Baltimore pre 1769, Loyalist, d. 5 July 1806 Baltimore.   (SRO.CS16.1.138)(CF.3.533)(DPCA213)

SOMERVILLE, JAMES, b. 23 Feb. 1742, merchant, res. Glasgow, sett. Fredericksburg and Caroline Co, Va, d. 25 Apr. 1798 Port Royal, Va, bd. Masonic Cemetery. (VG16)(WMQ.2.2.225)

SOMERVILLE, JAMES, b. 16 Oct. 1774, s. of Walter Somerville and Mary Gray, res. Glasgow, merchant, sett. Fredericksburg, Va, m. Mary Attwell, fa. of James, Margaret, Henry, Walter, Albert, Julia, Samuel, Robert, Mary, William and Jane, d. 29 Aug. 1858 Culpepper Co, Va.   (VG16)(N.A.-M932/982)

SOMERVILLE, WILLIAM, b. 1775, m. Mary -, sett. Rockbridge Co, Va.   (N.A.-M932/982)

SOUTAR, JOHN, joiner, res. Ellon, Aberdeenshire, Jacobite, tr. 22 Apr. 1747, fr. Liverpool to Va, on *Johnson,* arr. Port Oxford, Md, 5 Aug. 1747. (P.3.360)(MR133)(PRO.T1.328)

SOUTTER, ROBERT, b. 9 Dec. 1773, merchant, res. Dundee, Angus, m. Margaret Taylor 1806, fa. of James and Eliza, sett. Norfolk, Va, nat. 20 Mar. 1810 Norfolk, d. 24 Jan. 1842 Norfolk, Va.   (ANY.2.220)(LNA149)

SOUTAR, THOMAS, b. 1798, machinist, m. Mary -, sett. Richmond, Va. (N.A.-M932/982)

SPALDING, ALEXANDER, Jacobite, tr. 24 May 1716, fr. Liverpool to Md, on *Friendship,* arr. Md Aug. 1716.   (SPC.1716.311)(HM386)

SPARK, ALEXANDER, merchant, res. Arbuthnott, Kincardineshire, sett. Westmoreland Co, Va, pro. 25 Aug. 1767 Westmoreland.

SPARK, WILLIAM, res. Arbuthnott, Kincardineshire, sett. St Thomas, Surrey Co, Jamaica, pro. 25 Aug. 1767 Westmoreland Co, Va.

SPEDEN, WILLIAM, s. of Robert Speden, res. Bowden, sett. Washington, D.C. pre 1819. (SRO.SH11.7.1819)

SPEED, WILLIAM, Jacobite, tr. 24 Feb. 1747, fr. Liverpool to Va, on *Gildart,* arr. Port North Potomac, Md, 5 Aug. 1747.   (PRO.T1.328)

SPEIRS, ALEXANDER, b. 1714, s. of John Speirs, merchant and planter, res. Edinburgh, sh. 1740, sett. Elderslie, Va, m. (1) Sarah Carey (2) Mary Buchanan, d. 1782 Glasgow.   (SRA.B10.15.5943)

SPEIRS, JAMES, merchant and planter, res. Glasgow, sh. pre 1754, sett. Va. (SRA.B10.15.6653)

SPEIRS, JUDITH, da. of John Speirs, res. Edinburgh, m. David Bell, sett. Elderslie, Va, pre 1754.   (SRA.B10.15.6653)

SPENCE, HELEN, tr. 1696, fr. Newhaven, Midlothian, to Va.   (SRO.RH15.14.58)

SPENCE, JAMES, b. 1794, res. Glasgow, d. 1 Aug. 1831, Alexandria, Va. (Natl.Intelligencer3.8.1831)

SPENCE, JOHN, b. 1766, physician, res. Edinburgh, sett. Va, d. 1829.   (SA188)

SPENCE, PETER, s. of Peter Spence, surgeon, res. Linlithgow, West Lothian, sett. Va pre 1775.   (SRO.CS16.1.165)(SRO.CS.GMB301)

SPENCE, WILLIAM, b. 1751, baker, sh. Apr. 1774, fr. London to Md, on *Diana*. (PRO.T47.9/11)

SPENCER, JOHN, b. 1737, housecarpenter and joiner, runaway, Anne Arundel Co, Md, 1777.   (MdGaz5.6.1777)

SPOTSWOOD, ALEXANDER, s. of Dr Robert Spotswood and Catherine Elliot, sh. 1710, m. Ann Bryan 1724, Lt Governor of Va, Deputy Postmaster General of America 1730, fa. of John, d. 7 June 1740 Annapolis, Md.   (AGB.1.174)

SPRATT, DANIEL, res. Fife or Edinburgh, sett. Urbanna, Middlesex Co, Va, pro. 28 Dec. 1807 Williamsburg, Va.

SPRATT, ROBERT BEVERLEY, res. Fife or Edinburgh, sett. Urbanna, Middlesex Co, Va, pro. 22 Apr. 1805 Williamsburg, Va.

SPROULE, ANDREW, s. of John Sproule, res. Milton, Galloway, merchant, sh. 1735, sett. Gosport, Norfolk Co, Va, m. Annabella McNeil, Loyalist, d. 1776, bd. Portsmouth, Va, pro. 22 Jan. 1779 Edinburgh, pro. Mar. 1782 PCC.   (SRO.1.2.1777)(SRO.CC8.8.124) (PRO.AO13.31.244)

STAMPER, MARIANNA, b. 1749, sh.24 Apr. 1770, fr. Scotland to Va, on *Golden Fleece*, arr. Va. 13 June 1770.   (UNC.SHC.360)

STARK, JAMES, b. 1695, s. of John Stark, sh. 1710, sett. Londonderry, N.H., m. Elizabeth Thornton, sett. Stafford Co, Va, 1720, d. 1754, pro. 1754 Stafford Co.

STARRAT, MARGARET, b. 1804, arr. Baltimore 1823, with bros/sis (?) John, Thomas, Ezekial, Robert, Ann, Margery and Sarah.   (N.A.-M596)

STEEL, ALEXANDER, forger, tr. Feb. 1670, fr. Leith, Midlothian, to Va on *Ewe and Lamb*. (PC.3.650)

STEEL, MICHAEL, laborer, res. Logie Almond, Perthshire, Jacobite, tr. 22 Apr. 1747, fr. Liverpool to Va, on *Johnson*, arr. Port North Potomac, Md, 5 Aug. 1747. (P.3.332)(MR27)(PRO.T1.328)

STENHOUSE, ALEXANDER, physician, sh. 1756, sett. Baltimore, Loyalist, sett. Britain. (PRO.AO12.6.60)(PRO.AO12.109.276)(MdMag.2.135)

STEPHEN, ADAM, b. 1718, physician, edu. Aberdeen and Edinburgh Unis. 1740s, sh. 1748 to Md, sett. Fredericksburg, Va, 1754, d. 16 Sep. 1791 Martinsburg, Berkeley Co, Va. (RAV86)(SA188)(VaGaz10.8.1791)

STEPHEN, JAMES, res. Fife, m. Rebecca -, fa. of William, Mary and Alexander, d. 1802 Md, pro. 24 July 1802 Md.

STEPHEN, JOHN, b. 2 Sep. 1740, clergyman, res. Gaitly, sh. 1764, sett. Tobago and Md, d. 1784 Md. (EMA57)(FPA318)

STEVEN, JEAN, tr. Aug. 1756, fr. Aberdeen to Va, on *St Andrew*. (AJ451)

STEVENS, JAMES, miller, res. Balornock, Glasgow, sett. Halifax Co, Va, pre 1773. (VMHB.30.66)

STEVENS, JANE MARY, b. 1813, arr. Baltimore 1823. (N.A.-M596)

STEVENS, WILLIAM, b. 1815, arr. Baltimore 1823. (N.A.-M596)

STEVENSON, NATHANIEL, b. 1734, barber, sett. Northampton Co, Va, militiaman in Va Regt 1756. (VMHB.1/2)

STEVENSON, ROBERT, b. 1796, sett. Alleghany Co, Md. (N.A.-M432.277-299)

STEVENSON, WILLIAM, s. of James Stevenson, physician, edu. Glasgow Uni., sett. Va. (WMQ.2.21.177)

STEWART, ADAM, merchant, sett. Georgetown, Frederick Co, Md, 1755, Loyalist, sett. Ayr. (PRO.AO12.8.54)(PRO.AO12.109.272)

STEUART, ALEXANDER, res. Shetland Islands, sh. 7 Dec. 1774, fr. London to Va, on *Planter*, arr. Fredericksburg, Va, 10 May 1774. (PRO.T47.9/11)

STEWART, ALEXANDER, sett. Va pre 1766. (SRO.CS16.1.125)

STEWART, ALEXANDER, Jacobite, tr. 29 June 1716, fr. Liverpool to Jamaica or Va, on *Elizabeth and Anne*, arr. York, Va, 1716. (SPC.1716.310)(CTB.31.208)(VSP.1.186)

STEWART, ALEXANDER, b. 1713, footman, res. Perthshire, Jacobite, tr. 14 May 1747, fr. Liverpool to Md, arr. Port North Potomac, Md, 5 Aug. 1747, sett. Wicomico, Md, (P.3.336)(MR8)(PRO.T1.328)

STEWART, ALEXANDER, b. 9 Dec. 1725, s. of Rev. James Stewart and Elizabeth Campbell, res. Perthshire, sh. 1751, sett. Va and N.C. (F.6.169)(SCM.6.10)

STEWART, ALEXANDER, b. 1736, planter, sett. Stafford Co, Va, militiaman in Va Regt 1756. (VMHB.1/2)(L)

STEWART, ALEXANDER, thief, sett. Newcastle, Va, pre 1776. (VaGaz6.7.1776)

STEWART, ANTHONY, s. of James Stewart, merchant, res. Edinburgh, merchant, sett. Annapolis, Md, 1753, Loyalist. (SRO.CS17.1.2)(PRO.AO12..6.322) (PRO.AO12.109.274)(All Hallows OPR, Anne Arundel Co, 146)

STEWART, ARCHIBALD, b. 1789, res. Paisley, Renfrewshire, nat. 23 Feb. 1829, Norfolk City, Va.

STEWART, CHARLES, sh. 1742, sett. Caroline Co, Va. (WMQ.2.22.345)

STEWART, CHARLES, merchant, sett. Va pre 1756. (SRO.CS16.1.99)

STEWART, CHARLES, merchant, res. Orkney Islands, colonial official, sett. Norfolk, Va, 1755. (NLS.MS5025/46)

STEWART, CHARLES, d. 1803, Queen Anne Co, Md. (GM.73.1254)

STEWART, CHRISTINA, b. 1751, da. of John Stewart, Earl of Traquair, res. Peeblesshire, m. Cyrus Griffin, d. 1807 Va. (Bruton g/s)

STEWART, DANIEL, Jacobite, tr. 28 July 1716, fr. Liverpool to Va, on *Godspeed,* arr. Md Oct. 1716. (SPC.1716.310)(CTB.31.209)(HM388)

STEWART, DANIEL, s. of Daniel Stewart, res. Edinburgh (?), sett. Petersburg, Va, pre 1802. (SRO.RD3.296.828)(SRO.RD3.308.595)

STEWART, DAVID, b. 1616, sett. Anne Arundel Co, Md, pre 1661, d. 1696. (SCM.9.5)

STEWART, DAVID, Jacobite, tr. 24 May 1716, fr. Liverpool to Md, on *Friendship*, arr. Md Aug. 1716. (SPC.1716.311)(HM387)

STEWART, DAVID, nat. 27 Nov. 1792 Norfolk City, Va.

STEWART, DONALD, Jacobite, tr. 29 June 1716, fr. Liverpool to Jamaica or Va, on *Elizabeth and Anne,* arr. York, Va, 1716. (SPC.1716.310)(CTB.31.208)(VSP.1.186)

STEWART, DONALD, res. Strathie, Aberdeenshire, horsethief, tr. 1775, fr. Greenock, Renfrewshire, to Va, on *Rainbow*, arr. Port Hampton, Va, 3 May 1775. (SRO.JC27.10.3)(AJ1321)

STEWART, GEORGE, b. 1695, physician, sett. Annapolis, Md, 1720. (SA178)

STEWART, GEORGE HUME, res. Kilmadock, Perthshire, sett. Md 1722, m. Anne Digges, sett. Prince George Co, and Anne Arundel Co, Md, Loyalist, fa. of David and William, d. pre 1788. (PRO.AO12.6.229)(PRO.AO13.62.406)(PRO.AO13.62.390) (SRO.RD4.246.179)

STEWART, JAMES, b. pre 1713, gardener, runaway, Urbanna, Va, 1739. (VaGaz16.3.1739)

STEWART, JAMES, s. of Thomas Stewart of Kinnaird, sh. 1725 to Va. (SRO.GD38.3)

STEWART, JAMES, Jacobite, tr. 29 June 1716, fr. Liverpool to Jamaica or Va, on *Elizabeth and Anne*, arr. York, Va, 1716. (SPC.1716.310)(CTB.31.208)(VSP.1.186)

STEWART, JAMES, b. 1789, stonecutter, arr. Baltimore, Mar. 1820, on schooner *Only Daughter.* (PA41)

STEWART, JANET, sewing mistress, res. Corstorphine, Midlothian, infanticide, tr. 1771, fr. Port Glasgow to Md, on *Crawford*, arr. Port Oxford, Md, 23 July 1771. (SRO.JC27.10.3)

STEWART, JEAN, tailor's servant, res. Edinburgh, tr. 1773, fr. Port Glasgow to Va, on *Phoenix*, arr. Port Accomack, Va, 20 Dec. 1773. (SRO.JC27.10.3)

STEWART, JOHN, s. of Angus Stewart, res. Atholl, Perthshire, thief, tr. 28 Nov 1704, fr. Leith, Midlothian, to Md. (SRO.PC2.28.307)

STEWART, JOHN, sh. pre 1690, sett. Wadboo, S.C., and Va. (LJ34)

STEWART, JOHN, Jacobite, tr. 29 June 1716, fr. Liverpool to Jamaica or Va, on *Elizabeth and Anne*, arr. York, Va, 1716.(SPC.1716.310)(CTB.31.208)(VSP.1.186)

STEWART, JOHN, Jacobite, tr. 28 July 1716, fr. Liverpool to Va, on *Godspeed*, arr. Md Oct. 1716. (SPC.1716.310)(CTB.31.209)(HM388)

STEWART, JOHN, b. 1793, constable, m. Elizabeth -, fa. of John, Mary and Maria, sh. pre 1825, sett. Baltimore. (N.A-M432/277-99)

STEWART, JOHN, b. 1800, rigger, m. Betsey, sh. pre 1825, fa. of John, sett. Norfolk, Va. (N.A.-M932/982)

STEWART, JOHN, storekeeper, sett. Va pre 1771. (SFV41)

STEWART, Colonel JOHN, d. June 1794 Somerset Co, Md. (SM.55.655)

STEWART, JOHN, b. 1790, hack-proprietor, m. B. -, fa. of John and E., sh. pre 1828, sett. Baltimore. (N.A.-M432/277-99)

STEWART, MALCOLM, Jacobite, tr. 29 June 1716, fr. Liverpool to Jamaica or Va, on *Elizabeth and Ann*, arr. York, Va, 1716. (SPC.1716.310)(CTB.31.208)(VSP.1.186)

STEWART, MARJORY, res. Edinburgh, whore and thief, tr. 28 Nov. 1704, fr. Leith, Midlothian, to Md. (SRO.PC2.28.307)

STEWART, PATRICK, Jacobite, tr. 29 June 1716, fr. Liverpool to Jamaica or Va, on *Elizabeth and Anne*, arr. York, Va, 1716. (SPC.1716.310)(CTB.31.208)(VSP.1.186)

STEWART, RICHARD, b. 1754, baker, res. Edinburgh, sh. May 1774, fr. London to Md, on *Brothers*. (PRO.T47.9/11)

STEWART, ROBERT, Jacobite, tr. 29 Apr. 1716, fr. Liverpool to Jamaica or Va, on *Elizabeth and Anne*. (SPC.1716.310)(CTB.31.208)

STEWART, ROBERT, b. 1736, planter, sett. Stafford Co, Va, militiaman in Va Regt 1757.   (VMHB.1/2)(L)

STEWART, ROBERT, b. 1745, res. Edinburgh, sett. Baltimore, Md, m. Susanna -, d. 29 Oct. 1826.   (SG.14.38)

STEWART, ROBERT, merchant, res. Inveravon, Banffshire, sett. Petersburg, Va, pro. 13 Apr. 1816 Edinburgh.   (SRO.CC8.8.142)

STEWART, ROGER, merchant, sett. Portsmouth, Va, pre 1776, Loyalist, sett. Greenock, Renfrewshire, 1780.   (PRO.AO13.33.247)(SRO.CS16.1.179)

STEWART, WILLIAM, clergyman, edu. Glasgow Uni. 1718, sett. Manokin and Wicomico, Va.   (APC.192)

STEWART, WILLIAM, res. Ardshiel, Argyllshire, Jacobite, tr. 22 Apr. 1747, fr. Liverpool to Va, on Johnson, arr. Port Oxford, Md, 5 Aug. 1747, (d. 1786 Surry Co, Va?)   (P.3.348)(PRO.T1.328)(MR12)

STEWART, WILLIAM, res. Monteith, Stirlingshire, sett. Annapolis, Md, pre 1747. (MdHist.Mag.1.349)(LM.2.212)

STEWART Dr, res. Monteith, Stirlingshire, sett. Annapolis, Md, pre 1747. (LIM.2.212)

STILL, JOHN ALEXANDER, b. 1738, sett. Hanover Co, Va, pre 1776.   (VSL23816)

STINSON, JOHN, sh. 2 Nov. 1674, to St Mary's Co, Md, on *Bachelor of Bristol*. (MSA.ESB.152)

STIRLING, JAMES, clergyman, sh. 1737, sett. Md.   (EMA57)

STIRLING, JAMES, b. 1752, sh. 1774, m. Elizabeth Gibson 1782, fa. of Archibald, Loyalist, sett. Baltimore, d. 25 June 1820.   (BLG2926)(PRO.AO13.33)

STIRLING, JOSEPH, sh. 1740, sett. Caroline Co, Va.   (WMQ.2.22.345)

STIRLING, MABEL, gypsy, res. Roxburghshire, tr. 1 Jan. 1715, fr. Glasgow to Va. (GR530)

STIRLING, THOMAS, m. Christian -, fa. of Thomas and Eliza, sett. Calvert Co, Md, d. 24 Jan. 1685, pro. 27 June 1685 Md.   (MSA.Wills4.150)

STOBO, ROBERT, b. 7 Oct. 1726, s. of William Stobo, merchant and soldier, res. Glasgow, edu. Glasgow Uni. 1742, sh. 1742, sett. Williamsburg, Va, d. 19 June 1770 Chatham, England.   (DCB.3.600)(SRO.SC36.63.2)

STODDART, JAMES, surveyor, sett. La Plata, Md, 1650.   (DAB.18.63)

STOTT, EBENEZER, res. Kelton, Kirkcudbrightshire, sett. Petersburg, Va, pre 1814. (SRO.RD5.54.600)

STOTT, WATSON, merchant, sett. Petersburg, Va, pre 1841.   (WMQ.2.17.3)

STRACHAN, ALEXANDER GLASS, b. 29 July 1748, s. of Joseph Strachan and Elizabeth Glass, druggist and physician, res. Edinburgh, edu. Edinburgh Uni., sett. Petersburg, Va, pre 1772, m. Sarah Field. (SA188)

STRACHAN, DAVID, clergyman, sh. 1715 to Va. (EMA57)

STRACHAN, JAMES, b. 1728, res. Kincardineshire, edu. Aberdeen Uni., Jacobite, tr. 24 Feb. 1747, fr. Liverpool to Va, on *Gildart*, arr. Port North Potomac, Md, 5 Aug. 1747. (P.3.352)(JAB.2.444)(MR76)(PRO.T1.328)

STRACHAN, JAMES, b. 1756, laborer, sh. Nov. 1774, fr. Bristol to Md, on *Sampson*. (PRO.T47.9/11)

STRACHAN, JOHN, sh. Dec. 1698, fr. Liverpool to Va, on *Globe*. (LRO.HQ325.2.Fre)

STRACHAN, MARGARET, res. Aberdeen, thief, tr. Nov. 1667, fr. Aberdeen to Va. (ABR.ARC1667)

STRACHAN, MARGARET, tr. 1696, fr. Newhaven, Midlothian, to Va. (SRO.RH15.14.58)

STRACHAN, PATRICK, s. of Patrick Strachan and Jean Rait, tailor, res. Aberdeen, sh. 1711 to Va, d. 1723 Jamaica. (APB.2.153)

STRACHAN, PETER, physician, sett. Va 1745, Loyalist. (PRO.AO13.83.640)

STRACHAN, SUSAN, res. Aberdeen, m. John Mitchell, sett. Va pre 1797. (SRO.SH20.5.1797)

STRACHEY, JOHN, b. 1709, physician, sett. Va, d. 1759. (SA188)

STRANGE, JAMES, merchant, res. Glasgow, sett. Petersburg, Va, d. 15 June 1809. (SM.69.558)

STRATON, JANET, tr. 1696 , fr. Newhaven, Midlothian, to Va. (SRO.RH15.14.58)

STRATTON, JAMES, b. 1672, mason, res. Morayshire, Jacobite, tr. 24 Apr. 1747, fr. Liverpool to Va, on *Johnson,* arr. Port Oxford, Md, 5 Aug. 1747. (P.3.356)(PRO.T1.328)

STRAUGHAN, WILLIAM, b. 1613, sh. 28 May 1635, fr. London to Va, on *Speedwell*. (PRO.E157.20)

STRETTON, JAMES, b. 1651, sh. May 1683, fr. London to Md, on *Elizabeth and Mary*. (CLRO/AIA)

STROAK, WILLIAM, Jacobite, tr. 29 June 1716, fr. London to Jamaica or Va, on *Elizabeth and Anne,* arr. York, Va, 1716. (SPC.1716.310)(CTB.31.208)(VSP.1.186)

STUART, ANGUS, thief, tr. Mar. 1758, fr. Aberdeen to Va, on *Leathly*. (AJ533)

STUART, Lady CHRISTIAN ELIZABETH, b. 1741,da. of John Stuart, Earl of Traquair, and Christian Anstruther, m. Cyrus Griffin, sett. Williamsburg,Va, 1773, d. 8 Oct. 1807. (SRO.RD3.239.683)(SP.8.408)

STUART, DAVID, clergyman, sh. 1715, d. 1749 St Paul's, Va. (CCVC49)

STUART, DAVID, m. Margaret Lynn, sett. Augusta Co, Va, d. 1767. (RAV88)

STUART, EDWARD, sett. Millington, Kent Co, Md, pre 1776, m. Sarah Evans, fa. of William, Henry, Edward and John, d. post 1792. (MdHistMag.12.390)(MdGen.2.43)

STUART, JAMES, clergyman, sh. 1766 to Va. (EMA57)

STUART, Dr JOHN, sett. Baltimore 1748, fa. of Daniel, Elizabeth, Comfort, Ann, Mary and William, d. 1774 Sussex Co, Del. (SG.33.235)

STUART, JOHN, b. 1754, merchant, res. Glasgow, sett. Petersburg, Va, d. 1 Feb. 1814. (Blandford g/s)

STUART, ROBERT, Jacobite, tr. 29 June 1716, fr. Liverpool to Jamaica or Va, on Elizabeth and Anne, arr. York, Va, 1716. (SPC.1716.310)(VSP.1.186)

STUBBS, ROBERT, Jacobite, tr. 24 May 1716, fr. Liverpool to Md, on *Friendship,* arr. Md 20 Aug. 1716. (SPC.1716.311)(HM387)

SULLY, ELIZABETH, b. 1775, sh. pre 1795, mo. of Sarah and Charlotte, sett. Richmond, Va. (N.A.-M932/982)

SUTHERLAND, ADAM, Jacobite, tr. 22 Apr. 1747, fr. Liverpool to Va, on *Johnson,* arr. Port Oxford, Md, 5 Aug. 1747. (PRO.T1.328)

SUTHERLAND, ANDREW, arr. Philadelphia 1773, indented to Samuel Ingles, Va, 23 Sep. 1773. (RecIndent.Phila.)

SUTHERLAND, DANIEL, pickpocket and vagrant, tr. 1773, fr. Glasgow to Va, on *Donald,* arr. Port James, Upper District, Va, 13 Mar. 1773, runaway Apr. 1773. (SRO.B59.26.116.21)(SRO.JC27.10.3)(AJ1293)(SM.34.579)(VaGaz15.4.1773)

SUTHERLAND, G., b. 1792, sett. Washington, D.C. (N.A.-M432/56-57)

SUTHERLAND, JAMES, res. South Ronaldsay, Orkney Islands, sett. Fredericksburg, Va, pre 1774. (Spotsylvania Deeds H.17.3.1774)

SUTHERLAND, JOHN, s. of James Sutherland, physician, res. Winbreck, Orkney Islands, sett. St George's ph, Spotsylvania Co, Va, m. Susannah Brent 1756, d. 10 July 1751, pro. 1 July 1765 Spotsylvania Co, Va. (Spotsylvania Wills D213)(VMHB.19.94)

SUTHERLAND, WILLIAM, res. South Ronaldsay, Orkney Islands, sett. Fredericksburg, Va, pre 1774. (Spotsylvania Deeds H.17.3.1774)

SWAN, JOHN, s. of John Swan, merchant, res. Scarig, sett. Baltimore, pre 1792. (SRO.SH21.4.1792)

SWAN, JOHN, b. 1750, sett. Annapolis, Md, 1766, m. Elizabeth Maxwell 1787, fa. of James, d. 1824. (CAG.1.919)

SWAN, JOHN, clergyman, sett. Md and Ohio pre 1829. (NMC21)

SWAN, ROBERT, merchant, res. Torthorwald, Dumfriesshire (?), sett. Annapolis, Md, pre 1753, d. 1763, pro. 7 Oct.1763.   (SRO.CS16.1.89)(MSA.Wills32.152)

SWIFT, JOHN, nat. 7 Mar. 1809 Norfolk City, Va.

SWINTON, CHARLES, weaver, sh. 1714, fr. Glasgow to Potomac River, on *American Merchant*.   (TM202)

SWORD, HUMPHREY, Jacobite, tr. 29 July 1716, fr. Liverpool to Va, on *Godspeed*, arr. Md Oct. 1716.   (SPC.1716.310)(CTB.31.209)(HM389)

SYME, ANDREW, b. 1755, tutor and clergyman, res. Lanarkshire, sh. 1790, sett. Essex Co, Va; South Farnham ph, Va; and Bristol ph, Dinwiddie Co, Va, m. Jean Cameron 1806, d. 1839.   (WMQ.2.19.418)

SYME, GEORGE, merchant, res. Fife, sett. Richmond City, Va, nat. 24 Sep. 1799. (US D/C 1799.90)

SYME, JOHN, m. Sarah Winston, fa. of John, d. 1731 Va.   (ANY.1.140)

SYMES, WILLIAM, b. 1753, saddler, sh. Feb. 1774, fr. London to Va, on *Betsy*. (PRO.T47.9/11)

SYMS, WILLIAM, b. 1757, sett. Williamsburg, Va, pre 1776.   (VSL23816)

SYMINGTON, JAMES, b. 1798, merchant, arr. Baltimore 1824.   (N.A.-M596)

SYMMER, ALEXANDER, s. of Alexander Symmer, merchant, res. Edinburgh, sh. pre 1756, sett. Md.   (SM.18.524)

SYMMER, ANDREW, s. of Alexander Symmer, merchant, res. Edinburgh, sh. pre 1756, sett. Md.   (SM..18.524)

TAGGART, THOMAS, sh. 2 Nov. 1674, to St Mary's Co, Md, on *Bachelor of Bristol*. (MSA.ESB.152)

TAIT, JAMES, sh. 1774, canal builder and saltworks proprietor, sett. Cabin Point, Va, Loyalist, sett. Ayr.   (PRO.AO12.54.214)(PRO.AO12.109.288)(PRO.AO13.32.552)

TANKARD, WALTER, Jacobite, tr. 29 June 1716, fr, Liverpool to Jamaica or Va, on *Elizabeth and Anne*, ar. York, Va, 1716. (SPC.1716.310)(CTB.31.208)(VSP.1.185)

TAYLOR, ALEXANDER, b. 1709, laborer, res. Edinburgh, Jacobite, tr. 22 Apr. 1747, fr. Liverpool to Va, on *Johnson,* arr. Port Oxford, Md, 5 Aug. 1747. (P.3.362)(PRO.T1.328)

TANNOCH, JAMES, cordiner, res. Mauchline, Ayrshire, m. Robina Johnston, pro. 9 Apr. Baltimore.

TAYLOR, JAMES, s. of Robert Taylor, res. Aberdeen, sh. Sep. 1667 to Va.   (REA90)

TAYLOR, JOHN, m. Margaret -, fa. of James, Margaret and John, merchant, sett. Norfolk, Va, pro. 15 Feb. 1745 Norfolk, Va. (Norfolk Wills 1)

TAYLOR, JOHN, b. 1719, servant, res. Boharm, Banffshire, Jacobite, tr. 22 Apr. 1747, fr. Liverpool to Va, on *Johnson,* arr. Port Oxford, Md, 5 Aug. 1747. (P.3.366)(MR128)(PRO.T1.328)

TAYLOR, NATHANIEL, clergyman, res. Fife (?), sh. post 1703, sett. Marlborough, Patuxent, d. 1710. (F.7.665)

TAYLOR, ROBERT, robber, tr. 1771, fr. Port Glasgow to Md, on *Crawford,* arr. Port Oxford, Md, 23 July 1773. (SRO.JC27.10.3)

TAYLOR, R.L., nat. 22 Nov. 1809 Norfolk, Va.

TAYLOR, WILLIAM, b. 31 Dec. 1764, s. of Rev. William Taylor and Katherine Hay, res. Rhynd, Perthshire, sh. 1785 to Va, d. 6 Oct. 1793. (F.4.244)

TEGAR, JOHN, b. 1734, farmer, sett. Fairfax Co, Va, mi.itiaman in Va Regt 1756. (VMHB.1/2)(L)

TELFAIR, EDWARD, b. 1735, merchant and politician, res. Kirkcudbright, sh. 1758, sett. Va, fa. of Thomas, d. 1807 Ga. (TSA

TELFER, DAVID, s. of David Telfer, merchant, res. Kirkcudbright, sett. Va pre 1779. (SRO.RD2.225.1299)

TELFER, JEAN, widow of Rev. David Somerville, res. Strathaven, Lanarkshire, d. 6 June 1800 Lexington, Va. (GC1407)

TELFORD, JOHN, b. 1758, husbandman, sh. Mar. 1774, fr. Whitehaven, Cumberland, to Va, on Ann. (PRO.T47.9/11)

TEMPLETON, ISOBEL, da. of James Templeton, thief, res. Sorn, Ayrshire, tr. 1772, fr. Glasgow to Va, on *Brilliant,* arr. Port Hampton, va, 7 Oct. 1772. (SRO.JC27.10.3)(AJ1270)

TENNANT, JOHN, physician, m. Helen Katherine Balfour, in Canongate, Edinburgh, 2 May 1794, sett. Caroline Co, Va, d. pre 1818. (Canongate OPR)(SRO.RD5.274.574)

THOM, ALEXANDER, sett. Berryhill, fauquier Co, Va, 1746, m. Elizabeth Triplett, d. 1791. (CAG.1.621)

THOM, JOHN, s. of James Thom, res. Glasgow, thief, tr. 28 Nov. 1704, fr. Leith, Midlothian, to Md. (SRO.PC2.28.307)

THOMAS, JAMES, b. 1725, sailmaker, sett. Alexandria, Va, militiaman in Va Regt 1757. (VMHB.1/2)(L)

THOMAS, JAMES, b. 1730, farmer, militiaman in Va Regt 1753. (VMHB.1/2)

THOMSON, ADAM, physician, res. Edinburgh, sh. pre 1745, sett. Annapolis, Md, and Marlborough, Prince George Co, Md, d. 18 Sep. 1767 N.Y. (SRO.CS16.1.75)(SA183)(AP339)

THOMPSON, ALEXANDER, b. 1804, clerk, arr. Baltimore 1823, sett. Petersburg, Va. (N.A.-M596)

THOMPSON, ANDREW, s. of Thomas Thompson, mariner, res. Auchterhouse, Dundee, Angus, sh. 1625 to Va, on *Jacob of London*, pro. 1 Apr.1665. (Archdeaconry of London Reg.6.143)

THOMPSON, ANDREW, b. 1673, clergyman, edu. Marischal College, Aberdeen, 1691, res. Stonehaven, Kincardineshire, sh. 1712, sett. Elizabeth City, Hampton, Va, d. 1 Sep. 1719, pro. 3 May 1727 Edinburgh. (Elizabeth City g/s)(SRO.CC8.8.91)(EMA58)(OD15)

THOMPSON, DANIEL, Jacobite, tr. 29 June 1716, fr. Liverpool to Jamaica or Va, on *Elizabeth and Anne*, arr. York, Va, 1716. (SPC.1716.310)(CTB.31.208)(VSP.1.185)

THOMPSON, DAVID, merchant, res. Jedburgh, Roxburghshire, sh. pre 1749, sett. Yorktown, Va. (WMQ.11.155)

THOMPSON, DOROTHY, b. 1765, mo. of James, sett. Washington, D.C. (N.A.-M432/277-299)

THOMSON, DUNCAN, merchant, sett. Va pre 1780. (SRO.CS16.1.179)

THOMSON, GEORGE, Jacobite, tr. 24 May 1716, fr. Liverpool to Md, on *Friendship*, arr.Md. Aug. 1716. (SPC.1716.311)(HM387)(MdArch.34.164)

THOMSON, JAMES, s. of James Thomson, res. Aberdeen, clergyman and tutor, edu. Marischal College, Aberdeen, 1745-1748, sh. 1767, sett. Leeds ph, Fauquier Co, Va, d. 1812. (EMA59)(OD19)

THOMPSON, JAMES, res. Glasgow, prisoner, Suffolk Co, Va, 1771. (VaGaz1.8.1771)

THOMSON, JANE, b. 1779, sett. Baltimore. (N.A.-M432/277-299)

THOMPSON, JOHN, clergyman, edu. Marischal College, Aberdeen, 1715, sh. 1739, sett. St Mark's ph, Culpepper Co, Va, 1740, d. 1772. (OD16)(EMA58)

THOMPSON, JOHN, b. 1804, factory manager, m. Ann -, fa. of Mary, Anna, Edward, James and George, sett. Baltimore. (N.A.-M432/277-299)

THOMSON, MARGARET, res. Edinburgh, thief and whore, tr. 28 Nov. 1704, fr. Leith, Midlothan, to Md. (SRO.PC2.28.307)

THOMPSON, MARY, arr. Baltimore 1824. (N.A.-M596)

THOMPSON, ROBERT, b. 1788, farmer, m. Jane -, sett. Cecil Co, Md. (N.A.-M432/277-299)

THOMSON, THOMAS, sh. to Md, pro. June 1736 PCC.

THOMPSON, THOMAS, b. 1724, schoolmaster, sett. Winchester Co, Va, militiaman in Va Regt 1756. (VMHB.1/2)(L)

THOMSON, WILLIAM, b. 1730, tailor, res. Glasgow, Jacobite, tr. 24 Feb. 1747, fr. Liverpool to Va, on *Gildart,* arr. Port North Potomac, Md, 5 Aug. 1747. (P.3.372)(PRO.T1.328)

THOMPSON, WILLIAM, b. 1744, schoolmaster, sh. Aug. 1774, fr. London to Va, on *Beith.* (PRO.T47.9/11)

THOMSON, WILLIAM, nat. 26 Jan. 1804 Norfolk City, Va.

THORBURN, ELIZABETH, b. 1786, mo. of Alice and John, sett. Tyler Co, Va. (N.A.-M932/982)

THORBURN, JAMES, sett. Norfolk, Va, 1786, m. Martha Kirkby 1804. (CAG.1.393)

THORNTON, WILLIAM, physician and architect, edu. Edinburgh Uni. and Marischal College, Aberdeen, 1780s, sett. Washington, D.C. (SA226)

TILLERY, ANDREW, b. 24 Sep. 1710, s. of Andrew Tillery and Margaret Brown, horsehirer, res. Old Machar, Aberdeen, Jacobite, tr. 22 Apr. 1747, fr. Liverpool to Va, on *Johnson,* arr. Port Oxford, Md, 5 Aug. 1747. (P.3.374)(JAB.2.446)(PRO.T1.328)

TOD, GEORGE, s. of Charles Tod, res. Westshore, Orkney Islands, sett. Caroline Co, Va, pre 1765. (SRO.NRAS1246)(SRO.CS16.1.117)(SRO.SH23.1.1765)

TORRANCE -, assistant storekeeper, sett. Falmouth, Va, Loyalist, sett. Scotland. (SFV209/213)

TOWARD, JANET, res. Edinburgh, whore and thief, tr. 28 Nov. 1704, fr. Leith, Midlothian, to Md. (SRO.PC2.28.307)

TOWARD, JOHN, painter, sh. 1714, fr. Glasgow to the Potomac River, on the *American Merchant.* (TM202)

TRAIL, WILLIAM, b. 28 Sep. 1640, s. of Robert Trail and Jean Annand, res. Edinburgh, clergyman, edu. Edinburgh Uni. 1658, sh. 1682, sett. Potomac, Md, m. (1) Euphan Sword (2) Eleanor Trail, fa. of Mary, Sarah, James, William, Robert, Jean, Eleanor, Margaret and Elizabeth, d. 3 May 1714 Scotland. (F.1.302)

TRAVIS, CHARLES, b. 1733, planter, sett. Richmond, Va, militiaman in Va Regt 1756. (VMHB.1/2)(L)

TROKES, DAVID, merchant, d. 1813 Petersburg, Va. (EA.5131.13)

TROOPE, ROBERT, sh. 1651, sett. 'Scotland Yard', Charles Co, Md, 5 June 1663. (OPW35)

TROTTER, RICHARD, b. 1726, mason, sett. Essex Co, Va, militiaman in Va Regt 1756. (VMHB.1/2)(L)

TRUE, MARY, da. of Marbour (?) Blair, res. Glasgow, d. Apr. 1818 Charles Co. Md, bd. All Saints, Frederick Co, Md. (All Saints OPR)

TURNBULL, CHARLES, s. of George Turnbull and Elizabeth Turnbull, merchant, res. Glasgow, m. Rachel Robinson 1759, Charles ph, York Co, Va, sett. Dinwiddie Co, Va, pre 1777. (SRO.CS16.1.170)(SRA.B10.15.5943)(WMQ.2.16.99)

TURNBULL, PETER, b. 1759, sett. Va pre 1776. (VSL23816)

TURNBULL, ROBERT, s. of George Turnbull and Elizabeth Turnbull, merchant, res. Glasgow, sett. Dinwiddie Co, Va, pre 1775. (SRO.CS16.1.165)

TURNBULL, WILLIAM, servant, m. Elizabeth , da. of James Lyon, wright in Md, 15 June 1785 Edinburgh. (Edinburgh OPR)

TURNBULL of ASHIEBURN, -, res. Ancrum, Roxburghshire, tr. 1665 to Va. (F.2.100)

TURNER, CHARLES, clock cleaner, sett. Alexandria, Va, d. Jan. 1776. (VaGaz8.11.1776)

TURNER, JOHN, storekeeper, sett. Fauquier, Rocky Ridge, Va, 1768. (SFV135)

TURNER, WILLIAM, Jacobite, tr. 29 June 1716, fr. Liverpool to Jamaica or Va, on *Elizabeth and Anne*, arr. York, Va. 1716. (SPC.1716.310)(CTB.31.208)(VSP.1.185)

URQUHART, ALEXANDER, res. Tannachie, Forres, Morayshire, sh. pre 1770, sett. St Mary's Co, Md. (SRO.RS29.8.188)

URQUHART, JAMES, Jacobite, tr. 29 June 1716, fr. Liverpool to Jamaica or Va, on *Elizabeth and Anne,* arr. York, Va, 1716. (SPC.1716.310)(CTB.31.208)(VSP.1.186)

URQUHART, JOHN, clergyman, sh. 1732 to Md. (EMA61)

URQUHART, JOHN, b. 1788, sh. pre 1822, fa. of Ann and Christiana, sett. Tenn. and Isle of Wight Co, Va. (N.A.-M932/982)

URQUHART, JOHN, res. Ross and Cromarty, clergyman, edu. King's College, Aberdeen, 1782, sett. Cortlandt, N.Y., 1809-1814, then Va. (ANY.1.316)

VALLANCE, ROBERT, tr. 1728, fr. Glasgow to Md, on *Concord of Glasgow,* arr. 24 May 1728 Charles Co, Md. (SRO.JC27.10.3)

VAN HESTON, SOPHIA, res. Edinburgh, whore and thief, tr. 28 Nov. 1704, fr. Leith to Md. (SRO.PC2.28.307)

VASS, JAMES, res. Forres, Morayshire, sh. pre 1816 to Va, m. (1) Susanna Brook (2) Elizabeth B. Maury. (GM.1956.292)

VEITCH, JAMES, b. 1628, sh. 1651, sett. Calvert Co, Md, m. Mary Gakerlin, fa. of Nathan etc, d. 1685. (BLG2951)

VEITCH, JOHN, s. of Alexander Veitch, res. Peebles, sh. 1766, sett. Bladenburg, Md. (MSA.MHR.M1098)

VERNOR, JOHN, merchant, sh. Apr. 1684, fr. Port Glasgow to Va, on *Margaret of Morfin*. (SRO.E72.19.9)

WALES, MARGARET, b. 11 June 1651, da. of Alexander Wales, res. Dundee, Angus, sh. Aug. 1684, fr. London to Md.   (CLRO/AIA)

WALKER, ALEXANDER, b. 16 Aug. 1723, s. of William Walker, servant, res. Bervie, Kincardineshire, Jacobite, tr. 22 Apr. 1747, fr. Liverpool to Va, on *Johnson*, arr. Port Oxford, Md, 5 Aug. 1747.   (P.3.384)(PRO.T1.328)

WALKER, ALEXANDER, s. of Emanuel Walker, merchant, res. Port Glasgow, sett. Va pre 1749.   (SRO.CS16.1.81)

WALKER, ARCHIBALD, b. 1775, s. of Robert Walker and H. Gray, res. Dumfries, Dumfriesshire, d. 5 Feb. 1805 Petersburg, Va. (RaleighRegister 18.2.1805)(Dumfries g/s)

WALKER, CHARLES, s. of Dr James Walker, res. Peterhead, Aberdeenshire, m. Anne Craddock 1 Sep. 1772 Md, fa. of Thomas.   (BLG2636)

WALKER, DAVID, merchant, sett. Va 1766 and Portobacco, Md, 1770. (SRO.CS16.1.125)(SFV18)

WALKER, GEORGE, physician, sett. Md 1713, d. 1743.   (SA178)

WALKER, GEORGE, surveyor and merchant, res. Clackmannanshire, sett. Georgetown, Md, 1787.   (ANY.1.260)

WALKER, JAMES, physician, edu. Aberdeen Uni., sh. 1713, sett. Md, d. 1759.   (SA178)

WALKER, JEAN, b. 30 Oct. 1687, da. of William Walker, res. Old Aberdeen, sett. Va 1718. (VaGaz26.5.1768)

WALKER, JOHN, sh. 2 Nov. 1674, to St Mary's Co, Md, on *Bachelor of Bristol*. (MSA.ESB.152)

WALKER, JOHN, merchant, sett. Norfolk, Va, pre 1776, Loyalist, sett. Barbados. (PRO.AO13.32.643)

WALKER, JOHN, merchant, res. Glasgow, sett. Va and Nassau, Bahamas, d. 1784, pro. 13 Dec. 1784 Williamsburg, Va.

WALKER, ROBERT, res. Toeks, Dunottar, Kincardineshire, sh. 1730, sett. Rappahannock River, Va.   (VaGaz13.7.1775)

WALKER, ROBERT, res. Kingston, sh. pre 1775, m. Elizabeth Starke, fa. of Robert, Richard, David, Bolling, Freeman, Starke, Louisa, Martha, Mary and Clara. (HBV

WALKER, ROBERT, merchant, sh. pre 1795, nat. Richmond, Va, 13 Nov. 1802. (VSP.9.331)(VMBH.87.80)

WALKER, WILLIAM, merchant, sett. Portsmouth, Va, 1770, Loyalist. (PRO.AO13.32.648)

WALKINGSHAW, WILLIAM, merchant, sh. Dec. 1682, fr. Port Glasgow to Va, on *Supply of Chester.* (SRO.E72.19.8)

WALLACE, ALEXANDER, sh. 2 Nov. 1674, to St Mary's Co, Md, on *Bachelor of Bristol.* (MSA.ESB.152)

WALLACE, DAVID, s. of David Wallace and Margaret Hanton, res. Stonehaven, Kincardineshire, sh. 1723, planter, sett. James River, Va, m. - Hall, fa. of David, d. pre 1741. (Spotsylvania Deeds3.9.1751)(APB.3.92)

WALLACE, HERBERT, m. - Douglas, sh. pre 1738, sett. Va, fa. of James and William. (VG734)

WALLACE, JAMES, b. 1677, clergyman, res. Errol, Perthshire, sh. 1711, sett. Elizabeth Co, Va, m. Martha Westwood, d. 1712. (WMQ.3.168)(VG102)

WALLACE, JOHN, s. of - Wallace and Mary Smith, res. Edinburgh, d. 1788 Md, pro. 26 Mar. 1788 Md.

WALLACE, MARGARET, res. Edinburgh, whore and thief, tr. 28 Nov. 1704, fr. Leith, Midlothian, to Md. (SRO.PC2.28.307)

WALLACE, MICHAEL, b. 11 May 1719, s. of William Wallace of Galrigs, physician, sh.. 1734, sett. Falmouth, Va, m. Elizabeth Brown 1747, fa. of William, Gustavus, Michael, James, William, Rebecca, John and Thomas, d. Jan. 1767 Elderslie, Va, pro 4 June 1767 King George Co, Va. (VG696)(AGB.1.328)

WALLACE, MICHAEL, b. 1744, merchant, res. Lanarkshire, sett. Norfolk, Va, 1771, Loyalist, sett. Halifax, N.S., d. 1831. (PRO.AO12.55.106)(DCB.10.798)

WALLACE, ROBERT, res. Holmstone, Ayrshire, sett. Holmstone, Md, d. pre 1754. (HAF.1.210)

WALLACE, THOMAS, b. 1808, carpet weaver, m. Jane -, sh. pre 1830, fa. of Alexander, Agnes and Isabel, sett. Baltimore. (N.A.-M432/277-299)

WALLACE, WILLIAM, b. 1779, m. Catherine, sh. pre 1822, fa. of Isabella, William, Jefferson, Gustavus, Catherine, Barbara, Ellen and Julia, sett. Richmond, Henrico Co, Va. (N.A.-M932/982)

WALLACE, WILLIAM, sh. 2 Nov. 1674, to St Mary's Co, Md, on *Bachelor of Bristol.* (MSA.ESB.152)

WALTERS, ROBERT, b. 1734, planter, sett. Northumberland Co, Va, militiaman in Va Regt 1756. (VMHB.1/2)(L)

WANLESS, RICHARD, b. 1805, farmer, m. Sarah -, sh. pre 1830, fa. of William, Mary, Frances, Richard and John, sett. Ritchie Co, Va. (N.A.-M932/982)

WARD, KATHERINE, b. 1714, runaway, Baltimore Ferry, Pointon, Patapsco River 1734. (AmerWklyMercury25.7.1734)

WARDEN, EBENEZER, b. 1750, s. of Henry Warden, wright, res. Leith Mills, Midlothian, housebreaker and thief, tr. 1771, fr. Port Glasgow to Md, on *Matty,* arr. Port Oxford, Md, 17 Dec. 1771. (SRO.JC27.10.3)(REA69)

WARDEN, HUGH, merchant, res. Perth, sh. 1763, sett. Va, Loyalist. (SRO.CS16.1.157)(PRO.AO12.54.52)(PRO.AO12.109.310)(PRO.AO13.32.649)

WARDEN, JAMES, clergyman, sh. 1711, sett. Jamestown, Va, 1712/1713. (SCHR.14.144)

WARDEN, SAMUEL, clergyman, sh. 1712, sett. Va. (EMA64)

WARDROP, DANIEL, b. 1765, merchant, res. Glasgow, d. 1791 Va. (SRA.CFI)

WARDROP, JAMES, merchant, sett. Md, pre 1761. (SRO.CS16.1.110)

WARDROP, Mrs, d. 10 Sep. 1793 Ampthill, Richmond, Va. (VaGaz13.9.1793)

WARDROPE, JOHN, merchant, res. Glasgow, sett. Brunswick Co, Va, d. 31 Mar. 1789, pro. 25 July 1791 Edinburgh. (SRO.CC8.8.128)(SM.51.309)

WARE, WILLIAM, b. 1804, manufacturer, m. Ann -, fa. of Isabella, Sarah, William, Elizabeth and Margaret, sett. Baltimore. (N.A.-M432/277-299)

WARWICK, ANTHONY, storekeeper, sh. 1761, sett. Va and N.C., Loyalist. (PRO.AO12.100)

WARWICK, EBENEZER, b. 1786, farmer, sett. Hanover Co, Va. (N.A.-M932/982)

WATSON, CHRISTINA, b. 1790, sett. Ohio Co, Va. (N.A.-M932/982)

WATSON, GEORGE, b. 1723, s. of George Watson, weaver, res. Bervie, Kincardineshire, sh. 1745, sett. Md. (MdGaz4.5.1775)

WATSON, GEORGE, laborer, res. Banffshire, Jacobite, tr. 22 Apr. 1747, fr. Liverpool to Va, on *Johnson,* arr. 5 Aug. 1747 Port Oxford, Md. (P.3.390)(JAB.2.446)(PRO.T1.328)

WATSON, JAMES, Jacobite, tr. 29 June 1716, fr. Liverpool to Jamaica or Va, on *Elizabeth and Anne,* arr. York, Va, 1716. (SPC.1716.310)(CTB.31.208)(VSP.1.186)

WATSON, JAMES, b. 1754, runaway, Leedstown, Va, 1774. (VaGaz24.3.1774)

WATSON, JAMES, b. 1800, farmer, m. Martha -, sh. pre 1830, fa. of Margaret, Martha, Robert, Catherine and James, sett. Washington Co, Va. (N.A.-M932/982)

WATSON, JANE, sh. 2 Nov. 1674, to St Mary's Co, Va, on *Bachelor of Bristol.* (MSA.ESB.152)

WATSON, JOHN, merchant, res. Edinburgh, planter, Va, 1696-1713. (SRO.CS29.1752.3309)

WATSON, JOHN, res. Hamilton, Lanarkshire, sh. 2 Oct. 1684, fr. Bristol to Va, on *Bristol Merchant.* (BRO.04220)

WATSON, JOHN, nat. 11 Nov. 1803 Norfolk City, Va.

WATSON, Mrs MARGARET, sett. Wiccomico ph, Northumberland Co, Va, d. 1772, pro. 8 June 1772 Northumberland.

WATSON, WILLIAM, barber, sh. 1714, fr. Glasgow to Potomac River on *American Merchant.* (TM202)

WATSON, WILLIAM, arr. Baltimore 1786, fa. of Robert, sett. Pa. 1790. (OVG122)

WATT, ALEXANDER, Jacobite, tr. 29 June 1716, fr. Liverpool to Jamaica or Va, on *Elizabeth and Anne,* arr. York, Va, 1716.
  (SPC.1716.310)(CTB.31.208)(VSP.1.185)

WATT, CHRISTINE, res. Edinburgh, tr. 1696, fr. Newhaven, Midlothian, to Va. (SRO.RH15.14.58)

WATT, JAMES, b. 26 May 1740, s. of James Watt and Jean Clark, merchant, res. Panbride, Angus, sett. Caroline Co, Va, pre 1764.
(SRO.RD2.197.470)(SRO.SH22.11.1775)

WATT, JOHN, b. Feb. 1724, s. of John Watt, fisherman, res. Gamrie, Banffshire, Jacobite, tr. 22 Apr. 1747, fr. Liverpool to Va, on *Johnson,* arr. Port Oxford, Md, 5 Aug. 1747. (P.3.392)(JAB.2.446)(PRO.T1.328)

WATTIE, JOHN, farmer, res. Towie, Aberdeenshire, murderer, tr. 18 Jan. 1760, fr. Aberdeen to Va, on *Montrose of Aberdeen.* (AJ611/628)

WAUGH, WILLIAM, b. 1732, via Jamaica to Baltimore, Md, 1788, d. Nov. 1788 Md, bd. New Presb. Cemetery. (MdJournal18.11.1788)

WEATHERTON, WILLIAM, b. 1753, baker, sh. May 1774, fr. London to Md, on *Union.* (PRO.T47.9/11)

WEBSTER, DAVID, gunner's mate, res. Musselburgh, Midlothian, d. Va, pro. Feb. 1767 PCC.

WEBSTER, JAMES, Jacobite, tr. 24 May 1716, fr. Liverpool to Va, on *Friendship,* arr. Md Aug. 1716. (SPC.1716.311)(HM386)

WEBSTER, JAMES, weaver, res. Glamis, Angus, sett. Talbot Co, Md, d. 1743, pro. 3 Apr. 1744 Md.

WEBSTER, WILLIAM, b. pre 1745, brickmaker, runaway, Fairfax Co, Va, 1775. (VaGaz28.4.1775)

WEDDERBURN, DAVID, b. 1682, s. of Peter Wedderburn of Donside, sett. York River, Va. (SEV87)

WEEK, ALEXANDER, b. 1758, husbandman, sh. Mar. 1774, fr. Whiehaven, Cumberland, to Va, on *Ann.* (PRO.T47.9/11)

WEEMS, DAVID, b. 1706, s. of James Wemyss, sett. Marshes Seat, Md, 1721, m. Margaret Harrison, d. 5 May 1779. (MdGen.2.471)(VG350)

WEIR, GEORGE, facctor, sett. Va pre 1775. (PRO.T79/73)

WEIR, JAMES, sett. Dumfries, Prince William Co, Va, pre 1810, fa. of Robert. (CAG.1.403)

WEIR, JAMES, s. of Abraham Weir and Grizel Weir, merchant, res. Leadhills, Lanarkshire, sett. Fredericksburg, Va, 1785. (SRO.RD2.240.479)

WEIR, MARY, tr. 1 Feb. 1670, fr. Leith to Va. (ETR129)

WELSH, EUPHEMIA, b. 1780, sett. Baltimore. (N.A.-M432/277-299)

WELSH, JOHN, merchant, sett. Norfolk, Va, pre 1773, Loyalist. (PRO.AO13.32.691)

WEST, JAMES WALKER, b. 11 May 1705, physician, res. Peterhead, Aberdeenshire, sh. pre 1731, m. Susanna Gardner, d. 14 Jan. 1759 Baltimore, Md. (GKF613)

WEST, JAMES, b. 11 June 1791, s. of John West, res. Kirkcaldy, Fife, sh. 1815, sett. Wood Co, WVa 1817, d. 1851 Fox Township, Ohio. (OVG125)

WETHERLY, PETER, b. 1795, res. Cockburnspath, Berwickshire, nat. 6 Sep. 1824 Loudoun Co, Va. (LoudounSup.Ct.A124)

WHITE, ALEXANDER, Jacobite, tr. 29 June 1716, fr. Liverpool to Jamaica or Va, on *Elizabeth and Anne,* arr. York, Va, 1716. (SPC.1716.310)(CTB.31.208)(VSP.1.185)

WHITE, ALEXANDER, clergyman, sett. St David's, King William Co, Va, 1754-1775, m. Elizabeth Camm. (VMHB.82.101)

WHITE, ARCHIBALD, merchant, sett. Norfolk, Va, d. Glasgow,pro. 7 Oct. 1772 Glasgow.

WHITE, ARCHIBALD, res. Greenock, Renfrewshire, pro. 19 July 1765 Norfolk, Va.

WHITE, HECTOR, Jacobite, tr. 28 July 1716, fr. Liverpool to Va, on *Godspeed.* (SPC.1716.310)(CTB.31.209)

WHITE, HUGH, Jacobite, tr. 1716, on *Godspeed,* arr. Md 18 Oct. 1716 . (HM389)

WHITE, HUGH, nat. 20 Jan. 1795 Norfolk City, Va.

WHITE, JAMES, Jacobite, tr. 24 May 1716, fr. Liverpool to Va, on *Friendship,* arr. Md 20 Aug. 1716. (SPC.1716.311)(HM387)

WHITE, JOHN, Jacobite, tr. 29 June 1716, fr. Liverpool to Jamaica or Va, on *Elizabeth and Anne*, arr. York, Va, 1716.
(SPC.1716.310)(CTB.31.208)(VSP.1.185)

WHITE, JOHN, sett. Frederick Co, Md, pre 1766. (SRO.CS16.1.125)

WHITE, ROBERT, b. 1688, surgeon and physician, edu. Edinburgh Uni., sh. pre 1735, sett. Fredericksburg, Va. (SA188)(SRO.SH6.1.1762)

WHITE, ROBERT, Jacobite, tr. 24 Feb. 1747, fr. Liverpool to Va, on *Gildart*, arr. Port North Potomac, Md, 5 Aug. 1747. (PRO.T1.328)

WHITE, ROBERT, surgeon, res. Edinburgh (?), sett. Va pre 1760, fa. of John.
(SRO.SH6.1.1762)

WHITE, THOMAS, s. of Andrew White (1769-1841), res. Dunfermline, Fife, sett. Va.
(Kirkcaldy g/s)

WHITE, THOMAS, b. 1795, grocer, sh. pre 1825 to N.C., m. Sarah -, fa. of John, sett. Petersburg, Va. (N.A.-M932/982)

WHITE, WILLIAM, b. 1708, planter, sett. Fort Cumberland, Md, militiaman in Va Regt 1756. (VMHB.1/2)(L)

WHITE, WILLIAM, b. 1780, s. of David White and Mary Johnston, res Duns, Berwickshire, sett. Richmond, Va, nat. 11 Nov. 1801, d. 18 Oct. 1814.
(US D/C 1801)(Duns g/s)

WHITEFORD, JAMES, b. 1701, husbandman, res. Lanark, sh. Nov. 1730, fr. London to Md.
(CLRO/AIA)

WHITEHEAD, ALEXANDER, b. 1764, res. St Ninian's, Stirlingshire, clergyman and physician, edu. Glasgow Uni., sh. 1788, sett. Norfolk, Va, nat. 20 Jan. 1795 Norfolk City, Va, d. 1823. (WMQ.2.19.421)(FamilyVisitor6.12.1823)

WHITEHEAD, JAMES, res. St Ninian's, Stirlingshire, clergyman, edu. Glasgow Uni., sett. Elizabeth River ph, Va, Norfolk, Va, 1792, Baltimore 1805. (OD68)

WHITEHEAD, JAMES, b. 1756, cordiner, res. Edinburgh, sh. Dec. 1773, fr. London to Va, on *Elizabeth*. (PRO.T47.9/11)

WHITSON, ROBERT, b. 1803, weaver, sh. pre 1830, fa. of Jane, Elizabeth, James, Robert and John, sett. Hanover Co, Va. (N.A.-M932/982)

WIGHTON, MARGARET, da. of Alexander Wighton, m. James P Oldfield, merchant in Baltimore, 13 Apr. 1825 Glasgow. (S551.255)

WILKIE, JOHN, shipmaster, sh. pre 1776, sett. Gloucester Co, Va, Loyalist.
(PRO.AO12.102.203)

WILL, LAUGHLAN, res. Aberdeenshire, thief, tr. 1773 on *Donald*, arr. Port James, Upper District, Va, 13 Mar. 1773, runaway Apr. 1773.
(AJ1292)(SRO.JC27.10.3)(VaGaz15.4.1773)

WILLIAMS, FREDERICK, sett. Petersburg, Va, pre 1776, Loyalist, sett. Irvine, Ayrshire. (PRO.AO13.4.195/28.415)

WILLIAMS, GEORGE, b. 1755, baker, sh. Mar. 1774, fr. Hull, Yorkshire, to Md, on *Shipwright*.   (PRO.T47.9/11)

WILLIAMSON, ALEXANDER, res. Forres, Morayshire, clergyman, edu. King's College, Aberdeen, 1705, sh. 1710, sett. St Paul's, Kent Co, Md, m. Anne -. (ANQ.1.73)(EMA63)

WILLIAMSON, ALEXANDER, b. 1775, fa. of Angus and Elizabeth, sett. Baltimore. (N.A.-M432/277-299)

WILLIAMSON, ARCHIBALD, smith, sh. 1714, fr. Glasgow to the Potomac River, on the *American Merchant*.   (TM202)

WILLIAMSON, ARCHIBALD, d. 16 Apr. 1779 Va.   (Richmond g/s)

WILLIAMSON, BENJAMIN, b. 1793, carpenter, m. Harriet -, fa. of Virginia, J.B., Sarah, Elizabeth and Charles, sett. Washington, D.C.   (N.A.-M432/56-57)

WILLIAMSON, JAMES, res, Forres, Morayshire, clergyman, edu. King's College, Aberdeen, sh. 1712, sett. Shrewsbury, Kent Co, Md.   (ANQ.1.73)(EMA63)

WILLIAMSON, JOHN, planter, res. Haddington, East Lothian (?), sett. Va pre 1785. (SRO.SH17.9.1785)

WILLIAMSON, JOSEPH, merchant, sett. Rappahannock, Va, 1764 -1776, Loyalist. (PRO.AO13.32.700)

WILLIAMSON, JOSEPH, lawyer and clergyman, res. Edinburgh, sh. 1780, m. Sarah North, fa. of Joseph.   (CAG.1.951)

WILLIAMSON, ROBERT, physician, sett. isle of Wight Co, Va, pre 1663, m. Jane Allen, fa. of Robert.   (CAG.1.246)

WILLIAMSON, WALTER, s. of William Williamson of Chapeltoun, surgeon, res. Dunbartonshire, sh. pre 1756, sett. St Paul's, Staffod Co, Va, d. 1772, pro. 1776 Edinburgh.   (SRO.CC8.8.123)(SRO.SH14.8.1761)(SRO.CS16.1.99)

WILLIAMSON, WILLIAM, b. 1764, schoolmaster and clergyman, res. Edinburgh, sh. 1787 to N.Y., sett. Front Royal, Warren Co, Va.   (PV117)

WILLISON, JAMES, b. 15 Feb. 1751, s. of John Willison and Margaret Dunbar, res. Port Glasgow, sett. Cabin Point, Prince George Co, James River, Va, pre 1778, m. Mary L'Anson, fa. of John, Archibald, Lucy, Margaret and Mary, d. 1787 Surry Co, Va.   (VMHB.28.67)

WILLSON, DAVID, b. 1750, farmer, sett. Rockingham Co, Va, pre 1776. (VSA24296)

WILLSON, WILLIAM, b. 1694, runaway, Queen Anne Co, Md, 1720.
(Amer.Wkly.Mercury21.7.1720)

WILSON, Major, sett. James River, Va, pre 1693. (NEHGS.ScotsC.Soc.pp)

WILSON, ANDREW, founder, res. Aberfoyle, Stirlingshire, thief, tr. 1771, fr. Port
Glagow to Md, on *Crawford* arr. Port Oxford, Md, 23 July 1771.
(AJ1170)(SRO.JC27.10.3)

WILSON, ANDREW, tailor, res. Dumfries, Dumfriesshire, rioter, tr. 1771, fr. Port
Glasgow to Md, on *Matty*, arr. Port Oxford, Md, 17 Dec. 1771.
(AJ1232)(SRO.JC27.10.3)(SM.33.497)

WILSON, CUMBERLAND, s. of James Wilson, merchant, res. Kilmarnock, Ayrshire,
sett. Va 1760, Loyalist.   (PRO.AO13.33.367)

WILSON, DAVID, b. 1701, clerk, res. Edinburgh, sh. June 1721, fr. London to Va.
(CLRO/AIA)

WILSON, DAVID, b.1756, farmer, sett. Rockingham Co, Va. (VSA.Acc24296)

WILSON, GEORGE, physician, res. Stonecleugh, Edinburgh, m. Marianne Bannister,
1789, sett. Petersburg, Va, d. 13 Oct. 1799 London.
(SM.51.412)(EA3738.271)

WILSON, HENRY, Jacobite, tr. 24 May 1716, fr. Liverpool to Md, on *Friendship*, arr.
Md Aug. 1716.   (SPC.1716.311)(HM386)

WILSON, JAMES F., b. 1790, s. of Alexander Wilson, merchant, res. Inverness,
sett. New Orleans, d. 5 Oct. 1821 Va.   (BM.40.263)

WILSON, JAMES, b. 1794, baker, m. Agnes -, sett. Baltimore.   (N.A.-M432/277-299)

WILSON, JOHN, b. 1740, runaway, Anne Arundel Co, Md, 1770. (MdGaz13.9.1770)

WILSON, JOHN, b. 1782, farmer, m. Mary -, fa. of Lee and Archibald, sett. Harford Co,
Va.   (N.A.-M932/982)

WILSON, JOHN, shipmaster and merchant, res. Ayr, sett. Nansemond Co, Va, fa. of Janet
and Jacobina, d. pre 1771.   (SRO.CS16.1.168)(SRO.SH2.1771)

WILSON, MARY, res. Brechin, Angus, thief, tr. Oct. 1772, fr. Port Glasgow to Va, on
Phoenix, arr. Port Accomack, Va, 20 Dec. 1772, m. Charles Stewart.
(SRO.JC27.10.3)(AJ1293)

WILSON, PETER, b. 1751, runaway, Newcastle, Va, 1775.   (VaGaz28.7.1775)

WILSON, SAMUEL, nat. 20 Jan. 1806 Norfolk, Va.

WILSON, THOMAS, b. 1758, s. of William Wilson of Dullatur, advocate, res. Edinburgh,
   edu. Glasgow Uni. 1771, arr. Baltimore 1822, d. 27 June 1824 Georgetown, D.C.
(N.A.-M596)(GUMA97)

WILSON, WILLIAM, s. of James Wilson, merchant, res. Kilmarnock, Ayrshire, sett. Alexandria, Va, and Md 1768-1776, Loyalist. (PRO.AO13.33.367)

WINGATE, JOHN, b. 31 July 1741, s. of Thomas Wingate, res. Kincardine, clergyman, edu. Glasgow Uni. 1763, sh. 1771, sett. Dale, Va.
(FPA310)(MAGU71)(EMA64)

WISE, JOHN, b. 1798, clerk, m. Elizabeth -, fa. of Janet and Mary, sett. Richmond, Va. (N.A.-M932/982)

WISE, NINIAN, b. 1714, laborer, Jacobite, tr. 22 Apr. 1747, fr. Liverpool to Va, on *Johnson*, arr. Port Oxford, Md, 5 Aug. 1747. (P.3.406)(PRO.T1.328)

WISHART, JOHN, clergyman, sh. 1764 to Va. (EMA64)

WITHERSPOON, JAMES, merchant, sh. 1734, fr. Glasgow to Md, sett. Charles Co, Md. (MdGaz25.1.1749)

WITHERSPOON, JAMES, b. 17 Nov. 1751, s. of Rev. John Witherspoon and Elizabeth Montgomery, res. Paisley, Renfrewshire, sh. 1768, d. 1777 Brandywine, Md. (F.3.175)

WITHERINGTON, RICHARD, Jacobite, tr. 28 July 1716, fr. Liverpool to Va on *Godspeed*, arr. Md Oct.1716. (SPC.1716.310)(CTB.31.209)(HM389)

WODDROP, THOMAS, s. of Thomas Woddrop, shipmaster, res. Glasgow, sett. Va 1765. (SRO.CS16.1.122)

WODDROP, WILLIAM, s. of John Woddrop, merchant, res. Edinburgh, sett. Tappahannock, Va, pre 1772. (SRO.SH.22.1.1772)

WODDROW, ALEXANDER, s. of Rev. Robert Woddrow, merchant, sett. Va pre 1778. (SRO.CS16.1.173)(HAF.2.509)

WODDROW, ANDREW, planter, res. Glasgow, sh. 1768 to Va. (SNQ.10.140)

WOOD, ANDREW, nat. 22 Apr. 1805, Norfolk City, Va.

WOOD, DAVID, b. 1699, laborer, res. Kinneff, Kincardineshire, Jacobite, tr. 24 Feb. 1747, fr. Liverpool to Va, on *Gildart,* arr. Port North Potomac, Md, 5 Aug. 1747. (P.3.408)(MR112)(PRO.T1.328)

WOOD, DAVID, b. 1737, cordiner, sh. Apr. 1774, fr. London to Md, on *Diana.* (PRO.T47.9/11)

WOOD, JAMES, Jacobite, tr. 29 June 1716, fr. Liverpool to Jamaica or Va, on *Elizabeth and Anne*, arr. York, Va, 1716.
(SPC.1716.310)(CTB.31.208)(VSP.1.185)

WOOD, JOHN, merchant, res. Glasgow, sett. Flowr de Hundred, Va, pre 1783. (SRO.CS17.1.2)

WOOD, JOHN, b. 1775, author and cartographer, sh. 1800 to N.Y., sett. Richmond, Va, 1808, d. 15 May 1822. (Raleigh Register24.5.1822)(BM.12.250)

WOOD, WILLIAM, s. of Gabriel Wood, merchant, res. Greenock, Renfrewshire, sett. Baltimore, Md, HM Consol, d. 1812, pro. 10 Apr. 1821 Edinburgh, pro. Aug. 1816 PCC. (SRO.CC8.8.147)

WOODROP, WILLIAM, factor res. Glasgow, sh. pre 1770, sett. Essex Co, Va. (SRA.CFI)

WOTHERSPOON, JAMES, res. Colehill, Old Monklands, Glasgow, sett. Va pre 1738. (VaGaz15.9.1738)

WRIGHT, JOHN, clergyman, edu. Princeton Uni. 1752, sett. Va 1754-1762. (CCVC55)

WRIGHT, JOHN, b. 1745, runaway, King William Co, Va, 1769. (VaGaz7.12.1769)

WRIGHT, ROBERT, surgeon, *The Alexander,* Va 1761. (SRO.CS16.1.107)

WRIGHT, WILLIAM, Jacobite, tr. 29 June 1716, fr. Liverpool to Jamaica or Va, on *Elizabeth and Anne,* arr. York, Va, 1716. (SPC.1716.310)(CTB.31.208)(VSP.1.185)

WRIGHT, WILLIAM, b. 1707, postillion, res. Glasgow, sh. May 1725, fr. London to Md. (CLRO/AIA)

WRIGHT, THOMAS, nat. 26 Mar. 1794 Norfolk City, Va.

WYLIE, ROBERT, merchant, sett. Queen's Creek, Gloucester Co, Va, pre 1776, Loyalist. (PRO.AO13.87.295)

WYLLIE, WILLIAM, clergyman, sett. Va 1740 -1776. (SCHR.14.142)(WMQ.2.20.134)

YATES, FRANCIS, res. Fochabers, Morayshire, Jacobite, tr. 24 Feb. 1747, fr. Liverpool to Va, on *Gildart,* arr. Port North Potomac, Md, 5 Aug. 1747. (P.3.412)(MR124)(PRO.T1.324)

YEATES, BENJAMIN, b. 1702, res. Berwick, sh. 9 Apr. 1720, fr. London to Va. (CLRO/AIA)

YORSTOUN, JANET, gypsy, Roxburghshire, tr. 1 Jan. 1715, fr. Glasgow to Va. (GR530)

YOUNG, ANDREW, b. 1784, farmer, m. Agnes -, fa. of Elizabeth, Andrew, Nancy, Christiana, John, Margaret and Margaret, sh. 1830, sett. Ritchie Co, Va. (N.A.-M932/982)

YOUNG, EDWARD, b. 1772, storekeeper, sett. va, d. 1792. (VaHerald6.9.1792)

YOUNG, JAMES, merchant, res. Glasgow, sh. pre 1745, sett. Va. (SRA.CFI)

YOUNG, JAMES, b. 1718, merchant, sett. Albemarle Co, Va, militiaman in Va Regt 1756. (VMHB.1/2)(L)

YOUNG, JAMES, tr. Mar. 1751, fr. Aberdeen to Va or West Indies on *Adventure of Aberdeen*. (AJ170)

YOUNG, JAMES, b. 1799, s. of Alexander Young and Jean Quarrier, biscuit maker, res. Uphall, West Lothian, sett. Richmond, Va, pre 1815, d. 2 Aug. 1815 Richmond. (Uphall g/s)(SRO.RH1.2.804.3)

YOUNG, THOMAS, b. 1810, blacksmith, m. Ellen -, fa. of Margaret, Ellen, Elizabeth and Isabella, sh. pre 1830, sett. Harford Co, Md. (N.A.-M432/277-299)

YOUNG, JOHN, b. 1758, res. Edinburgh, sh. pre 1783, m. Elizabeth Ogleby, Va 1783, fa. of Robert and Alexander, d. 1800. (WMQ..2.19.381)

YOUNG, JOHN, b. 1805, boatbuilder, sh. pre 1830 to N.B., m. Euphemia -, fa. of Christina, William, John, Thomas, James, Isabel, Jane, Euphemia, Elizabeth and Jesse, sett. Md. (N.A.-M432/277-299)

YOUNG, MARGARET, b. 1787, sett. Richmond, Henrico Co, Va. (N.A.-M432-277/299)

YOUNG, PHILIP, b. 1787, clergyman, arr. Baltimore 1826. (N.A.-M596)

YOUNG, ROBERT, b. 1798, tallow chandler, sett. Alexandria, Va. (N.A.-M932/982)

YOUNG, THOMAS, b. 1782, teacher, sett. Wythe Co, Va. (N.A.-M932/982)

YOUNG, WILLIAM, s. of William Young, res. Glasgow, sett. Northampton Co, Va, pre 1749. (SRO.SH22.5.1749)

YOUNG, WILLIAM, Jacobite, tr. 31 July 1716, fr. Liverpool to Va, on *Anne*. (SPC.1716.310)(CTB.31.209)

YOUNGER, JASPER, b. 1793, implement maker, m. Margaret -, sh. pre 1825, fa. of Francis and Jasper, sett. Baltimore. (N.A.M432-277/299)

YOUNGER, JOHN, sh. 2 Nov. 1674, to St Mary's Co, Md, on *Bachelor of Bristol*. (MSA.ESB.152)

YOUNGER, MARY, sh. 2 Nov. 1674, to St Mary's Co, Md, on *Bachelor of Bristol*. (MSA.ESB.152)

YUILLE, GEORGE, factor, sett. Va pre 1755. (Col.Inst.Williamsburg Ms)

YUILLE, JOHN, b. 1719, s. of Thomas Yuille of Darleith, d. 1746 Williamsburg, Va. (Bruton g/s)(SRA.B10.15.5959)(SRA.CFI)(VaHist Colln.11.67)